History Of The Ancient Order Of Hibernians From The Earliest Period To The Joint National Convention At Trenton, New Jersey, June 27, 1898, With Biography Of The Rt. Rev. James A. Mcfaul

Thomas Francis McGrath

Yours truly

J. F. McGrath

HISTORY

OF THE

ANCIENT ORDER OF HIBERNIANS

FROM THE EARLIEST PERIOD

TO THE

JOINT NATIONAL CONVENTION

AT

TRENTON, NEW JERSEY, JUNE 27, 1898,

WITH BIOGRAPHY OF THE

Rt. Rev. James A. McFaul,

BISHOP OF TRENTON, ARBITRATOR FOR THE A. O. H. OF AMERICA, AND
THE A. O. H. BOARD OF ERIN.

T. F. McGRATH, CLEVELAND, O.

PRESS OF J. B. SAVAGE,
CLEVELAND.

OPINIONS OF

RT. REV. BISHOP JAMES A. McFAUL

AND

NATIONAL OFFICERS.

I am in receipt of your book, "A History of the A. O. H." You deserve great credit for the pains you have taken to accomplish this task. The work is a proof of the love you bear the organization and the Irish race.—Jas. A. McFaul, Bishop of Trenton, N. J.

Your history of the A. O. H. I have perused it with much pleasure.—John S. Foley, Bishop of Detroit, Mich.

I am in receipt of your interesting history of the A. O. H. It is good. The historical records of our order. —John T. Keating, National President.

I received your copy of the history of the Ancient Order of Hibernians. It will be read with great interest by every member of the order and will be a great incentive to every loyal member of the organization to redouble his efforts to make the order more powerful and influential in the elevation of our race at home and abroad.—James O'Sullivan, National Secretary.

I have read your history of A. O. H. It is the only history of the order ever written and should be in the home of every member of the order.—T. Donoghue, Ex-State Delegate of New York, a member of 40 years' good standing.

A new book bearing the following title has just been published, "History of the Ancient Order of Hibernians, from the Earliest Period to the Joint National Convention at Trenton, N. J., June 27, 1898." It is a work of intense interest to the immense membership of the largest Irish society in the world. It supplies a need which has been apparent for a long time, and will be hailed with delight by all who will have the privilege of recurring to its pages. That every member of the order will secure a copy may be looked upon as certain. The author, Mr. Thomas Francis McGrath, of Cleveland, Ohio, has dealt with the History in a masterly way, showing at the same time culture and research.—Irish American Review, Philadelphia, Pa.

Our readers will be interested to learn that a history of the Ancient Order of Hibernians has just been written and published by Thomas Francis McGrath, of 206 Gordon Ave., Cleveland, Ohio. Mr. McGrath gives an interesting sketch of the famous society since it was founded some hundreds of years ago to protect the priests and schoolmasters in Ireland from the vengeance of the English; tells of its introduction into the United States in 1836, and of its history here up to and including the joint national convention of the two wings of the order in Trenton last June; treats at length of the trouble which began in 1883, and ended in disruption, and the proceedings which resulted last year in the uniting of the divisions, and gives in full the decision of Bishop McFaul, the arbitrator between the contenders.—The Boston Pilot.

A History of the Ancient Order of Hibernians. We have read this history through and are surprised at the amount of information it contains. In it you will find a detailed account of the trouble that caused the split in the ranks and also a fine account of the cause of the reunion. The early formation of the order makes interesting reading, and in the years that we have been members of the order we remember of no publication that gives such facts pertaining to the history of the Ancient Order of Hibernians. Every member of the order should possess himself with a copy.—The Emerald, the official organ of the A. O. H. for the State of New Hampshire.

A book has just been put upon the market which will prove of much value and historical interest to all members of the A. O. H. It is a "History of the Ancient Order of Hibernians from the Earliest Period to the Joint National Convention at Trenton, N. J., June 27, 1898, with a biography of Rt. Rev. James A. McFaul, Bishop of Trenton, arbitrator for the A. O. H. of America and the A. O. H. Board of Erin. The work is approved by the Rt. Rev. Bishop McFaul; Rt. Rev. Bishop Foley of Detroit, national chaplain; John T. Keating, N. P.; James O'Sullivan, N. S., and many others.

This book supplies what may be called a long felt want. Perhaps there is no organization or association of Irishmen in existence which better deserves to have its story told in print and its record perpetuated than the Ancient Order of Hibernians. Certainly there is none that can present a more patriotic, a more honorable record—a record of service to Ireland.

An idea of the field covered can be gathered by scanning the contents. Starting with the date of birth of the order about the time of Cromwell's infamous edict of "To hell or to Connaugh," it tells the story of the "Defenders," Massacre of Mullaghmast, the death of Rory Oge, Donald O'Driscoll's successor, the death of Owen O'Moore, the confederation of Kilkenny, the meeting at Knockcrofty, where the Celtic Irish and the Lords of the Pale united, etc., etc.

The history of the A. O. H. is practically the history of Ireland for 300 years. The defenders of their altars in the mountain fastnesses and the sentinels on the hilltops of Erin are hallowed and dear to every Hibernian. No descendants of the Gael, no Hibernian, no believer in the motto "For God and Country," but will find this timely and instructive work from Mr. McGrath's eloquent pen as enlightening as a history and as fascinatingly interesting as a novel.—The Evening Tribune, Lawrence, Mass.

Mr. T. F. McGrath of Cleveland has compiled a very complete history of the Ancient Order of Hibernians from the institution of the order in Ireland to the present day. This book gives a very interesting account of the old order, dealing with the causes leading to the secession of a portion of the members and their subsequent unification at Trenton in June last. The book will prove quite interesting to members of the order.—The Ohio Pilot.

A new book which has supplied a long felt want has just appeared in the "History of the Ancient Order of Hibernians from the Earliest Period to the Joint National Convention at Trenton, N. J., June 27, 1898." The author is Mr. Thomas Francis McGrath of Cleveland, O., a prominent member of the order. We have received a copy of the book and have read it with much interest and pleasure, and we hope that it will have a wide circle of readers, especially among the constituents of the Irish World, for, as we need hardly say, the A. O. H. has always been promptly and generously to the front in every good work for the old land and the old cause undertaken by the Irish World and its friends.—The Irish World.

PREFACE TO SECOND EDITION.

In placing this work in the hands of the members of the Ancient Order of Hibernians, I feel that it is supplying a want long felt. It has been my endeavor to give a history of the order so that it can be remembered by its readers and at the same time be a handy book of reference. It is the only work of the kind ever attempted. It tells of the organization of the order in Ireland and of the various vicissitudes it has gone through on this side of the ocean. No man can understand the condition of Irish feeling or the status of Irish parties without becoming interested in the history of Ireland. The present edition has been prepared with the view of placing in the hands of every Hibernian a history of his organization. And now that the order is reunited through the kind offices of the Rt. Rev. Bishop McFaul, and that all Hibernians are in friendship, I trust the A. O. H. will continue to grow in numbers until it will take the position it so richly deserves—the leading Irish Catholic organization in the world and the pride of all patriots. My first reliance has been on my own recollections of events for the past twenty-five years. Besides I have collected information from those whom I know to be reliable, well informed and honest, and have consulted the best authors on Irish history to make this work an authority on Hibernianism. The present work contains far more matter than the very limited first edition. Anything omitted in this volume which appeared in the previous edition has been eliminated through a spirit of harmony and in the endeavor not to rethrash old straw.

—The Author.

RT. REV. JAMES A. McFAUL.

SKETCH OF BISHOP McFAUL.

Bishop James Augustine McFaul was born near the village of Larne, County Antrim, Ireland, June 6th, 1850. His parents immigrated to America when he was but six months old and settled in New York City where they remained for about four years. At the end of that time they went to Bound Brook, N. J., where they lived out their happy, peaceful lives until God called them, a few years since, to enjoy their reward in Heaven. In this beautiful country the early years of our good Bishop were passed. He attended the neighboring schools of Weston and Millstone and early attracted the marked attention of his teachers for persevering industry in the pursuit of knowledge. When his parents settled at Bound Brook, Catholics were few in that part of the State. There was no church at Bound Brook, and so to hear Holy Mass the journey to New Brunswick or Raritan had to be made. How faithful his parents were in performing this duty is a tradition throughout the whole neighborhood. Never, when circumstances did not render it impossible, were they absent from the Holy Sacrifice. On stormy days the mother and father would gather the children around them, as they could not reach the distant churches, they would kneel (at least during the time of the Mass), and devoutly reciting the beads, endeavor to be present in spirit at the divine Mysteries. Under such training it was impossible that the future Bishop should not acquire that spirit of strong, enduring faith which is characteristic of him. At the early age of nine years, he was prepared by a good Benedictine Father, Rt. Rev. Bishop Seidenbush, for his First Holy Communion, and was confirmed in St. Peter's Church, New Brunswick, by the lamented Archbishop Bayley. The Benedictines continued their labors at Bound Brook and gathered the few Catholics of the neighborhood together. The house is still standing where the first Mass was said. It was used for a church for many years, and in it young James received first communion. Here the subject of our sketch also served Mass, and was so prudent and docile in his bearing as to attract the attention of Father William Walter, O. S. B., who advised him to devote the talents God had given him to the service of the church. Acting on his advice, the young man entered St. Vincent's College at Beatty, Westmoreland County, Pennsylvania, where he remained for four years. He then entered St. Francis Xavier's College, New York City, where he completed his classical course, and fitted himself for the seminary. His theological studies were made at Seton Hall College, South Orange, N. J., where he was ordained to the Holy Priesthood on May 26, 1877. His first assignments were to Paterson, then to Orange (taking the place of sick priests), until he was permanently appointed to St. Patrick's Church, Jersey City. Afterwards he was stationed at St. Patrick's Cathedral, Newark, and later at St. Peter's, New Brunswick. Finally, he was sent to be assistant to the late lamented Vicar-General Antony Smith, at St. Mary's in Trenton, shortly before the division of the State into two dioceses. The See of Trenton was erected in 1881, and Michael Joseph O'Farrell was appointed its first Bishop. He chose St. Mary's Church as his cathedral, and was thus early brought into contact with its young, able and vigorous assistant. It did not take long for him to know what manner of man Father McFaul was, and in the first days of his work as a Bishop was laid the foundation of an affectionate confidence between these two, which grew the stronger with the passing years. In 1884 Fr. McFaul was made pastor of St. Mary's, Star of the Sea, Long Branch. Here he labored for six years. During this period he paid off the very heavy indebtedness of the church and built also the beautiful Church of St. Michael at Elberon. In the meantime, good old Father Antony Smith died, and the Bishop, deprived of his inestimable services, turned to the man upon whose devotion he could count implicitly, and Fr. McFaul was summoned to Trenton. In course of time he was made the Vicar-General of the diocese. How loyal he was to Bishop O'Farrell everyone knows. The Bishop's interest was his interest. He discharged with scrupulous fidelity every commission given to him. He supported the Bishop in everything and encouraged and consoled him in trial and sorrow. Very few know the labor his position imposed upon him during the last years of Bishop O'Farrell. But now, God, who knows all things, has rewarded it, and he is the chosen successor of his dead friend.

And now who is Bishop McFaul? He is a man who has filled every position in the church, from assistant priest to his present place. He has spent his hours in the confessional. He has gone among the people for many years, day and night, administering the last sacraments to them, and therefore he knows them. He knows their circumstances; how much they can do and suffer, and hence he will be their friend. If a young assistant goes to him to tell him of his difficulties, he knows how to sympathize with him, for he has experienced them. If a pastor, harrassed by the cares of his parish, weighed down by a heavy debt, goes to him, he knows how to console him, for he has felt the same burdens. If the burden of supporting a school disheartens the pastor, he can reanimate him, for he has known it. He knows the duties of a priest perfectly, and who else should be a Bishop? All those who have the happiness of acquaintance with Bishop McFaul know that above all things he is fair and just; and so the priests of the Diocese of Trenton rejoice today. He knows every one of them, and there is not among them a single one for whom he has not a warm place in his heart. We look forward to the future with hope and joy! There is a noble work to be done in this young diocese, and we turn with unbounded gratitude to the Great Pope Leo, who has shown his sympathy for the priest more than once, and who has now given us as our chief pastor, the priest of our own choice. To our Bishop we tender not only the loyalty of good priests, but the affection of friends who have known him and loved him. He is in the prime of manhood, full of strength of mind and body. May he rule the fair church of Trenton for many, many years.

SKETCH OF P. McGARRY, N. D.

P. McGarry, the ex-National delegate of the Ancient Order of Hibernians (Board of Erin), is the proprietor of the Washington Steam Boiler Works in Chicago, Ill. He was born at Whitehouse, a suburb of Belfast, County Antrim, Ireland, on July 2d, 1845. He attended the local school there and had for a teacher the late Joseph G. Biggar, M. P. He learned the trade of iron shipbuilding and boilermaking in Harland & Wolff's on the Queen's Island, being the first Roman Catholic to serve a five years' apprenticeship under Harland & Wolff. He joined the Fenian Brotherhood in 1863, when he was 18 years of age. Mr. McGarry comes from a great Nationalist family, his grandfather and father both taking part in all the patriotic movements in Ireland. He was a prominent figure in connection with the Orange riots in Belfast in 1864, and in the great strike of the Orangemen against the Catholics in the Queen's Island shipbuilding yards, arising out of the 1864 riots, when it was agreed to settle it by arbitration. As the leader of the Catholics he appointed the late Joseph G. Biggar (his old teacher), then an obscure bacon merchant, and the late A. J. McKenna, editor of the "Northern Star," a Nationalist newspaper, to act for the Catholics. Biggar handled the subject so well that the Nationalists shortly after elected him to represent Smithfield Ward in the Belfast City Council, and shortly afterwards he was elected to the British parliament by the Nationalists of the County Cavan, where he became Parnell's lieutenant, and enjoyed the reputation of being the best hated Irishman who ever entered the British House of Commons and whose name, next to that of the illustrious Parnell, will ever be honored by all true Irish Nationalists as true Irish patriots.

On the 2d of July, 1871, he came to New York, being just twenty-six years old. He soon went west and settled in Chicago. He joined the Ancient Order of Hibernians in 1881, and has always been an ardent admirer and friend of the late Dr. Cronin. He is now President of the Confederated Irish Societies of Chicago.

In Irish politics he is a strong Parnellite, and hopes to live to see the "Old Green Flag" floating over the Albert Memorial in Belfast. He was elected National Secretary of the A. O. H. (Board of Erin) at the convention held in Tammany Hall in May, 1894, and was re-elected by acclamation in May, 1895, and elected National Delegate in Philadelphia in May, 1896.

THE ANCIENT ORDER OF HIBERNIANS.

When clouds obscured fair freedom's ray
   All o'er our native Island,
And tyranny's fierce hand held sway
   O'er valley green and highland.
When Erin's final hope had fled
   And spiritless each warder
There, rose like meteor blazing red,
   Our glorious "Ancient Order."

Hibernians of world fame
   Who Erin love and honor,
Who guard with zealous care her name
   Nor stain yet brought upon her
Defenders of her faith are you
   And loyal, too, each brother
And to the Church of Rome e'er true
   And to your Island Mother.

From flame-swept town and hearthstone cold,
   From ruined shrine and chapel;
From whitened bones and warriors bold,
   Who died in foeman's grapple;
From memories of bitter woes,
   From years of desolation;
Your gallant Ancient Order rose
   To save the Irish nation!

And boldly did you take your stand,
   In these dread days of Erin,
When mother Church and Motherland
   Alike the chains were wearin'.
When in the Isle of saints had ceased
   The song of sacred mass
And like wolf the holy priest
   Was chased to mountain pass.

And thinking of these penal days
  We mourn the brave who perished
And raise our voices in their praise
  Who faith and country cherished.
Those days of gore and ruthless sword
  Of pitch cap, rack and halter
Produced the men who could afford
  To die at freedom's altar.

By tyrant laws, proscribed and banne'd,
  In stealth the Order struggled;
And by its aid into the land
  Was many a "soggarth" smuggled;
And lonely vale and mountain pass,
  Apart from Church and steeple,
Beheld the hurried midnight mass
  Said for the faithful people.

God rest those men who, unafraid,
  'Mid tears and tribulation,
In secrecy and silence laid
  The Order's first foundation.
Few though they were, but stout of heart;
  God grant that we inherit
Their virtue and at least a part
  Of their undaunted spirit.

But stay—I know that men as true
  Today your ranks are filling;
And noble deeds to dare and do
  As ready are and willing.
Years pass and men who live depart,
  But dies the Order never!
Its freedom loving Celtic heart
  Beats now the same as ever.

The chains are falling link by link,
    Our country's cry is heeded;
The right of Irishmen to think
    At least has been conceded.
Yours be the credit, you who fought
    Distrust and foul suspicion,
And to unfriendly people taught
    Your patriotic mission.

A little part of centuried wrong
    Some years ago was righted.
An English Church vexatious long
    By English law was blighted.
'Tis not enough—you must not rest
    Nor cease your earnest trying
'Till o'er your land with home rule blest
    The old Green Flag is flying.

Hibernians! O illustrious band!
    For valor famed and virtue,
You feared not England's bloody brand
    Vain were her laws to hurt you—
All men may honor Erin's Isle
    And hearty thanks accord her,
For from her consecrated soil
    Has sprung your Ancient Order.

THE BATTLE OF FONTENOY.

Thrice, at the huts of Fontenoy, the English Column
    failed,
And, twice, the lines of Saint Antoine, the Dutch in
    vain assailed;
For town and slope were filled with fort and flanking
    battery,
And well they swept the English ranks and Dutch
    auxiliary.
As vainly through De Barri's wood the British
    soldiers burst,
The French artillery drove them back, diminished
    and dispersed,
The bloody Duke of Cumberland beheld with anxious
    eye,
And ordered up his last reserve, his latest chance to
    try.
On Fontenoy—on Fontenoy, how fast his generals
    ride!
And mustering come his chosen troops, like clouds at
    even-tide.

Six thousand English veterans in stately column
    tread,
Their cannon blaze in front and flank, Lord Hay is at
    their head;
Steady they step adown the slope—steady they climb
    the hill;

Steady they load—steady they fire, moving right onward still,
Betwixt the wood and Fontenoy, as though a furnace
blast;
Through rampart, trench, and palisade, and bullets
showering fast;
And on the open plain above they 'rose and kept their
course,
With ready fire and grim resolve, they mocked at hostile force;
Past Fontenoy—past Fontenoy, while thinner grow
their ranks—
They break, as broke the Zuyder Zee through Holland's ocean banks.

More idly than the summer flies, French tirailleurs
rush 'round:
As stubble to the lava tide, French squadrons strew
the ground;
Bomb-shell and grape, and round-shot tore, still on
they marched and fired—
Fast, from each volley, grenadier and voltigeur retired.
"Push on, my household cavalry!" King Louis madly
cried;
To death they rush, but rude their shock—not un-
avenged they died.
On through the camp the column trod—King Louis
turns his rein;
"Not yet, my liege," Saxe interposed, "the Irish troops
remain!"
And Fontenoy, famed Fontenoy, had been a Waterloo,
Were not these exiles ready then, fresh, vehement, and
true.

"Lord Clare," he says, "you have your wish, there are
    your Saxon foes!"
The marshal almost smiled to see, so furiously he
    goes!
How fierce the look these exiles wear, who're wont to
    be so gay,
The treasured wrongs of fifty years are in their hearts
    today—
The treaty broken, ere the ink wherewith 'twas writ,
    could dry,
Their plundered homes, their ruined shrines, their
    women's parting cry—
Their priesthood hunted down like wolves, their
    country overthrown!
Each looks as if revenge for all were staked on him
    alone.
On Fontenoy, on Fontenoy, nor ever yet elsewhere,
Pushed on to fight a nobler band than those proud
    exiles were.

O'Brien's voice is hoarse with joy, as halting he com-
    mands,
"Fix bay'nets—charge,"—Like mountain storm rush
    on these fiery bands!
Thin is the English column now, and faint their vol-
    leys grow,
Yet must'ring all the strength they have, they made a
    gallant show.
They dress their ranks upon the hill to face that battle
    wind;
Their bayonets the breakers' foam; like rocks the men
    behind!

One volley crashes from their line, when through the
    surging smoke,
With empty guns clutched in their hands, the head-
    long Irish broke,
On Fontenoy, on Fontenoy, hark to that fierce huzza!
"Revenge! remember Limerick! dash down the Sas-
    senagh!

Like lions leaping at a fold when mad with hunger's
    pang,
Right up against the English line the Irish exiles
    sprang.
Bright was their steel, 'tis bloody now, their guns are
    filled with gore;
Through shattered rank, and severed piles, and
    trampled flags they tore;
The English strove with desperate strength, paused,
    rallied, staggered, fled—
The green hill-side is matted close with dying and with
    dead.
Across the plain and far away passed on their hideous
    wrack,
While cavalier and fantassin dash in upon their track.
On Fontenoy, on Fontenoy, like eagles in the sun,
With bloody plumes the Irish stand—the field is
    fought and won!

THE GREEN ABOVE THE RED.

Full often when our fathers saw the red above the
    green,
They rose in rude but fierce array, with sabre, pike
    and skeen,
And over many a noble town, and many a field of
    dead,
They proudly set the Irish green above the English
    red.

But in the end, throughout the land, the shameful sight
    was seen—
The English red in triumph high above the Irish
    green;
But well they died in breach and field, who, as their
    spirits fled,
Still saw the green maintain its place above the Eng-
    lish red.

And they who saw, in after times, the red above the
    green,
Were withered as the grass that dies beneath the forest
    screen;
Yet often by this healthy hope their sinking hearts
    were fed,
That, in some day to come, the green should flutter
    o'er the red.

Shure it was for this Lord Edward died, and Wolfe
    Tone sunk serene—
Because they could not bear to leave the red above the
    green;
And 'twas for this that Owen fought and Sarsfield
    nobly bled—
Because their eyes were hot to see the green above the
    red.

So when the strife began again, our darling Irish green
Was down upon the earth, while high the English red
    was seen;
Yet still we held our fearless course for something in
    us said,
Before the strife is o'er you'll see the green above the
    red.

And 'tis for this we think and toil, and knowledge
    strive to glean,
That we may pull the English red below the Irish
    green;
And leave our sons sweet liberty, and smiling plenty
    spread,
Above the land once dark with blood—the green
    above the red.

The jealous English tyrant has banned the Irish green,
And forced us to conceal it like a something foul and
    mean;
But yet, by Heaven! he'll sooner raise his victim from
    the dead
Than force our hearts to leave the green and cotton to
    the red.

We'll trust ourselves, for God is good, and blesses
    those who lean
On their brave hearts, and not upon an earthly king or
    queen;
And, freely as we lift our hands we vow our blood to
    shed,
Once and forever more to raise the green above the
    red.

SKETCH OF JAMES O'SULLIVAN.

James O'Sullivan, the National Secretary, was born in Ballygarvan Parish, County Cork, Ireland, August 29th, 1851, and was educated in the Irish National schools. He served an apprenticeship in the grocery business in the city of Cork, and in 1870 immigrated to this country and settled in Westerly, R. I., where he learned the trade of granite cutting. In October, 1871, he became a member of Division No. 1 of Westerly, and subsequently served as President and Secretary of that body. He was one of the organizers of Company B, Third Regiment, C. N. G., and served seven years as a member of that organization and was for four years its First Lieutenant. In 1882 he moved to Philadelphia, where he worked at his trade for four years. In 1886 he entered the civil service examination for the position of letter carrier in the Philadelphia Post Office, and was appointed by Postmaster Harrity in 1886. He was removed from the Postal Service in 1892 because of entering a protest against the interpretation of the Eight Hour Law for letter carriers. He then secured a position with the Postal Record, then published in New York, where he was employed until October, 1893, when he was appointed Inspector of Stations in the Philadelphia Post Office by Postmaster Carr. One year later he was promoted to the position of Superintendent of City Delivery Division, which position he now holds. He became connected with Division No. 7 of Philadelphia, and

JAMES O'SULLIVAN,
NATIONAL SECRETARY, PHILADELPHIA.

afterwards was one of the organizers of Division No.
13, of which he is now President. He served for several years as Secretary of the County Board of Philadelphia and attended the National Convention of the
order held in Louisville, Ky., in 1888; in New Orleans,
La., in 1892, and in Detroit, Mich., in 1896, Trenton,
N. J., 1898. He has been delegate to every State Convention in Pennsylvania since 1886, and has always
taken an active interest in the affairs of the organization. He has always been connected with labor organizations, and was at one time Vice-President of the
Federation of Trade and Labor Unions of the United
States and Canada, to which position he was elected
at Chicago, Ill., in 1884. He was also the first Deputy
Grand Knight of the Knights of Columbus in Pennsylvania. His well known connection with every patriotic
Irish organization and with labor organizations has
made him popular with those who know him, and in
his position as National Secretary he has maintained
the same popularity which he has merited by his distinguished services for all the organizations with which
he has been connected in the past.

THE HISTORY OF THE
Ancient Order of Hibernians.

By Thos. F. McGrath.

The Ancient Order of Hibernians, as its name indicates, is a society composed exclusively of Irishmen by birth or descent, and practical Roman Catholics, organized in Ireland for the preservation of the Catholic Church and the protection of the priest and schoolmaster, who were hunted like wolves, with a price set upon their heads and of those who would grant them a shelter or refuge. Of these days of persecution and suffering, Edmund Burke says, that the ingenuity of the human intellect never devised an instrument so calculated to exterminate a race or degrade a nation as the system of British tyranny did to the Irish people. There has been a great deal said as to when and where the Ancient Order of Hibernians was first organized. Some authorities place it at 1642, when Pope Urban the Eighth sent his blessing to the Irish people and encouraged them in their fight for God and country. Again, it is given as 1651, in Connaught, after Cromwell's infamous edict of "To Hell or to Connaught." The history of the Ancient Order of Hibernians is practically the history of Ireland, as its members took an active part in all the struggles and efforts of the old Celtic chiefs to throw off the hated Saxon yoke. According to such authorities as MacGeoghegan's and Mitchell's, Wright's, Leekey's, O'Holleran's, and Robinson's History of Ireland, it was organized in 1565 by one Rory Oge O'Moore in the County of Kildare, Province of Leinster, Ireland. In 1565 the Earl of Sussex issued a proclamation making the penalty death to any priest found in the Province of Leinster. It was then that Rory Oge O'Moore organized the Defenders. He made arrangements with the clergy to erect rude altars in the mountain fastnesses, and there have the people attend the Holy Sacrifice of the Mass. Without printed constitutions or a code of laws for their guidance they met together, not in gilded and upholstered halls, with rich carpets, but in the mountain fastnesses with the canopy of heaven for a shelter and the stars their only guide to the trysting place. Strong hands grasped in friendship and true hearts beat in unison, bound together by sacred ties and united for a common purpose, they resolved to resist to the utmost every encroachment of despotism upon the liberties and rights of the people and pledged eternal friendship, hallowed by their country's misfortune. Rory sent out fleet-footed and trusted men to inform the Catholics of the country where the priest would read the next Mass. He placed sentinels on the hilltops to give warning to the people of the approach of sacreligious intruders. Those sentinels stood on the hills and mountains while the winter winds howled and moaned around them with the sleet cutting into their unprotected faces.

They found a place to shelter the hunted priest. Sometimes it would be in an isolated cabin in the mountain's glens, where he would be welcomed with a Cead Millie Failtha regardless of the danger incurred for harboring a priest, but often it would be in the cold and dismal caves in the mountains.

In 1577 Sir Francis Cosby, commanding Queen Elizabeth's troops in Leix and Offally, concocted a fiendish plot to murder the chief families of the Irish clans with the full knowledge and approval of Sir Henry Sidney, the Lord Deputy of Ireland. Cosby feigned great friendship for the Irish and invited them to a grand feast in the rath of Mullaghmast. The O'Nolans, O'Kellys, O'Moores, etc., responded to the invitation, and as they entered the rath they were seized and butchered by the blood-thirsty Sassenach. One hundred and eighty of O'Moore's kinsmen were massacred that day. Rory tracked Cosby and his minions with a sword of vengeance, and when they least expected, he would swoop down upon them and with fire and sword exact a terrible revenge. Cosby was slain at the Yellow Ford, near Armagh, at the bloody battle of Glenmalure, with the red flag of Eng-

land in the dust and Lord Gray de Wilton and his
Saxon army flying before the terrible charge of the
Irish under the command of Feach McHugh O'Byrine
of Ballinacor. The avenging sword of the Defenders
sought out Cosby and swiftly sent him before his God
to answer for his crimes.

The annals commemorate the death of Rory Oge as
follows:

Rory Oge, son of Rory, son of Conall O'Moore, fell
by the hand of Brian Oge, son of Brian McGilla
Patrick, June 30th, 1578. After the death of Rory,
Donald O'Driscoll was elected chief of the Defenders,
who continued to protect the priest and harass the Red
Coats until December 24th, 1594, when with six of his
men he was escorting the Rev. Father O'Connor to
the trysting place near Bray, County Wicklow, where
he was to celebrate the midnight Mass. They were
surprised by a company of English soldiers, and, after
a bloody fight, Donald and his companions were killed.
Donald's head was taken across the sea and placed on
a spike on the Tower of London. Thus died the
founders of the Ancient Order of Hibernians—fighting for church and country. Donald was succeeded by
Owen O'Moore, son of Rory Oge, who continued in the
same line as his father, besides assisting the old Celtic
chiefs in their efforts to drive the British tyrants out of
Ireland. Owen was with Hugh O'Neil at the siege of
Armagh and on August 10th, 1595, the Defenders dis-

tinguished themselves by their bravery at the battle of
Clontribet, and as a token of merit they were detailed
by O'Neil to lay siege to Porteloise, a fort held by the
English in Leix. After a five days' siege the fort sur-
rendered. The Defenders now joined O'Neil in the attack on Portmore Castle and continued with him until
he drove the English and Scotch from the north and
west of Ireland. The people of the north and west enjoyed two years of peace and prosperity under O'Neil's
government, but in 1601 Queen Elizabeth sent the
butcher, Sir Peter Carew, to Ireland as Lord President. With the view of breaking O'Neil's power he
forged letters purporting that they came from Earl
Desmond, offering to betray his confederate, O'Connor. Those letters were shown to O'Connor and with
an offer of friendship and a thousand pounds from
Carew if he would forstall Desmond and hand him a
prisoner to the English. This O'Connor did. Carew
next induced Nial Garv O'Donnell and Art
O'Neil to take up arms against Hugh O'Neil. Carew
having the Irish divided, placed himself at the head of
British troops and put man, woman and child to the
sword, old and young, not even sparing the innocent
babe in its mother's arms. Ireland being under the
dominion of the English once more, the Defenders
took to the mountains, there defying England and her
hirelings. Owen now commenced to increase the
membership of his organization by uniting with other

Irishmen, who like himself, refused to submit to British rule in Ireland. Branches sprung up all over the northern and western parts of the country. They were known by different names, such as Tories, Rapperees, Defenders, etc.

England offered large rewards for the capture of Owen O'Moore, dead or alive, who continued to defy them until he was captured through the treachery of a traitor, one Corney Doyle, on the night of May the 12th. Owen and Captain O'Brien were returning to their rendezvous after leaving Father O'Roarke in the cabin of a friend. They were fired upon by British soldiers, who lay in ambush awaiting their return. O'Brien was instantly killed, while Owen was danger-ously wounded and taken prisoner. Two days later he was taken before a magistrate and given a hurried trial, after which he was sentenced to be hung, drawn and quartered. He was executed on the morning of May 16th, 1619, four days after his arrest. The Defenders continued under different leaders from the death of Owen until they became a part of an oath-bound or-ganization, known as the Confederation of Kilkenny. In 1641 the prelates and laymen of the church issued a proclamation calling upon all Catholics to take the oath. Sir Phelim O'Neil was appointed to the com-mand of the old Irish, who were tall and huge of frame. Lords Gormanstown and Mountgarret had charge of the Anglo-Irish, who were weak and low of

stature. The Lords of the Pale or Anglo-Irish are
the descendants of Strongbow and other adventurers,
who invaded Ireland from 1169 and at the time of the
Reformation stood true to the Roman Catholic
Church. Hence they were called the gentry of the
Pale. The Lords of the Pale now became convinced
that their kindly feeling towards England could not
protect them when their tenants on their own estates
were being mobbed and murdered by the blood-thirsty
demon, Coote, who could smile and become facetious
when an infant was writhing on the pike of a soldier,
and his barbarities in Wicklow are beyond description.
His threat of not leaving a Catholic in Ireland began to
gain some truth. Finglas, Clontarf and Santry were
the scenes of the most wanton and brutal murders.
Thus it was that the old Celtic Irish and the Lords of
the Pale met on the hill of Crofty and plighted a
solemn vow and swore to bury in oblivion the feuds
and dissensions which had for four hundred years
wasted their strength and now left them a prey to the
designs and hatred of the common enemy. At the
meeting in Knockcrofty, in the County of Meath, were
present Sir Phelim O'Neil, the Earl of Fingall, Lords
Slane, Neeterville, Gormanstown, Trimbleston,
Mountgarret, Dunsany, Colonel Hugh McMahon, the
Very Rev. Heber McMahon, Vicar General of Clogher, Sir Connor McGinniss, etc. Lord Gormanstown
presided. Delegates were elected to attend the Na-

tional Synod in the City of Kilkenny, October 14th, 1642, it being the first annual meeting of the Federation. At this meeting there were eleven spiritual and fourteen temporal peers and 226 commoners, representing the Catholics of Ireland. Lord Mountgarret was chosen president at the annual meeting and six persons as delegates for each province.

FOR MUNSTER.

The Viscount Roche, Edmund Fitzmaurice, Sir Daniel O'Brien, Robert Lambert, Dr. Fennell and George Comyn.

FOR ULSTER.

The Archbishop of Armagh, the Bishop of Down, Colonel Hugh McMahon, Phillip O'Rielly, Heber McGinniss and Turlough O'Neil.

FOR CONNAUGHT.

The Bishop of Clonfert, the Viscount Mayo, the Archbishop of Tuam, Sir Lucas Dillon, Patrick Darcy and George Brown.

FOR LEINSTER.

The Archbishop of Dublin, Nicholas Plunket, Richard Belling, James Cusack, Lords Gormanstown and Mountgarret.

Those delegates represented four-fifths of the people of Ireland. They formed the National government under whose legislature the Catholics struggled for three years against bigoted and tyrannical England for the right to worship God according to their conscience. Had the Catholics abandoned all that they were taught to believe sacred and forswear it in public, there is no system of impiety, blasphemy or atheism into which they might not throw themselves and profess it openly with the sanction of the British government, provided they would abjure the Roman Catholic faith. The Catholics, however, adhered to the faith of their ancestors, taught them by the holy St. Patrick, and defied the British government and its hirelings in their persecutions and confiscations, and stood true to the Church of Rome. In 1642 the Defenders lost their identity as a national organization. They became part and parcel of the Confederationists, but as an organization they continued to hold together and were assigned to the command of Phelim O'Neil. Pope Urban the Eighth sent Father Scarampi with a purse of $30,000 and his blessing to the Irish Catholics. King Charles the First now became alarmed at the action of the Irish and decided to treat with them for peace. He appointed the Marquis of Ormond as peace commissioner, urging him to use all his powers in diplomacy (treachery) to bring the Irish to terms. At the first conference held in Ormond's Camp at Sigginstown, September 15th, 1643, a compromise treaty was effected as follows:

First—The Catholics of Ireland are to enjoy the free and public exercise of their religion.

Second—They are to hold and have secured to them all Catholic churches not now in the hands of the Protestants.

Third—The Catholics shall be exempt from the jurisdiction of the Protestant clergy.

Fourth—The Catholics agree to send 10,000 men to assist King Charles at Chester. The old Celtic Chiefs were forced to accept the terms, as the Lords of the Pale threatened to leave the Federation and take up arms for King Charles if the terms were rejected. Mr. Nugent Robinson, in referring to the treaty, says: "The Irish by signing the treaty of Sigginstown lost their golden opportunity. The tide which set in so gloriously for Irish independence rolled back its sobbing waves slowly and sadly toward the English coast and has never since returned with the same hopeful freedom and overpowering strength." The treaty being a compromise, was not satisfactory to the old Celtic chieftains, as they were fighting for country and conscience. Before 1644 the English ruthlessly and dishonorably violated the treaty and the persecutions of the Catholics continued with increased vigor and hatred. October 21st, 1645, John Baptist Rinuccini, the Envoy of Pope Innocent the Tenth, landed in Kenmare Bay with supplies, besides $36,000, 2,000 muskets, 2,000 pike heads, etc., sent by Father Luke Wadding. Rinuccini sent the supplies and arms to Owen Roe O'Neil, urging him to strike another blow for God and country. O'Neil was not slow in accepting the invitation, for on June the 1st, 1646, he marched with 5,000 foot and 400 horse to attack General Monroe, who was then at Armagh. Monroe having a much superior force than O'Neil came forth to give battle on the morning of the 5th. O'Neil kept him engaged for four hours, when Monroe resolved to retreat to Armagh. Owen Roe, seeing the advantage gained, gave the command to charge. With a cry of vengeance the Irish dashed down upon the enemy and after a fierce and bloody struggle the English fled, leaving 3,000 dead upon the field. Monroe fled so precipitately that he left his hat, sword and cloak upon the field. The Irish had 70 killed and 200 wounded. Thus ended the battle of Benburb, a glorious victory for church and country. Owen Roe O'Neil died suddenly at Cloughoughter Castle, County Cavan, November 6th, 1649, while on his march south against Cromwell, who had landed in Ireland August 14th, 1649. The murders and massacres that followed from the siege of Drogheda to Hugh Dubh O'Neil's evacuation of Clonmell, were ferocious, savage and brutal. On and after September 11, 1654, rewards of five pounds sterling were offered for a priest's or wolf's head. Any person giving shelter to a priest should suffer death and the loss of their property. Any person knowing the place of concealment of a priest and not disclosing it to the authorities was publicly whipped and suffered the loss of both ears.   Everything that the ingenuity of the human intellect could devise was resorted to to crush the people and stamp out of existence the Catholic Church of Ireland.

A. M. Sullivan, in his splendid work, the Story of Ireland, quoting from Cassell's History of Ireland, says: "The eighteenth century was the era of persecution in which the law did the work of the sword. Then was established a code framed with almost diabolical ingenuity to extinguish natural affection, to foster perfidy and hypocrisy, to petrify conscience, to perpetuate brutal ignorance, to facilitate the work of tyranny, by rendering the vices of slavery inherent and natural in the Irish character, and to make Protestantism almost irredeemabley odious as the monstrous incarnation of all moral perversions.   Having no rights or franchises; no legal protecton of life or property; disqualified to handle a gun even as a common soldier or a gamekeeper; forbidden even to acquire the elements of knowledge at home or abroad; forbidden even to render to God what conscience dictated as his due; what could the Irish be but abject serfs? What nation in their circumstances could have been otherwise? Is it not amazing that any social virtue could have survived such an ordeal? That any seeds of good, any roots of national greatness could have outlived such a long tempestuous winter?"

In 1695 the following laws were enacted under Lord

Capel: Catholic gentlemen were fined 60 pounds ($300.00) for absence from Protestant form of worship. They were forbidden to travel five miles from their houses, to keep arms, to maintain suits at law, any four justices of the peace could without further trial banish any man for life, if he refused to attend the Protestant services.   Any two justices of the peace could call any man over 16 years of age before them, and if he re-refused to renounce the Catholic religion, they could bestow his property to the next of kin.   No Catholic could employ a Catholic schoolmaster to educate his children, and if he sent his child abroad for education, he was fined 100 pounds ($500), and the child could not inherit any property either in England or Ireland. Any Catholic priest who came to the country should be hanged. Any Protestant suspecting another Protestant of holding property in trust for any Catholic, might file against the suspected trustee, and take the property from him.   Any Protestant might take away the horse of a Catholic, no matter how valuable, by simply paying five pounds ($25.00).   Any Catholic gentleman's child, no matter how young, by becoming a Protestant could take possession of his father's estate and property, and have a guardian appointed.

Any Protestant seeing a Catholic tenant on a farm that in his opinion yielded one-third more than the yearly rent, could, by swearing to the same, take possession of the farm.   Horses and wagons belonging to

Catholics were in all cases to be seized for the use of the militia.

Those were days that tried men's souls when the sons and daughters of Erin would steal into the mountain glens and valleys under the cover of night to be present at the holy Sacrifice of the Mass, there to kneel in prayer while the cold winter winds howled and shrieked around them. The Defenders stood as sentinels to give warning of the approach of the bandogs of the law who were seeking the head of the priest that they might claim the five pounds reward offered for it by the English government.

On one occasion a congregation of Roman Catholics were assembled in a church in Dublin to adore the living God. The Protestant justices hearing of it, dispatched to the chapel a host of sacreligious ruffians of whom, to their eternal dishonor, the leaders were the archbishop, the mayor and recorder of Dublin. They entered the chapel in the midst of divine service, dragged the priest from the altar, hacked and hewed the images and other ornaments and like common robbers purloined the crucifixes, copes and chalices and other valuables. According to Sheridan a ruffian is a brutal, boisterous, mischievous fellow, and would any but a ruffian head a licentious band of mercenary soldiers in an attack upon an unarmed and defenceless body of men, women and children in the solemn act of worshipping the living God, or deface and destroy his altars

and purloin the ornaments consecrated to his worship?
Were the question taken on this point among a million
of candid men there would, I feel confident, be an
unanimous negative vote.*

Matters continued in this condition until 1745, when
the Catholics were granted the right of public worship.
Priests and friars went around unmolested, enjoying
a freedom they were denied for over a century.   Although the penalty of death for being a priest was
withdrawn and the right granted to the people to worship God in public, persecutions of the Catholics continued for over a hundred years longer, as in 1847,
when famine and pestilence ravaged our fair land,
when the tongue of the nursing child stuck to the roof
of its mouth from thirst and died on its mother's breast.
The base and treacherous hand of England could be
seen using hunger as an instrument of torture, trying
to get the unfortunate Catholic to forswear his religion
and sell his birthright for a mess of pottage. The Defenders now turned their attention to the persecuted
farmer, who was evicted from his holding on every
pretext that the ingenuity of the agent of an absentee
landlord could devise, and the farm turned into pasture
land to raise cattle for the English market.   The unfortunate farmer is driven to squat upon the bogs and
marshes trying to raise a crop upon the cut-away bogs,
and trying to make soil by scraping down the barren

---

*M. Carey's Ireland Vindicated.

rock from the mountain side. The condition of the
peasantry was most pitiable. The little plots of potato
ground were let at a rental of six pounds sterling per
acre, but this was not paid in coin; it was worked out
at the rate of six pence per day, so that for one acre of
potato ground a man had to work 240 days for the
landlord, leaving him only 73 days to toil for himself
and family, pay tithe to the Protestant clergyman and
contribute to the support of the parish priest. The Defenders organized branches throughout the north and
west of Ireland. Their object was the protection of the
laborer in his wages and to prevent wherever possible
the ejectment of farmers from their holdings, who were
unable to pay oppressive rents and tithes, to prevent
land grabbing, and the putting of farms and houses up
to the highest bidder. In 1760 kindred organizations
made their appearance in the south of Ireland, known
as White Boys, Levellers, etc. The country was in a
deplorable condition. Farmers were evicted with their
families, and without industries or other resources to
procure an existence. Can it be wondered at that
crimes were committed? Is it reasonable to expect
that the Catholics could be satisfied with magistrates
and landlords who acted towards them only through
the medium of their prejudices and bigotry. Lord
Chesterfield, speaking of the unsettled state of the
country, in the fifth volume of his letters, says it can be
ascribed to the sentiment in every human breast, that

asserts man's natural rights to liberty and good usage, and which will and ought to rebel when provoked to a certain degree.

Committees were appointed by the British parliament to inquire into the cause of Irish disturbances. Sir George Cornewall Lewis, in his book, "Causes of Irish Disturbances," at page 49 cites the evidence of an inspector of police taken before this committee:— Question. To what do you attribute the long disturbances prevailing among the lower order in Munster? Answer. I think a great deal of disturbance has arisen about the rents. The land during the war was set very high in most parts of Ireland and in peace there was a great reduction in the price of produce and the landlords were proceeding to distress the tenantry by demanding those high rents which the produce of the land did not enable them to pay and I think that that caused a number of persons to be turned out of their farms and from that arose a number of outrages from the dispossessed tenants. Another witness is asked what was the object of these movements. Answer: It appears that it originated from the conduct of a gentleman on the estate of Lord Courtenay in the County of Limerick. He was very severe toward the tenants and the people who were in wealth previous to his coming were reduced to poverty and they thought proper to retaliate upon him and his family and upon those who took their land. Mr. Leslie

Foster, a member of parliament, when asked his opinion, says: I think the proximate cause is the extreme physical misery of the peasantry coupled with their liability to be called upon for the payment of different charges which it is often practically impossible for them to meet. The immediate cause of these disturbances I conceive to be the attempt to enforce these demands by the various processes of law. The next to be examined, who was Chief Justice Blackburne of the Queen's Bench, who says in reference to an eviction on the estate of Lord Stradbroke: The agent, attended by the sheriff, went upon the land and dispossessed a numerous body of occupants, they prostrated the houses leaving the people to carry away the timber. The number of persons that were thus deprived of their houses on that occasion was very large. I am sure that there were about forty families, but I cannot tell you the number of individuals. They were persons of all ages and sexes and in particular an old woman almost in the extremity of death. Q. What do you conceive became of them? A. I should think they have been received from charity up and down the country.

Sir George Cornewall Lewis, in summing up the evidence, says: All the above witnesses agree in a remarkable manner with regard to the causes of the Whiteboy disturbances. All trace them to the miserable condition of the peasantry—to their liability to certain charges, the chief of which is rent, which they are very often unable to meet, and to their anxiety to retain possession of land which is to them a necessary of life, the alternative being starvation. With the dread of this alternative before their eyes it is not to be wondered at that they make desperate efforts to avert it. That crime and disturbance should be the consequence of actual ejectment is still more natural.

The wretched condition of the mass of the Irish peasantry, their inability to obtain employment for hire and their consequent dependence on land drive them to a system of combination for self-defense against ejectment from their holding to be driven to utter destitution; to a state in which himself and family can only rely on a most precarious charity to save them from exposure to the elements, from nakedness, and from starvation. It is natural that the most improvident person should seek to struggle against such fearful consequences as these, that they should try to use some means of quieting apprehensions which would themselves be sufficient to embitter the life of the most thoughtless; and it is to afford this security that the Ribbon combination was formed.

The Ribbonmen's association may be considered as a vast trades union for the protection of the Irish peasantry, the object being not to regulate the rate of wages or the hours of work, but to keep the actual occupant in the possession of his land and in general to regulate the relation of landlord and tenant for the benefit of the latter.

Mr. Baron Fletcher, reviewing the causes of the disturbed state of Ireland, in his address to the grand jury in the County of Wexford in 1814, said in part: Ribbonism is the product of oppression. The mere pittance which the high rents leave the poor peasantry is taken from them by large county assessments. Roads are frequently planned and made not for the general good of the country but to suit the particular views of a neighboring landholder at the public expense. Such abuses shake the very foundation of the law. They ought to be checked. Superadded to these mischiefs are the permanent and occasional absentee landlords residing in another country, not known to their tenantry but by their agents who extract the uttermost penny of the value of the lands. If the lease happens to fall they sell the farm by public auction to the highest bidder, no gratitude for past services, no preference of the fair offer, no predilection for the ancient tenantry, be they ever so deserving. But if the highest price be not acceeded to, the depopulation of the entire tract of country ensues. What then is the wretched peasant to do? Chased from the spot where he had first drawn his breath, where he had first seen the light of heaven, incapable of procuring any other means of existence, vexed with those exactions I have enumerated and harassed by the payment of tithes, can we be surprised that a tenant of unenlightened mind, of uneducated habits, should rush upon the perpetration of crime, followed by the punishment of the rope and the gibbet? Nothing remains for them thus harassed and thus destitute, but with strong hand to deter the stranger from intruding upon their farms and to extort from the weakness and terrors of their landlords (from whose gratitude or good feeling they have failed to win it), a kind of preference for the ancient tenantry.

In 1771 the Steel Boys made their appearance in the north of Ireland. They were the predecessors of the Orangemen. 1780 came the Protestant and Peep O'Day Boys. 1795 came the Orangemen. The British government looked upon every Irish Catholic as being a rebel and treated him as such. The magistrates encouraged the Orangemen in their persecutions of the Catholics, whose houses they burned, murdered the inmates, wrecked their churches and desecrated their altars. The Catholics were driven from the place of their birth, where they first saw the light of heaven, and were arrested and punished for crimes committed by the Orangemen. Such unheard of cruelty and unmitigated acts of barbarity as was practiced by judges and Orangemen are without a parallel in the annals of any country in Christendom, save in Ireland herself in the days of Elizabeth and Cromwell. It is absurd to imagine that justice could be fairly administered when the administration of justice was in the hands of Orangemen, who were opposed to everything Roman Catholic, and are sworn to do all in their power to extermine the Papist of Ireland, and yet the Catholics were expected to be loyal to a government which not only deprived them of their civil rights, but places the execution of the laws in the hands of their bitterest enemies. It now became necessary that the Catholics should combine for self-preservation against the common enemy. The Defenders of the north and the White Boys of the south joined hands and adopted the name of Ribbonmen. They used two pieces of ribbon as the symbol of their organization—green and red. The green denoted unity, and the red blood for blood. This organization rendered valuable aid to the unfortunate Catholic, who goes to the Orange agent a few shillings short in his rent and begs for a few weeks' time to make up the deficiency. This bigoted Orangeman takes the money and hurls it at the unfortunate man's head and orders him to return with the full amount in two hours or he would eject him from his holding. This insolent agent displays his bigotry by pouring invective upon the poor man's head, whose only crime is his poverty. His spirit is broken down with the struggles and sufferings of life, yet he hears his honesty impugned, his efforts ridiculed and his character blackened. There cannot be any sympathy between these men, one is the oppressor, the other the oppressed. This struggling man is told he is to have no home, no house to shelter himself, his wife and children to be turned out upon the cold world without the

means to sustain their physical existence. He has sold
his wheat, oats and meal at a ruinous loss to try to
make up the rent to satisfy this tyrannical agent. Is it
any wonder that crimes were committed? That landlords and agents were assassinated when the people
had to deal with such demons as Lord Leitrim and his
kind, who would drive the people to desperation and
rob their daughters of their honor? One day the bailiffs and constabulary appeared near Ballymena,
County Antrim, to eject a poor and feeble old woman,
the Widow McGuire, from her little farm. The people
from the neighboring parishes assembled and determined if possible to prevent the ejectment, but resistance was of little avail, as the bailiffs and constabulary
were there in force and well armed. The bailiffs led
the poor old woman out of her cabin and her feeble and
trembling limbs, gray hair and miserable appearance,
added to her great age, produced a strong impression
upon the spectators. Next came her little grand-
children and their mother in tears. The bailiffs cast
their bed and bedding with what little furniture they
possessed into the road and levelled the house to the
ground. Thus was evicted the Widow Mollie Mc-
Guire, whose name afterward became so famous from
being signed to all threatening letters and notices sent
out by Ribbonmen and others. The Orangemen posted
notices on the doors of Catholic families ordering them
to leave the place. If they did not leave at the time

specified on the notice they would assemble at night, burn down the houses and force the families to fly for their lives. The Orangemen, encouraged by the magistrates, continued their hellish pastime of burnings and murdering. In 1796 they either murdered or drove from their homes in the county of Armagh 7,000 people. The wretched people had no place of shelter to fly to. Some of them took to the mountains, others were put in prison and died. The young men were packed off to the seaport and drafted on board of an English man-o'-war. Is it any wonder that the Ribbonmen held midnight meetings and devised plans by which they would protect themselves from murderers and the hirelings of a bigoted government, who advocated the extermination of the Papist by fire and sword? In 1808, during the administration of the Duke of Richmond, a party of Orangemen fired into an assemblage of Catholic men, women and children who were enjoying themselves around a garland pole at Corinshiga, a mile and a half from the town of Newry. One man by the name of McKeown was killed and several wounded. One of the magistrates, a Mr. Waring, sent the depositions of the Catholics to the officials at the castle in Dublin, asking the government to issue a proclamation offering a reward for the apprehension of the murderers. The secretary, Mr. Traill, replied that the government declined to take any steps in the matter.

In July of the same year the Orangemen murdered the Rev. Father Duane at Mountrath. In 1809 they murdered a Mr. Kavanagh in his own house, beating out his brains in the presence of his wife and children. Again at Balieborough in the county of Cavan the Orangemen attacked the house of the parish priest, fired several shots and left the priest for dead. Not satisfied with this they wrecked the chapel and insulted and wounded every Catholic that they met that day. Still the government refused to take any steps to protect the Catholics or puish the guilty Orangemen. Is it any wonder that the Ribbonmen sometimes took the law in their own hands and retaliated on those miscreants who were encouraged in their acts of crime against the Catholics by the government?

Edmund Burke says the crimes of the English against the Irish people may justly be regarded one of the blackest pages in the history of persecutions. Again, in speaking of the disturbed condition of the country, he says: "These rebellions were not produced by toleration, but by persecutions. They arose not from just and mild government, but from the most unparalleled oppressions." After one hundred and sixty years of penal laws and persecutions, God, as if by miracle, preserved the faith, virtue, vitality and power of the Irish race. Branches of the Ribbonmen began to spring up in England and Scotland under the name of the Hibernian Society and the Hibernia Sick and

Funeral Society, as the name Ribbonmen was out-lawed by the British government. In 1825 the name in Ireland was changed from the Ribbonmen to that of St. Patrick's Fraternal Society. It is not to be sup-posed that all these changes took place in harmony, as there was a large number of the members who rebelled against those changes and withdrew from the order and continued under the name of Mollie McGuires and Ribbonmen, especially in the county Antrim.

In those days one hundred pounds were offered by the English government to any person who would give private information where a body of Ribbonmen might be found. Although the Irish were poor and crushed by the minions of England, yet there was not one among them who would be Judas enough to take the blood money offered by a blood-thirsty govern-ment. This grand and noble society cemented its members together in the bonds of friendship, unity and true christian charity. There were no sick benefits connected with the order at that time. But the mem-bers were at all times to assist each other in every way possible when a member would arrive in England or Scotland and had a traveling card or the password and sign and if he was in distress he would receive imme-diate aid from the brothers he would meet. As each district or parish master, as they were then called, had on hand a fund of money from which he would assist the members who were in distress. There was work found for the new arrival and he was made to feel that he was a member of an organization that had for its object friendship, unity and true christian charity. The men who organized, fought and died for the Ancient Order of Hibernians are gone, but their memory still lives. Star after star sinks and leaves darker the gloom which lowers over the land of the shamrock—the country that produced a Swift, Burke, Grattan, Flood, Curran, Goldsmith, Davis, Sterne, Moore, Emmet, Wolftone, Fitzgerald, Sarsfield, Montgomery, O'Connell, Mitchell, Meagher, Parnell, Biggar, Sexton, Griffin, Davitt, Daly, Sir Charles Russell and a bright galaxy of illustrious characters. A country which has furnished almost every nation in christendom with statesmen and warriors, driven from their native soil by lordly despotism, rampant injustice and religious intolerance. A land which has produced the men on whom the destinies of Europe often depended in the field and in the cabinet.

The people and the peoples' leaders are passing away, but the Ancient Order of Hibernians continue to grow and assist the Catholic Church in her onward march for the salvation of mankind. Wherever the A. O. H. may be established there you will find its members as missionaries aiding the sick and those of their race when in distress. Thousands of emigrants who have emigrated to this land of liberty have been assisted in procuring employment and aided in every way possible by the members of the Ancient Order of Hibernians. In 1836 some of the members who had emigrated to America wished to organize a branch of the order in New York city. They communicated their desires to their brothers in Ireland and in June they received the following instructions from the men in Ireland, to wit:

Brothers, Greeting—Be it known to you and to all it may concern, that we send to our few brothers in New York full instructions with our authority to establish branches of our society in America. The qualification for membership must be as follows:

First—All members must be Roman Catholics and Irish or Irish descent, and of good and moral character, and none of your members shall join in any secret societies contrary to the laws of the Catholic Church, and at all times and at all places your motto shall be:

"FRIENDSHIP, UNITY AND TRUE CHRISTIAN CHARITY."

You must love without dissimulation, hating evil, cleaving to good. Love one another with brotherly love, without preventing one another, let the love of brotherhood abide in you, and forget not hospitality to your emigrant brother that may land on your shores, and we advise you, above all things, have natural charity among yourselves.

Also be it known unto you that our wish and prayer is that when you form your society, in many cities or towns, you will do all that is in your power to aid and protect your Irish sisters from all harm and temptation. As the Irish woman is known for her chastity all over the world; some of them may differ from you in religion, but, brothers, bear in mind that our good Lord died for all, therefore be it known unto you that our wish is that you do all that you can for the Irish emigrant girls, no matter who they may be, and God will reward you in your new country, and doing this you will keep up the high standing and honor of the Irish in America.

We send these instructions to you, hoping you will carry them out to the best of your ability. Be it known unto you that you are at liberty to make such laws as will guide your workings and for the welfare of our old society, but such laws must be at all times according to the teachings of the Holy Catholic Church, and the obligation that we send you, and all of your workings must be submitted to any Catholic priest, when called for. We send you these instructions, as we promised to do, with a young-man that works on the ship, and who called on you before. Send a copy to our late friend that you spoke of and who is now working in Pennsylvania. Hoping the bearer and this copy will land safe, and that you will treat him right, we remain your brothers in the true bonds of friendship, this 4th day of May, in the year of our Lord, 1836.

> PATRICK McGUIRE, County Fermanagh.
> JOHN RIELLY, County Cavan.
> PATRICK McKENNA, County Monahan.
> JOHN DERKIN, County Mayo.
> PATRICK REILLY, County Derry.
> PATRICK BOYLE, County Sligo.
> JOHN FARRELL, County Meath.
> THOMAS O'RORKE, County Leitrim.
> JAMES McMANUS, County Antrim.
> JOHN McMAHON, County Longford.
> PATRICK DUNN, County Tyrone.
> PATRICK HAMILL, Westmeath.
> DANIEL GALLAGHER, Glasgow.
> JOHN MURPHY, Liverpool.

TERENCE DONOGHUE,
EX-STATE DELEGATE, NEW YORK.

I am indebted to that veteran Hibernian, Terence Donohue, ex-State Delegate of New York, for the foregoing communication.

SKETCH OF TERENCE DONOGHUE.

Mr. Donoghue was born in Ballyconnelly County, Cavan, Ireland, July, 1841. He became a member of the order in 1858 and has always been a hard worker for the cause of Ireland and the elevation of the Irish race at home and abroad.

Mr. Donoghue is a thorough Irishman and a true Hibernian, and has always been a hard worker in the ranks of Hibernianism. He has ever been ready to aid a fellow countryman in distress and has sacrificed time and money for the elevation of the order in his forty years' membership in the society. He has made some very able speeches in defense of the Ancient Order of Hibernians and the Catholic Church when they were assailed by the A. P. A.'s, (a new name for Orangemen). Mr. Donohue is a true and consistent Irishman and has rendered me valuable aid in compiling this history of the Ancient Order of Hibernians.

The necessity for protection from a tyrannical government no longer existed. Their purpose being to unite all Irish Catholics in a bond of unity, friendship and true christian charity, to help the needy, console the afflicted and bury the dead, to aid and protect the

Irish emigrant and extend to him the hand of friendship in this great land of the free.   To protect Irish emigrant girls, irrespective of their religious belief, with love and respect for all, to protect them from those vultures who are seeking to ruin innocent young girls by leading them into those dens of infamy which unfortunately are to be found in large cities and seaports.

By acting as missionaries to the sons and daughters of Erin, who might land on the shores of this grand republic, so that the honor of the daughters of Erin might be upheld as a monument of chastity to our race at home and abroad.   How well the twig from the parent tree flourished is evidenced by the fact that branches or divisions sprung up in New York, Pennsylvania, Ohio, Illinois and all states in the Union, that by 1883 the A. O. H. had a membership of nearly 60,-000, with over a million dollars in its treasuries to succor its members in sickness, and to aid the widows and orphans.   The order continued to grow and prosper without anything of note occurring until 1876, when an organization that existed in Luzerne and Schuylkill Counties, Pennsylvania, known as Mollie McGuires, became in bad repute owing to some murders being committed in the coal regions, and it was alleged that they were committed by the Mollie McGuires. Several arrests followed, and among those arrested were a few members of the A. O. H., who were accused of the awful crime of murder, for which the fair name of the A. O. H. suffered in the eyes of the church; yet the officers and rank and file of the members of the order were as free from any knowledge of the crimes about to be committed as the unfortunate victims themselves. It is true that some of those convicted were known as members of the Ancient Order of Hibernians, but it does not follow that the rank and file of the order had any knowledge that those crimes were about to be committed. It is impossible for officers or members of divisions to know whether an aspirant for membership is connected with any secret organization that may be under the ban of the church, when such candidate for membership will conceal the fact when asked if he is a member of such an organization.

It is possible for a person to be known for years in a community to be of good moral character and a practical Catholic (as far as appearances go) and not be known as a member of any secret organization that encourages the taking of life. Hence the possibility of such persons getting into the A. O. H. or any other society.

The writer knew the president of a division who was highly esteemed by his parish priest. He attended Mass regularly and to all appearances lived the life of a good Catholic, and was recognized as such by all his brother members and Catholic friends. Yet it accidentally became known that he was a member of the order of Free Masons. Hence it is unjust to condemn a whole community for the acts of a few who may live in it. The national and state conventions throughout the country held in 1876 repudiated the Mollie Mc-Guires and their acts.

McMahon in his story of the anthracite regions, 1873 to 1876, says: It is not my intention to favor the law breakers or in any manner to shield crime or do I wish to paliate the crimes of the Mollies; I know that many of them are guilty of heinous violations for which they deserve punishment. But it must be confessed that many outrages are perpetrated by outside parties and sometimes by minor officials of the company with the view to promote their own interests and with the idea which is always ratified that the suspicion will at once be attached to the Mollie McGuires. Alleviating circumstances may also be found in the fact that some mine bosses, by their stubborn and willful partiality, have driven men to sheer desperation. I have known men who were compelled to quit the country because they happened to incur the displeasure of one boss. The lofty idea of superiority claimed by the higher classes over the miners tend to excite among the latter a strong prejudice. A miner must have good judgment as well as muscle and if he does not continually exercise his brains at his work he will soon have them crushed out beneath tons of coal and rock. Has not the miner to gain a living for himself and his family? Is not all his time taken up with his labor? Does he not undergo greater exposure and danger than any other class of workingmen? Where then is the justice in giving special privileges to grinding monopolies, whereby they are enabled to tyrannize over their employes and combine to invent systems, while they may seem to make trade flourish, it but tends to make the rich more wealthy and the poor almost slaves. But the time came which produced heart-rending scenes in the coal regions. McParlan (alias McKenna) became an informer. Men were arrested and hurried to their doom; many fled from their homes in fear; wives were weeping for their husbands, children for their fathers, mothers for their sons. The name Mollie McGuire became a reproach and many true minded men who knew nothing of the wicked deeds of their fellow members were regarded with suspicion. People did not stop at this but condemned the whole society as being criminal. As if a family that grieves over the untimely fate of a prodigal should be sneered at. As if the unwarranted acts of a few enthusiasts in a community should reflect discredit on the laws which they were able to transgress. People said, and said rightly, that no grievance could justify the extreme measures which were resorted to. But it will be admitted that there were grievances, that there were strong incentives, that it was not the nature of the society to produce criminals and that outside of this particular locality the Ancient Order of Hibernians claimed the respect of all classes.   The great body of the order always respected its constitution and by-laws, the spirit of which is expressed in the following verse and preamble:

"These laws, though human, spring from love divine;
 Love laid the scheme—love guides the whole design.
 Vile is the man who will evade these laws
 Or taste the sweets without sufficient cause."

The members of this order do declare that the intent and purpose of the order is to promote friendship, unity and true christian charity among its members, by raising or supporting a stock or fund of money for maintaining the aged, sick, blind and infirm members, for the legitimate expenses of the order, and for no other purpose whatsoever.

The motto of this order is friendship, unity and true christian charity:

Friendship, in assisting each other to the best of our power.

Unity, in uniting together for mutual support in sickness and distress.

True christian charity, by doing to each other and all the world as we would wish they should do unto us.

Of the power and right of the church to condemn secret societies there is, and can be, no question. She is the divinely-appointed guardian of faith and morals, and, as such, is empowered to anathematize any society or association whose doctrines or practices might taint the one or corrupt the other. In fact, it has been for more than a century the settled discipline of the Catholic Church to put outside her fold members of secret societies. Her decrees against Freemasonry, etc., are founded on the principle that these organizations are bound together by oath for purposes hostile to the church or state, and that such unholy fellowship is unlawful and entails on its members exclusion from her communion.

Whether the A. O. H. is under the ban of the church or not is, therefore, one of fact, and must be decided by reference to the authentic announcements of the Holy See and the disciplinary teachings of the archbishops and bishops of this country in council assembled. That the church has condemned secret societies is a fact, but it is also a fact that by the term "secret societies" she did not mean the A. O. H., or trades unions, or other organizations whose sole object is mutual protection and benefit. In a decree of the Sacred Congregation of the Inquisition, communicated by order of the Pope to the Archbishops and Bishops of the United States on July 13, 1865, we have the authoritative definition of the term "secret societies." The tenor of it is as follows: "The secret societies, of which mention is made in the Pontifical Constitution, are all those which propose to themselves something opposed to the church or the state." Let us judge the A. O. H. by this standard and see if it can, in any way, be included in the associations contemplated in the Pontificial Constitutions. The preamble to the constitution and by-laws of the Ancient Order of Hibernians is but a simple exposition of christian duty:

The Ancient Order of Hibernians is composed of practical Catholics who would lay down their lives for the faith. They are descendants of martyrs and the most stalwart defenders of Catholicity. During the trials of Know-Nothingism they were defenders of our churches, and they are today the most reliable opponents of imported Orangeism and anti-Catholic hate. They are the bone and sinew of the church, glorious confessors of the faith and most patriotic American citizens. Long live the Ancient Order of Hibernians!

Up to and including 1878 the constitution called for all national conventions to be held in New York city. But in 1879 the national convention was held in the city of Boston, Mass., by order of the national delegate Hart. As there was no record on the minute-book stating where the national convention should be held, some of the New York and New Jersey counties refused to send delegates to the Boston convention and would not recognize the officers elected thereat. But at the convention held in the city of Philadelphia, Pa., May 11 to 15, 1880, the trouble was happily adjusted on the following terms:

COMPROMISE.

As understood by the Committee on Grievance of the A. O. H. on the one side, the presidents of divisions of New York and New Jersey on the other, and ratified and adopted by the A. O. H. of America in convention assembled in the city of Philadelphia, May 11-15, 1880: 1st. The New York and New Jersey members not in friendship do recognize through their presidents, now present, the Philadelphia convention and the national officers elected there as the only officers of the A. O. H. in America. 2nd. We agree to carry out in spirit and letter the principles of harmony as understood by the committee of conference of both sides and ratified by the convention, to wit: That state and county officers now acting must not throw any illegal obstacles in the way of a settlement of the difficulties which now exist. 3rd. Said divisions will present themselves with roll books through their five division officers to the county delegate, who shall at once admit said division or divisions, provided there are none of the expelled names as expelled by the convention of 1878. 4th. Split divisions or divisions bearing the same number will come together with their respective roll books. Both books are to be considered as one roll book. A chairman and a secretary pro tem. be elected by both sides, who will preside at such meeting, the roll books to be given to the secretary-elect and a committee of two from each side who shall be appointed to assist him in giving the standing of each member as his name is called. This done the new division or consolidated one will proceed to elect division officers. Said officers will be the only ones entitled to vote at the state convention. 5th. That a meeting of said split divisions be duly advertised for at least two days previous to the holding of the same. 6th. State and county officers of New York will see that these instructions are carried out, if not already done. 7th. If the state convention of New York should be held in violation of these rules, and those men not given an opportunity to return as above cited, the same will be considered null and void.

Should this be acceptable to the divisions not in friendship, they will call upon the proper officers and become reconciled to harmony and friendship.

Trusting that the aforesaid is plain and easily understood, and that friendship, unity and true christian charity will prevail among all men of our race, creed and nationality.

Believe me yours fraternally,

PETER KIERNAN, N. D.

New Orleans, La., May 31st, 1880.

The Ancient Order of Hibernians continued to grow stronger until it became the most powerful and influential Irish Catholic organization in the world. It not only became a benefit to its members but to society in general. The members, as a body, also as individuals, contributed funds to many charitable institutions for the benefit of mankind, having a good will for all and malice to none. The various divisions of the order donated money for the erection of schools and orphan asylums for the homeless children of our race. Year after year the A. O. H. responded most liberally to the appeals for aid from the suffering people in Ireland, when the bishops and priests appealed to the Catholics in America to aid the starving people in the west of Ireland, (driven to starvation by a relentless and tyrannical system of landlordism, which is abetted by a bigoted government). The representatives of the Ancient Order of Hibernians telegraphed from New York City to the Archbishop of Dublin to draw on the bank of Eugene Kelly & Co. for $2,000.00 in the name of the Ancient Order of Hibernians. The order gave thousands of dollars towards the erection of a memorial church in Rome, dedicated to the memory of St. Patrick. When Brother Francis and others made the appeal for aid in the interest of the deaf and dumb and orphan children of Dublin, Ireland, the A. O. H. responded promptly and liberally. The Rev. Father Flynn, acknowledging the same, said: "May my blessing with the blessing of God and the blessing of two hundred and sixty-eight little children attend the members of the Ancient Order of Hibernians and their families." The A. O. H.

contributed funds to the land league.   It sent $3,000 to that sterling Irishman, Charles Stewart Parnell, to aid him in his fight in the English parliament for home rule for Ireland, when the six hundred scoundrels united to quell the eloquent pleadings of Charles Stewart Parnell.   These are only a few of the many charitable and patriotic acts of the A. O. H.   There is not an organization in the world in which the officers and members are so united in the work of charity as the Ancient Order of Hibernians.   What is more purely patriotic than the princely gift of $50,000 given by the members of the Ancient Order of Hibernians for the endowment of a Gaelic chair in the Catholic University at Washington, D. C., for the preservation of our language, history and literature? But unfortunately there came a time when the members of the A. O. H. disagreed.   At the national convention held at Cleveland, Ohio, May 16th, 1884, it was decided to amend the constitution so that persons who were Irish by either parent would be eligible to membership in the Ancient Order of Hibernians.   That was the first step towards the unfortunate split, which rent the order asunder for nearly fourteen years.   Another cause for dissatisfaction was the case of Hugh Murray, county delegate for New York Co.   Mr. Murray presented a bill for $265.00 which the various New York divisions had paid to emigrant brothers who had placed their cards in the aforesaid divisions.   At that time it was constitutional to pay five dollars to a member from across the water who would deposit his card in any division, provided said card was properly signed and authenticated, and upon the presentation of such card at the next annual convention the amount would be refunded to the division.   But the Cleveland convention repudiated Mr. Murray's claim.*

After the convention adjourned some of the delegates returned home very much dissatisfied.   They called meetings in their respective counties, which were well attended and the result was a meeting at Emmet's Hall, 232 West 30th street, New York City, August 12th, 1884. At that meeting it was decided to send John Nolan to Ireland to attend the quarterly meeting of the Board of Erin, for the purpose of laying the action of the Cleveland convention before them.

The result of Mr. Nolan's attendance at the Board of Erin meeting was that the quarterly communications were sent to Hugh Murray, county delegate for New York county, thus ignoring the officers elected at the Cleveland convention. The principal members of the Board of Erin at that time were Gallagher of Patrick, Scotland; Harkins, Greenock, Scotland; Kelley, Darlington, England; Reid, Liverpool, England; Devlin, County Tyrone, Ireland; Crilly, Belfast, Ire-

---

* Bro. Terence Donoghue ex-state delegate of New York states that the records of Hugh Murray's claim being a just legal one are still on the New York record book for 1884.

land; McKernan, County Fermanagh, Ireland; Rooney, Glasgow, Scotland.

The national officers elected at Cleveland were Henry F. Sheridan of Chicago, Ill., N. D.; P. H. Mc-Nelis of Indianapolis, N. S.; John McSorley of East Cambridge, Mass., N. T. The Board of Erin notified Mr. Sheridan that he and his colleagues were charged with having changed the ritual and of being members of a secret society, etc. Mr. Sheridan then called a meeting of his officers and directors. They met at the Gilsey House, New York City, August 11th, 1884, and there decided to issue the following circular to all the divisions of the A. O. H. in America:

GILSEY HOUSE CIRCULAR.

Office of National Delegate, Ancient Order of Hibernians, United States of America. ·

Chicago, Ill., August 26th, 1884.

To the Officers and Members of the Ancient Order of Hibernians, of the United States of America:

Brethren—Since the adjournment of the national convention, held at Cleveland, Ohio, May 16th, 1884, a conspiracy has been unearthed in the City of New York, which has been in secret operation for the past eighteen months, headed by the county delegate, Hugh Murray, of New York County, and aided by one Mr. Nolan, an ex-member of the Board of Erin.

The working of these conspirators terminated on

the 13th inst., in the shape of a mock convention held in Emmet Hall, New York City, and electing officers and seceding from the organization in general—proceedings unwarranted, unconstitutional, and in direct violation of our obligation. The secessionists held that all national conventions must be held in New York City; that the national officers must be residents thereof, and that the brotherhood outside of the same city are incompetent to manage the affairs of the society. Consequently to fathom these uncalled for actions, the directory and national officers met on the 11th inst., at the Gilsey House in New York City and held a consultation for the purpose of ascertaining the true state of affairs, and reporting the result of their investigation in circular form to the order in general. It was developed at said meeting that a fund of $800 had been raised previous to the assembling of the Cleveland convention, to defray the expenses of Mr. Nolan to Europe, with instructions that he should use his influence with the Board of Erin and have said board recognize him as national delegate, providing that the secessionists should elect him to that office on his return to America. In this scheme the conspirators were successful, and the usual quarterly communication was not received at the appointed time by the legally elected officer.

The Board of Erin has given no cause why the parcel was not forwarded as formerly. But instead of

pointing out its objections, if it had any, it fell help-
lessly into the trap set for it by the New York City
traitors, who are now vigorously at work trying to
scatter firebrands into the ranks of 50,000 Hibernians
who were moving along without a ripple. and whose
progress for the past two years is unparalleled.

The exposition of such weakness on the part of the
Board of Erin convinces the directory and national officers that said board is unfit to preside at the head of
an organization of the magnitude of ours, therefore the
directory and national officers have unanimously
agreed to sever the link that bound them to that head,
which they have looked to as a faithful friend and
father.

The principal objection to our society by the church
authorities, was the invisible Board of Erin. This objection will no longer exist. Financially the board has
been a drain on the order in this country; intellectually, a disgrace. But to all these we have submitted like
dutiful children until we are satisfied that our separation from such a head (that has sacrificed a whole organization for a few New York favorites) is for the best
interests of the society, and will unquestionably result
in a religious, intellectual and financial advantage to
the order.

The national officers and directory will issue the
usual quarterly communications promptly and they
will be in the future, as they have proven in the past,

the true and faithful servant of the Ancient Order of Hibernians of the United States.

Very fraternally,

HENRY F. SHERIDAN, National Delegate.

P. H. McNELLIS, National Secretary.

JOHN McSORLEY, National Treasurer.

JEREMIAH CROWLEY, Chairman.

JOHN S. O'CONNOR, Secretary.

CORNELIUS HORGAN, Treasurer.

M. A. SHEA, P. B. MURPHY,

National Directors.

In answer to the above circular the national officers of the A. O. H. Board of Erin, issued the following:

CIRCULAR.

Office of National Delegate, Ancient Order of Hibernians, United States of America.

New York City, Oct. 6, 1884.

To the Officers and Members of the Ancient Order of Hibernians in the United States:

Brethren—The conspiracy which seized the government of our order at Cleveland has unfurled the flag of secession. In an address issued on the 20th of August, 1884, it has not only dared to ask you to go, but has cooly assumed that you will, as a matter of course, follow it into separation from that parent to which every true Hibernian in every part of the globe looks today in loving reverence. The rebellion which that self-seeking politician, Mr. Alexander Sullivan, has set going thus, through his tool, Mr. Sheridan, does not stop at even treason to our affections as an order and our traditions as a race. It aggravates that treason by flaunting in our face wanton and indecent outrage on the parent which has for five hundred years kept the sea-divided Gael "one in name and one in fame," the ancient and venerable Board of Erin!

The address signed by Messrs. Sheridan, McNellis and McSorley, confesses that "the usual quarterly communication was received at the appointed time." In issuing a quarterly communication to the divisions in this country the expelled national delegate, Mr. Sheridan, stands convicted thus out of his own mouth of not only insult to the Board of Erin, but also of fraud upon every member of the order in these United States. Guilty by his own confession of that crime, Mr. Sheridan and his associates go on in a further attempt to deceive you by an address of cunning falsehoods. In correction of their misrepresentations, we feel bound to give you the explanations we go on now to make:

Informed of the design to capture the order in the interest of politicians, the Board of Erin instituted private inquiry. In the face of concurrent evidence of the existence of that design, the board proceeded in patient forbearance. Its reluctance to act, would, however, have been carried into weakness from the moment at which evidences had been laid before it that the conspiracy had gone-into the crime of issuing "false information." That act of rebellion against the board and of fraud upon the order here left the board no escape from the duty of action; but even then, the duty was discharged in the caution and moderation which confined itself to the call of the convention which was held in New York on the 12th of last August, under instructions basing all further steps on the result of an investigation by the convention, as to the fact of the issue of that false information. That respect of the rights of the brethren in the United States having resulted in a verdict of guilt, the convention exercised the authority of our beloved and venerable parent in Ireland to punish the convicts, Messrs. Mc-Nellis and McSorley, by suspension, and Mr. Sheridan by expulsion. The order here could do no less if it were not willing to be made a subject of fraud; nor could the Board of Erin have required less, unless it were willing to submit to the disruption of our worldwide unity by the attempt of a few individuals here at high handed secession.

The addresses of Messrs. Sheridan, McNellis and McSorley is full of attempts at deceit. Besides those which it will be seen to contain under the light of the explanation just given, a few had better be pointed out specially. Referring to the Board of Erin and us, the

address states that we "hold that all national conven-
·tions must be held in New York city." This attempt
to introduce sectional jealousies into the order, is made
in willful falsehood. The convention ordered by the
Board of Erin had to be held somewhere, and the
board, following what was an actual condition of the
constitution up to 1876, directed that it be held at that
great centre of the nation, the city of New York. The
address makes another appeal to sectionalism in that
design upon our "unity" in which it asserts "that the
national officers must be residents of New York." The
work of reorganization necessary to rid the order of
the treason which had grasped it by the throat, demands in the opinion of the Board of Erin and of the
late convention in New York, that one of the national
officers, the national delegate, shall reside in New
York, as the centre of action, during his term of office. The addresses of Messrs. Sheridan, McNellis
and McSorley is, however, none the less false when it
implies that residence in New York is a condition in
the case of any other national officer or in the case of
even the national delegate until he shall have entered
on the discharge of his duties. All the national officers may be chosen under the new constitution as
freely as under the old, from the brethren in any part
of the United States. The attempt in splitting the order into fragments, by arousing sectional prejudices,
receives its most pointed illustration in the declaration

of Messrs. Sheridan, McNellis and McSorley's address that the work of purification proceeds in any such contemptible insolence as that of holding "that the brotherhood outside of said city" of New York "are incompetent to manage the affairs of the society." Our denunciation of that audacious falsehood can not be made without indignation at so outrageous an insult to your intelligence as men and to your love of fraternal unity as Hibernians.

The men who confess to have made you subjects of one fraud, attempt now to make you subjects of many similar impositions. Your self-respect and intelligence insulted by them thus, these rebels against our traditions and affections as Hibernians carry their treason into a most scandulous attack upon our venerable parent across the Atlantic. To rebellion they add wanton and wicked insult. They declare the body which has maintained the unity of our race throughout the globe for twenty generations to be no longer "a faithful friend and father," but a nuisance which they denounce as "intellectually a disgrace!" With an impudence of even laughable coolness, they assume the right to speak by an authority binding on the individual judgment, conscience and affections of all Hibernians to the extent of the declaration that they, these so-called "national officers have unanimously agreed to sever the link that bound them to that head," the Board of Erin! False to their trust as officers, they

subject you to deceits; false to their obligations as
Hibernians, they assail your unity by appeals to your
sectional prejudices; false to the memories of your
race, they villify the intelligence and intellect of your
brothers beyond the sea, in the person of the Board of
Erin, and close their outrages upon you by cooly asking you to join them in spitting in the face of that
virtuous and loving parent, who holding the "sea-
divided Gael" together as one family all the world over,
has come down to us from the mists of ages clothed
with a purity and love and grandeur which may well
serve to inspire us with the pride of a noble descent
and strength of universal unity.

If anything beyond what we have already said were
necessary to show you that Messrs. Sheridan, Mc-
Nellis and McSorley violated all that is true in Hibernianism, we might dwell on their course towards Bro.
James E. Dunn. As publisher of a newspaper looking
for its support to the members of the order, that
gentleman's interests would have made him all things
to all men. Disregarding those interests, he dared to
do his duty, as an earnest and honest Hibernian, by de-
nouncing the attempt to make the order a utensil of
self-seeking politicians. His unselfish and courageous
course in the conduct of the A. O. H. Emerald has won
the admiration of all true Hibernians; but has exposed him to an infamous attempt on the part of the
men who had captured the government of the order at

Cleveland, to silence him by ruining his business! They first struck at him by ordering that he remove from the name of his journal the initials of the order. The tyranny that sought thus to crush the freedom of your press, they followed up by a movement for his expulsion from the order. Placing him on trial in his division, the constitutional tribunal of that division, the Standing Committee, gave him a unanimous acquital. Mr. Alexander Sullivan having packed the meeting at which the acquittal was announced, protracted the proceedings until few but their personal supporters remained, and then taking the case out of the constitutional course of an appeal to the County Board, carried a motion for Bro. Dunn's expulsion from the division. The despotic malice which has persecuted that gentleman thus, goes on in its attempt to destroy his journal and the freedom of the A. O. H. press by selecting him for vindictive mention in the address of the so-called national officers and concurs thus in showing that these men are indifferent to all the principles of the order, not more so to its "unity" than to its "christian charity." That these designs will not bear the light is confessed vividly in their dread of an honest and independent journal.

Choose now, brethren, between Messrs. Sheridan, McNellis and McSorley, and the ancient and venerable Board of Erin. If you refuse, as we are convinced you will, to follow those designing politicians into the rebellion which they seek to thrust upon you, you have but to place yourselves by divisions in communication with us to receive that true information which will hold you in fraternal fellowship with the men of our race in every part of the world. In the name of the Board of Erin, by whose authority we act, we invite you earnestly to renew your allegiance to the order by opening correspondence with us through the heads of your several divisions, or through your county delegate.

Hoping that you may feel bound in the only way left by Messrs. Sheridan, McNellis and McSorley, to maintain the order in its world-wide "unity," we remain in "true christian charity."

Yours fraternally,

JOHN NOLAN, National Delegate.

WM. SHERIDAN, National Secretary.

JOHN J. REILLY, National Treasurer.

(Have circular read at regular meeting of your division. But it is not for publication in your local press.)

Thus was inaugurated a split in that old and historic organization, the Ancient Order of Hibernians. Law suits now followed by both sides for division and county property and the right of using the name The Ancient Order of Hibernians.

One took the name of the A. O. H. Board of Erin, while the other branch assumed the name of the A. O. H. Benevolent Society of America, as is shown by

Judge Brown's dismissal of the case of the American Board against the Board of Erin. Judge Brown, in reviewing the case, said in part: "My conclusion is that this new organization calling itself The Ancient Order of Hibernians Benevolent Society and changing from the original, I noticed in the session laws and after the words Hibernians is the apostrophe, indicating the possessive case. I am satisfied from the examination of the act and of all the evidence in the case, and listening to the arguments of the counsel, I find that the evidence indicates in the first place that for many years prior to any of these charters, a voluntary association of Irishmen had existed known as the Ancient Order of Hibernians, whose headquarters was in Ireland, and I do not think that the controversy which has thus arisen can be settled here.

"The question here is one purely of law, and the view which I take of it requires me to render judgment for the defendants with costs." The Hon. Justice Bartlett also concurred in the view of Judge Brown.

The chasm that now separated the both branches of the order continued to grow wider with little prospect of closing it. The A. O. H. of America were in possession of the same merchandise as the Board of Erin, and were displaying it among the A. O. H. Board of Erin members in Philadelphia and other cities.

Again the Board of Erin sent John Nolan, their National Delegate, and Patrick H. Sheridan, National

Secretary, to the quarterly meeting of the Board of
Erin to learn the cause of both sides receiving the
same merchandise in the United States. After some opposition by John Crilly and others Nolan and Sheridan
were admitted to the meeting and all delegates present
took oath with the exception of four; namely, Crilly,
Rooney, Reid and Devlin, who refused to take oath
that they did not send or had any knowledge of any
person or persons sending the merchandise to any person in the United States connected with the American
Board. Their refusal to take the oath placed them under
suspicion, and they were placed on trial on the charge
of sending the merchandise to members of the A. O.
H. B. of A., and at the next meeting they were found
guilty and expelled. On June 4th, 1887, representatives of the A. O. H. B. of A. entered into a written
contract with persons in Great Britain and Ireland to
represent them on that side of the Atlantic. (Statement made by John C. Weadock to writer at Dooner's
Hotel, Philadelphia, Pa., March 5th, 1897). Thus occurred the split in Europe. The following circular,
issued by National Delegate Peter Kiernan in 1881,
will give my readers an idea of the esteem in which
Mr. Nolan was held by the national officers three years
prior to the trouble of '84:

Office of National Delegate, Ancient Order of Hibernians, United States of America.

New Orleans, La., Dec. 1st, 1881.

Brethren: At the urgent solicitation of the Honorable Board of Erin, I beg to address your generous sympathies, and appeal to your hereditary consanguinity, for assistance in behalf of an honored brother member of that august body.

It is now, brethren, about six and twenty years since brother John Nolan first took his seat on the Board of Erin. He was then young and blooming, direct from the careful training of a paternal home, the blessing of his aged parents, of whom he was the hope and stay. A professed Catholic, a zealous patriot, with a mind bold, independent and decisive. For over a quarter of a century his majestic form has never been absent from the quarter gathering, or appointed place of rendezvous; though often a narrow gauntlet he had to run, through rocks, sands, and snows, he has always been proof against peril, and empowered with ubiquity.

Some years ago he settled in Manchester, England, following the business of wine and spirit merchant, which gave him a living, and no more. All our friends made his home their headquarters. English spies haunted the house, and the cloud of Saxon displeasure began to hover around and soon settled on his devoted head. England's bigotry and hatred for an

Irishman, together with her cursed laws, deprived him of his license more than two years ago. Repeated entreaties have been made, and petitions presented, for a renewal of the license, and sternly rejected. Clinging to the hope of one day or other to get a renewal, his hoardings became exhausted, and this noble Celt and brave Hibernian is now reduced to the almost humiliation of a beggar's position. Brothers, the day may soon come when our ashes shall be scattered before the winds of heaven, the memory of what you do cannot die; it will carry down to your posterity your honor, or your shame.

In the presence, and in the name of that ever-living God, I do therefore conjure you to not hesitate to give your mite. Freely have your purses opened before to all calls of charity. Generously did you contribute when the saffron plague swept over the South land, alleviating the distress of your stricken brethren. Nobly did you give to struggling Ireland, our oppressed motherland.

Ah, but now dear friends, within England's cruel borders is one of our own fraternity, suffering by her tyrannical and hated laws.

Let us, then, in God's name, and in the name of humanity, send a Christmas gift—labeled and sealed with our monogram. "To Brother John Nolan, from the Ancient Order of Hibernians, in America."

Your very truly and fraternally,
PETER KIERNAN, National Delegate.

P. S.—Send your donations direct to Bro. J. J. Sheehan, National Treasurer, Fitchburg, Mass., who will acknowledge and receipt for the same.

P. K.

We are happy, brothers, in having an opportunity of giving our concurrence, both in sentiment and principle, of the proposed appeal. We think it should meet with a generous response, and with the most perfect unanimity.

Yours in friendship,

M. J. COSGROVE, National Secretary.
J. J. SHEEHAN, National Treasurer.
MATT. CURRAN, Chairman National Directory.
P. H. McNELLIS, Secretary National Directory.
P. McGINNISS, Treasurer National Directory.

Conference committees were elected in 1888, but failed in their purpose. In 1890 other committees were appointed on unity. They met in Jefferson Hall, Brooklyn, N. Y., February 15th, 1891, only to disagree. In 1894 another committee was appointed by both national conventions. The A. O. H. Board of Erin were in session in New York City, and the A. O. H. of America in Omaha, Nebraska. The committees never met, but the following correspondence was entered into between P. J. O'Connor, N. P. for the A. O. H. of America, and James J. Hagerty, N. D. for the A. O. H. Board of Erin:

Office of National President, A. O. H. of America.

Savannah, Ga., June 11, 1894.

Mr. James Hagerty, New York City:

Dear Sir —I understand you were elected National Delegate at the convention held by the A. O. H. last month in Tammany Hall, New York City. You will doubtless remember the telegram sent from Omaha to your convention by the A. O. H. of America, which I now have the honor to represent, inviting your members to join with and return to us under the banner of "Friendship, Unity and True Christian Charity." It affords me great pleasure to repeat said invitation and indulge in the hope that the time is near at hand when all true and worthy Hibernians will be united in one brotherhood. I will be glad to hear from you thereon, and receive any suggestions which you consider likely to achieve that grand result. Hoping to be favored with an early reply, and sending best wishes, I remain, yours very truly,

P. J. O'CONNOR, National President.

Office of National Delegate, A. O. H., Board of Erin.

New York City, July 26, 1894.

P. J. O'Connor, Esq.:

Dear Sir —Your letter received and contents noted. You will remember the telegram sent from Tammany Hall, New York City, on May 11th, to your convention at Omaha, Neb., by the A. O. H., which I have now the honor to represent. I should have answered your letter sooner but one of your members thought I would meet you in New York after the state election was over.   At our convention we appointed a committee of five with the national officers to meet a likewise committee from your side to settle the difficulty existing with both organizations, if possible.   I will be glad to hear from you.   Hoping to be favored with an early reply, with best wishes, I remain, yours very truly,

JAMES HAGERTY, N. D.

Office of National President, A. O. H., of America.
Savannah, Ga., October 18, 1894.
Mr. James Hagerty, New York:
Dear Sir —I wrote you on the 8th ult. in reference to the proposed meeting of the conference committees for the purpose, if possible, of bringing about union among all Hibernians.   Up to the present time you have not favored me with a reply.   I would like very much to have my letter answered, so that I may thoroughly understand the exact position and terms of your side.   If a conference is to take place I want its result to be binding, and consequently it is necessary to have a perfect understanding beforehand.   You suggested the conference this time and I am, therefore, entitled to know the position that will be taken and the terms exacted by your committee.   As soon as these are ascertained our course will be determined.   Our side is desirous for the existence of only one Hibernian organization and will do whatever is fair and honorable

to bring it about. I sincerely trust that you will answer my last letter without further delay. With best wishes, I remain, fraternally,

P. J. O'CONNOR, N. P.

Office of National Delegate, A. O. H., Board of Erin.
New York City, November 10, 1894.

Mr. P. J. O'Connor:

Dear Sir—Your communication of October 18th, received, also yours of the 8th inst. in reference to the proposed meeting of the conference committee for the purpose, if possible, of trying to bring about a union of all Hibernians. You say you want to thoroughly understand the exact position and terms of our side, if a conference is to take place, and that you want the result to be binding, and consequently you say it is necessary to have a perfect understanding beforehand. I agree with you that it is: First, I find by our resolutions that part of the work of the conference would be to unite the board in Ireland, if such exists, but if you recognize no board across the water, as I see by the declaration of the New York State convention on your side, that you ceased all connections with the other side of the water, then I think it would be easy to come to a proper understanding to unite and cement the members of the old order in the country and have us all receive fatherly instruction from our centered Catholicity. Would you be kind enough to inform me if such is the case, so that I may make necessary propositions to you for a union or on what grounds we can unite. With best wishes, I remain, yours fraternally,

JAMES HAGERTY, N. D.

Office of National President, A. O. H., of America.
Savannah, Ga., December 3, 1894.
Mr. James J. Hagerty, New York, N. Y.:

Dear Sir —I received your favor of the 10th ult., but absence from the city prevented an earlier reply. I desire to say in answer thereto that our order has European affiliations, and that the New York State convention did not make any declaration to the contrary. Having satisfied you upon said subject there is no reason why you cannot, as you agreed to, make necessary propositions of the grounds upon which you claim we can unite without further delay. Hoping to hear from you soon, and sending you best wishes, I remain very truly yours,

P. J. O'CONNOR, N. P.

Office of National Delegate, A. O. H., Board of Erin.
New York City, December 26, 1894.
Mr. P. J. O'Connor:

Dear Sir —Your letter of the 3rd received and contents noted. The cause of my delay in answering was: You said to me that you had affiliations with a board on the other side. It then became my duty to make inquiries of our members on the other side of the water on what conditions the members of the B. of E. expelled the members that sent you the merchandise after they were notified not to communicate with your side, and Mr. M. F. Wilhere was served with the like notices also, and his money returned to him; the amount was $75.00. The answer to my inquiries was that they were expelled for life and that they never could get back, specially some of them, as I am further told that they do not come up to the standard that is required by the constitution and could not be admitted to our old order. This obstacle stands in the way of union on the other side of the water, and I understand you have a contract with such men since 1886. As you are ready to ignore the men that promised the new board, and if we can unite in an honorable way, as you are ready to stand by the old Board of Erin, that we all, in this country, receive our friendship from the old and honorable board that has stood by the church and fatherland for centuries, or will you submit to me the names of your delegates on the other side of the water so I can see if any of them are the men expelled for life for wrong-doing, and, in return, if you so require, I will furnish you with the names of our leading delegates and also their addresses. Hoping that the day is not far when we all will, on both sides, see our way clear to a proper understanding as members of the A. O. H., in this country as well as at home, as I want to see my countrymen united if possible. Hoping this will meet with your wishes, I am, as ever, respectfully yours,

JAMES HAGERTY, N. D.

Office of National President, A. O. H., of America.

Savannah, Ga., Feb. 1, 1895.

Mr. James J. Hagerty, New York City:

Dear Sir —Since the reception of your last letter, I attended our Supreme Court three hundred miles from here and had up to the present very little time to attend to private matters. Said letter does not carry out your promise. You assured me that if I satisfied you upon one subject, which was done, you would "make necessary propositions" of the grounds upon which union can be predicated. You did not do so in your last letter. I am anxious to bring this affair to a focus and, therefore, respectfully suggest that you state in writing, without delay, your demands or the concessions you will ask in order to bring about union and harmony once more. By so doing you will greatly oblige, Yours very truly,

P. J. O'CONNOR, N. P.

Office of National Delegate, A. O. H., Board of Erin.

New York City, April 23, 1895.

Mr. P. J. O'Connor, N. P.:

Dear Sir —Pardon me for delaying so long in answering your communication of February 1, 1895, as most of the time since I have been sick and had other business to attend to. In answer I would say to you that you did not answer the very important questions I put to you in my letter of December 26, 1894. That was the names of those you were associated with on the other side of the water, or if you and yours were ready to give up such affiliations, and you and us were to become united. Are you ready and willing to recognize the old and only board on the other side of the water, known as the B. of E.? These are questions if properly answered and accepted by your side, would open the way to unite our scattered ranks in this country and let us say that we could thank God there is only one A. O. H. in any part of the world. If we can agree on these points, I consider it would be an easy matter to settle our trouble in this country in an honorable and upright way. By calling each country together, dividing up the offices, letting each division elect its own officers and where there would be two divisions of the same number giving a higher or lower to one of them. States act in the same way, and as for the national officers, I don't think you or I would stand in the way of unity, as I am ready to resign at any time if that will have the desired effect to unite our people. Hoping, dear sir, you will give an early reply, as our convention meets on May 14, and it is my desire to lay the whole matter before that convention. Most respectfully yours,

JAMES J. HAGERTY, N. D.

Office of National President, A. O. H., of America.

Savannah, Ga., May 7, 1895.

Mr. James Hagerty, New York City:

Dear Sir —I regret that your last communication did not contain the exact terms to be demanded by you, which you promised to give me some time ago if I would furnish you certain information. I complied with your request, but you have not fulfilled your promise. Our affiliations on the other side are with the legal and constitutional board. It seems to me we ought to adjust the alleged differences between us here first, and other matters can then be easily made to conform thereto.

Our officers and directors have full authority in the premises, and if your convention confers similar powers upon your representatives, and they submit a definite proposition to me, I will see that it receives proper consideration.

Regretting that matters have not been satisfactorily arranged before this, I remain, fraternally,

P. J. O'CONNOR, N. P.

THE A. O. H. GAELIC CHAIR.

A resolution drawn up by Thomas Addis Emmet Weadock, of Bay City, Michigan, and introduced at the national convention of the Ancient Order of Hibernians of America, held at Hartford, Connecticut, May 16, 1890, by John McDevitt, asking the members of the A. O. H. to raise the sum of fifty thousand dollars for the endowment of a Hibernian chair in the Catholic University at Washington, D. C., for the purpose of teaching Irish language, history and literature. The national president, Hon. M. F. Wilhere, in issuing his annual report, invited every division of the order to discuss the questions involved in the resolution and take a vote on the proposition so that the delegates to the national convention to be held at New Orleans, La., May 13th, 1892, could vote thereon. At the New Orleans convention it was decided to assess the members seventy-five cents each to raise the $50,000, but on account of the panic of 1893 the assessment was not levied. Again at the national convention held at Omaha, May 8th, 1894, the national officers and directors were authorized, as soon as they deemed it expedient, to levy an assessment for the purpose of establishing an A. O. H. chair in the Catholic University at Washington, D. C. On May the 12th they met in Omaha and decided that every member of the order

RT. REV. JOHN S. FOLEY, National Chaplain.
BISHOP OF DETROIT, MICHIGAN.

be assessed seventy-five cents each. In a few months
the money began to come in from every state in the
Union and Canada, to-wit:

STATE.	MEMBERS.	AMOUNT
Alabama	59	$ 44.25
Arkansas	3	2.25
California	776	582.00
Colorado	252	189.00
Connecticut	4,509	3,381.75
Delaware	641	480.75
District of Columbia	155	116.25
Florida	26	19.50
Georgia	632	474.00
Illinois	2,342	1,756.50
Indiana	1,477	1,107.75
Indian Territory	16	12.00
Iowa	1,344	1,008.25
Kansas	444	333.00
Kentucky	458	343.50
Louisiana	362	271.50
Maine	1,167	875.25
Maryland	676	507.00
Massachusetts	10,326	7,744.50
Michigan	2,221	1,665.75
Minnesota	2,171	1,628.25
Missouri	914	685.50
Montana	300	225.00
Nebraska	361	270.00
Nevada	80	60.00
New Hampshire	956	717.00
New Jersey	3,263	2,447.25
New York	6,694	5,020.50
Ohio	3,648	2,736.00
Oregon	126	94.50
Pennsylvania	12,412	9,309.50
Rhode Island	936	702.00
South Carolina	339	254.25
Tennessee	98	73.00

STATE.	MEMBERS.	AMOUNT
Texas	100	75.00
Utah	169	126.75
Vermont	18	13.50
Virginia	200	150.00
Washington	204	153.00
West Virginia	533	399.75
Wisconsin	1,331	998.25
Wyoming	40	30.00
CANADA.		
New Brunswick	185	138.75
Ontario	375	281.00
Prince Edwards Island	32	24.00
Quebec	371	278.25
Doctor Kenny of Montana donated		2.00

Before the close of the National convention held at Detroit, Michigan, July 14, 1896, the $50,000 was collected and in the hands of the treasurer, the Rt. Rev. John S. Foley, Bishop of Detroit and National Chaplain of the A. O. H.

The endowment of the chair took place on October 21st, 1896, in the assembly room of the McMahon Hall of Philosophy. The exercises were attended by the board of directors and the visiting archbishops, the acting rector, the professors, and the students of all the schools. A large delegation came from the Baltimore, Alexandria, and Washington branches of the Ancient Order of Hibernians, and many visitors from the city assisted. There were present Archbishops Williams of Boston, Corrigan of New York, Riordan of San Francisco, Ryan of Philadelphia, Feehan of Chicago, Chappelle of Santa Fe, Elder of Cincinnati, Katzer of Milwaukee, Ireland of St. Paul, Kain of St. Louis, Hennessy of Dubuque; Bishops Foley of

Detroit, Maes of Covington, Horstmann of Cleveland, and Farley, auxiliary bishop of New York. The delegation of the Ancient Order of Hibernians occupied places on the platform with the archbishops and bishops. They were: Mr. P. J. O'Connor, of Savannah, Ga., National President; Mr. J. C. Weadock, of Bay City, Mich., National Vice-president; Mr. Jas. O'Sullivan of Philadelphia, National Secretary; Mr. T. J. Dundon, of Columbus, Ohio, National Treasurer. Besides these gentlemen there were the National Directors, Messrs. M. F. Wilhere, of Philadelphia, Pa.; T. J. Mahoney, Omaha, Neb.; J. P. Murphy, Norwich, Conn.; and M. J. Burns, Indianapolis, Ind. Mr. Thomas A. E. Weadock, ex-congressman from Michigan, accompanied the delegation, and made the opening discourse. Cardinal Gibbons presided and Very Rev. Dr. Garrigan, acting Rector of the University, introduced Mr. Thomas Addis Emmet Weadock, ex-congressman from Bay City, Mich., who reviewed the history of the movement; Judge M. F. Wilhere, of Philadelphia, Pa., during whose presidency of the order the movement was inaugurated, and Mr. P. J. O'Connor of Savannah, Ga., the national president of the order, made very able and patriotic addresses.

The money was handed to Cardinal Gibbons in the form of a draft from the Peninsular Savings Bank, of Detroit, on New York, payable to the order of Bishop Foley, of Detroit, for $50,000. Cardinal Gibbons, as chancellor of the university, received the gift.

After the exercises the delegates were entertained at Caldwell Hall. Dr. Shahan, who had taken a lively interest in this chair, addressed them. Very Rev. Dr. Garrigan, the acting rector, thanked them also in very appropriate terms, and pointed out the varied benefits that would come from this foundation.

In the evening the delegates were given a reception at Carroll Institute by the local organizations of the Ancient Order, and upon its conclusion a banquet was served, at which some fifty guests sat down. The next day the delegates were taken to see the points of interest in and about Washington, and in the evening an informal reception and lunch were tendered them at the residence of Thomas E. Waggaman, Esq., the treasurer of the university. They departed October 23 for their homes, having left lasting impressions on the minds and hearts of all who met them, as of men stalwart in faith and patriotism, high-minded and warmly devoted to the most elevated interests of Holy Church in the United States.

Since the endowment of the chair the Rev. Father Henebry, a graduate of Maynooth College and a priest of the diocese of Waterford, Ireland, has been appointed as teacher of Celtic language, literature and antiquities. His courses of instruction are old Irish grammar, middle Irish texts, selections from the Leahar Ne-huider modern Irish grammar and composition, etc.

On August 2d, 1895, James J. Hagerty, N. D., A. O. H., Board of Erin, and Terence Donoghue, S. D., New York, were invited to meet the national officers and directors of the American board at the Continental Hotel, New York, which they accepted, and the following conference took place. The minutes of the conference were forwarded to Mr. James J. Hagerty, at his request, by P. J. O'Connor, N. P., A. O. H., of America, May 9th, 1896.

Office of National Delegate, A. O. H., B. of E.
New York, May 18, 1896.

Mr. P. J. O'Connor, N. P.:

Dear Sir—I hope this short note will find you enjoying good health. My dear sir, I would feel much obliged if you would send me a copy of the minutes taken at our conference last August at the Continental Hotel, New York. I am told you have sent them around to your state officers, and I would like to have a copy for our national convention, that all may see the same. The reason why I ask for this is that your national officers and national directors had a stenographer taking the minutes, and as I wish to make a correct report of what had taken place. I remain yours fraternally,

JAMES J. HAGERTY.

P. S.—Please reply as soon as possible as I leave New York May 10th for our national convention. If not, please forward on Philadelphia.

JAMES HAGERTY, N. D.

Law Offices of O'Connor & O'Byrne.

Savannah, Ga., May 9, 1896.

Mr. James J. Hagerty, Philadelphia, Pa.:

Dear Sir—Your favor of recent date was duly received. In compliance with your request I send you by this mail a manifold copy of the minutes taken at our conference last August in the Continental Hotel, New York City. I did send two or three copies thereof to members who made special request for the same. I earnestly hope that all true and patriotic Hibernians will soon be united in one grand brotherhood. Hoping you are well and prospering, I remain, fraternally,

P. J. O'CONNOR,

N. P., A. O. H. of America.

MINUTES OF THE AMERICAN BOARD.

Continental Hotel, New York, N. Y., Aug. 2, 1895.

Pursuant to adjournment the meeting of the National Directory of the Ancient Order of Hibernians was called to order at 11 o'clock a. m., National President, P. J. O'Connor presiding. The following members of the directory being present:

P. J. O'Connor, National President, Savannah, Ga.; M. J. Slattery, National Secretary, Albany, N. Y.; Thos. J. Dundon, National Treasurer, Columbus, O.; Maurice F. Wilhere, Philadelphia, Pa.; Edward Sweeney, Cincinnati, O.; John W. Clark, Milwaukee, Wis.;

and the following proceedings were then had. Messrs. Hagerty and Donohue, representing the Board of Erin, A. O. H., were admitted into the room and introduced to each member of the directory, whereupon President O'Connor said:

Gentlemen, we had better come to order.

At the last national convention of our order a resolution was passed reading as follows:

"Resolved, That all action heretofore taken, expelling members for taking part in the secession movement be rescinded and that we invite them and all members of the so-called B. of E., A. O. H., to return and join with us under fair and honorable conditions, which our national officers and board of directors are hereby authorized to negotiate, they being constituted a committee to meet and treat with the committee already appointed by that body."

In compliance with that resolution, after learning that Mr. Hagerty represented the so-called Board of Erin, Ancient Order of Hibernians, I addressed him a communication extending the invitaton which is referred to in that resolution. He and I had some correspondence in reference to the matter, and on May 7th last I wrote him a letter with the express purpose of having him receive it before the convention of his branch, and I received no reply to it. We understand here from one or two members of the order that Mr. Hagerty had said that he had not received my communication. It was thought strange because it had not been returned, as it doubtless would have been had it not been received by him. The matter was submitted to the meeting here the other day and we determined in view of the fact that there was some misunderstanding about the receipt of my communication, that we send Mr. Hagerty a copy of that letter, and request that a committee from his body meet us at some convenient time and place for the purpose of seeing whether or not we could bring about an adjustment of the alleged differences that exist between us, and effect a union. We received a telegram from Bro. Sullivan, our County President, stating that a committee would meet us here at half past eleven o'clock today.

Now I would like to know if Mr. Hagerty received my communication, and if he did, if he submitted it to the convention, and what, if any, action was taken by his convention in reference to the matter. Will Mr. Hagerty be kind enough to inform us concerning this matter?

Mr. Hagerty—First and foremost, gentlemen, I do not remember of stating to anybody that I did not receive your communication, and I desire to know who is the author of that statement.

President O'Connor—The authors are Councilor Langan and Bro. Sullivan.

Mr. Hagerty—I require no one to apologize for me, because I generally speak the truth. I did have all of

your communications and my answers thereto read at
the Tammany Hall meeting.   You refused to answer
some questions in reference to the state convention,
held by your body at Syracuse, N. Y., in reference to
statements made by Archbishop McQuaid, and in connection with that I asked you if you recognized or had
any head on the other side of the water, and you told
me that you had, and also you asserted that you were
the legal body in this country.   You hold, I presume,
all of my letters, or copies of them, which will speak
for themselves.

I wish to say, however, that it is very unpleasant for
me to speak to you on this occasion for the reason that
I have not been well, and for more than a week past I
have been almost deaf through the effects of medicine
which I have been taking.   At the outset I wish it understood that anything which may take place at this
meeting is not for publication, and I am particularly
anxious that it shall not go to the press.   It has never
been my policy since I have held office in our order to
have our proceedings appear in the press, and I want
it understood, Mr. Chairman, that anything we do here
today is not for publication, and unless we can have
that understanding we will not undertake any negotiations with you.   I have always been of the opinion
that the airing of these matters in the press has been
detrimental to the order throughout the land.

President O'Connor—Then it is your desire that

anything which takes place here today is not to be published?

Mr. Hagerty—That is our wish. We ask this for the reason that we do not think that it helps our order to have their proceedings published, because we already have enough enemies throughout the country, and this would but give them the opportunity to further scandalize us, if the proceedings of this meeting were for newspaper publication.

Mr. Clark—Mr. Chairman, I move that whatever takes place here today is not for the press or for publication.

The motion was duly seconded by Mr. Dundon.

President O'Connor—Do I understand that that motion would prevent a circular being prepared, printed and sent out, in reference to this conference?

Mr. Hagerty—I have come here at very short notice, and I notified the state delegate on my side of the house to be present here with me, and I think that we are not prepared to say anything for publication at this time, when we have not had to exceed five minutes' consultation prior to our coming here.

To further complicate our matters I missed my train at Flatbush and that took up time which I had expected to have with my associate for consultation, and I do not think it would be treating us fairly to allow any conference that we may have to be published either in the press or by circular. We have come here for the purpose of ascertaining whether it is feasible or not to unite the two parties. I do not suppose that there can be a settlement of the matter at this meeting, but if you have any proposition to submit to us, it can be taken by us and submitted at our next national convention. Representatives of our body are not here in the city at this time, and it would be a great expense to bring them here to confer with you now. And as for Bro. Donahoe and myself, I will say that we are not now in a position to agree to anything. But if you have any proposition for us we will submit them to our next national convention. We wish to hear your propositions, and we hope, gentlemen, that anything that takes place here today will not be published, and that by reason of our meeting with you that you will not attempt to take any advantage of us.

Mr. O'Connor—We do not desire to take the slightest advantage of you gentlemen.

Mr. Donahoe—Before this motion prevails, I wish to say one word. If I understand the matter properly, Mr. Hagerty's idea is mine. It is simply this. There is some trouble in the order and it has been aired in the public press to the great delight of all the enemies of our race and our church, and I think that if good common sense prevails here and if the judgment of the gentlemen here be sound that anything which takes place at this meeting will not find a place in the public press.

President O'Connor—Before proceeding further I certainly think that we ought to have a reply to the question which I asked you, and that is as to whether you did submit this matter to your convention, and if you did what action did your convention take in the premises?

Mr. Hagerty—I have already stated that your communications and my answers thereto were each and all of them read at the Tammany Hall convention. I further expected to hear from you before our national convention, but you did not answer. If I had received a favorable letter it would have done a great deal of good and would have been of benefit to all of us. You did not answer my question as to what people you represented on the other side of the water. I asked you to give the names of the people that you claim to represent and stated to you that in return I would give you the names of those that we represented on the other side. ·

President O'Connor—Your letters are here. My question is what action did your convention take?

Mr. Hagerty—You will pardon me. We have come here at your request to endeavor to settle our alleged differences and I defy any man to go forth and state that I ever claimed that I did not receive your letter. I did state, however, that there was a letter some months previous that was mislaid, and that was my reason for the delay. As for Mr. Sullivan, I never met him to my knowledge until I met him at Patchogue, and I do not think he will claim that I made any such statement to him there.

Mr. Clark—Did your convention give you any authority to appoint any committee whatever to meet with us to settle the difficulty?

Mr. Hagerty—No, sir. I have already stated that we have no power or authority whatever until our next national convention meets. There has been no committee appointed.

Mr. Clark—Then you have no power or authority to act?

Mr. Hagerty—No, sir.

President O'Connor—Didn't your convention instruct you not to communicate any further with me?

Mr. Hagerty—That is the fact. If your letter had reached me before our convention there would have been different action taken, I can assure you.

President O'Connor—Then you admit that you received my letter?

Mr. Hagerty—Yes sir; I received it. There were certain obstacles that stood in the way, which were afterwards removed, except one perhaps, and that is one which you have placed in the way.

President O'Connor—Is the obstacle to which you refer that of the eligibility of members of the order?

Mr. Hagerty—It is. Several of our members would object to any affiliation with a body where both of the parents are not either Irish, or Irish descent. I understand that under the provisions of your constitution, were either parent Irish or of Irish descent, that that would make a person eligible to membership.

Mr. Clark—You can have a copy of our constitution and from that you can ascertain what it is.

Mr. Hagerty—On our side we think it is not the proper thing to name a body of men "Ancient Order of Hibernians" when it would be possible to admit the son of an Englishman, who happens to have an Irish mother, into its membership.

President O'Connor—You are business men and you will recognize the force of what I am about to state; and that is that there would be hardly sense or reason in our having a conference here unless the parties to that conference are duly authorized to act . and will be bound by whatever takes place here.

If your organization has not given you, or any other committee, any authority in the premises, so that your action would be binding, it seems to me that everything that we might do here, in the way of bringing about an adjustment of our differences, would be fruitless and amount to nothing.

Mr. Hagerty—If you have anything to suggest you may submit it in writing and we will in turn submit that to our colleagues. You certainly could not expect us upon so short notice to attempt to make laws for our colleagues when we have no such authority. And you certainly do not think it just and right to place us in that position at this time.

President O'Connor—Did I understand you to say that your convention had instructed you to have no further communication with me?

Mr. Hagerty—Yes, sir; I said that.

President O' Connor—Then there was no authority given you by your convention to meet with us?

Mr. Hagerty—No committee has been appointed for that purpose. If anything is done at this meeting it would have to be submitted to our next convention for ratification. My colleagues would first have to pass upon it before it would be binding.

President O'Connor—Then you would have no authority to take binding action in the matter?

Mr. Hagerty—If this objectionable clause in the constitution, to which I have referred, was removed, I do not see why we could not settle our difficulties.

President O'Connor—We are in a position to act and have received full authority from our national convention.

Mr. Hagerty—You, of course, have more authority than we have at present. I could not say at this time what we might do until I would have time to see my colleagues. I came here on a few minutes' notice and I do not think you could expect me to give you definite answers at this time.

President O'Connor—We have remained here for two days to attempt to adjust this matter.

Mr. Hagerty.—We were not aware of your coming here.

President O'Connor—You would have been if you had answered my letter.

Mr. Hagerty—If you had answered the questions which I put to you I would have answered your letter.

President O'Connor—I did not refuse to answer your questions at all.

Mr. Hagerty—I asked you certain questions which you never answered. You wished to lay down a basis upon which we could get together and I asked you what was the name of your delegate on the other side, or the name of the authority that you recognized there, and I said that if you would furnish me with the name that I, in turn, would send you the names of ours.

President O'Connor—My questions were not answered.

Mr. Hagerty—Did you answer the question in relation to your representative on the other side which I asked you?

President O'Connor—I answered all questions that I deemed it necessary to answer.

Mr. Hagerty—I thought that was a very important question and I should have had an answer to it. You claim that they are thus and so on the other side, and I claim that they are thus and so I wanted to know who were your representatives on the other side, and I said that I would give you ours in return. I thought that that was a very important question and I should have had an answer to it.

Mr. Wilhere—There is no use, in my judgment, in our threshing over this old straw. We are either here to do business or not for business; we are either here with authority or without authority. Our national president has very properly stated to you the object of this meeting and has read in your hearing the resolution of our national convention and we are here with authority. We are here not only with authority, but with a desire, an intense desire, with honest purpose to bring about an adjustment of this difficulty on such a basis as will work good to both branches. Now, in my humble judgment, there is but one question before us who reside upon the American soil, whether born here or not, but who reside upon the American soil, and that one question is, upon what equitable basis can we settle and adjust whatever differences that may exist between us here in this country; to attempt to predicate any adjustment in bringing contending factions together in Europe is idle and useless, and I think our conference would be fruitless unless we have enough strength of character, enough patriotism, enough liberalism, to lay down a basis of re-union and re-organization here that we, in America, shall settle our own differences before we attempt to settle any disputes that may have taken place on the other side. And if you will pardon a thought that comes into my mind, as I said yesterday, if after we have settled our differences and have got together for the good and for the common interests, then if it should be necessary, Bro. Hagerty, and those whom he represents, and members of our order, could go to the other side and settle any differences that may be there. If it can be shown that there is an organization sending the goods and merchandise to Bro. Hagerty and those whom he represents, who have no authority to do so, that matter could easily be adjusted, and I am free enough to say, that it is my honest judgment and opinion, having a thorough knowledge of the matter, and having met both of these gentlemen in conference eight years ago upon this very question, and I remember that both these gentlemen now present were then present, and, as I said, it is a matter of truth, and an actual matter of fact, that the organization which my friend, Mr. Hagerty, represents has no Board of Erin at all, save and except two or three men who have deserted the order, or were properly and legally expelled from the only genuine Board of Erin, with which we have been treating ever since the 4th day of June, 1887, now more than eight years. But I repeat there is no use again threshing the old straw. There is no use of our attempting bringing about a reconciliation and a reunion here in America based upon the question as to whether Mr. Hagerty or ourselves have the current merchandise from the genuine Board of Erin. We are here, if you will pardon the repetition, on American soil, and have a constitution and system of laws for our own guidance. When I joined this order, twenty-five years ago, I did not take my obligation from the Board of Erin. I did not take my obligation, nor neither did these brothers who are here, if they joined upon the American soil, as I did, take any obligation from the Board of Erin whatever. We took the obligation under the constitution of the Ancient Order of Hibernians of the United States, and we are bound by that constitution, and we are to be guided and directed by its principles alone.

The Board of Erin, from the very foundation of this order in America, has merely occupied the same relation to the organization in the United States of America that it occupies today to us, and to you, Mr. President, as the representative of our organization; and that is that we interchange cards, we receive merchandise from them, and we accept that in good faith, in order to have a common merchandise in use throughout the world; and the Board of Erin have treated with you, Mr. President, and those whom you have succeeded as the representative of the American organization of the Ancient Order of Hibernians in the United States, and you have a concurrent jurisdiction with them in all matters pertaining to the making of merchandise, and in all national questions that may arise.

Now as to the American organization. We have had some differences for the past eleven years, which we all agree have been unfortunate. The differences having arisen here between ourselves—bcause there were no differences in Europe at the time—the differences should be settled by ourselves.

Mr. Hagerty and Mr. Donahoe, representatives of the official head of their side of the organization here in this country, at the time of their convention, or at the time their alleged convention was meeting in Emmet Hall, on the 12th of August, 1884, when they seceded from our organization—at that time there was no division, no split in Europe, no differences in Europe whatever. But they seceded from our organization. Every national officer, every state officer and every regularly elected officer remained true to our organization, except Hugh Murray, the county delegate of New York. In Emmet Hall, at that convention, there was but one man who was constitutionally eligible to sit in a national convention, and that man was Hugh Murray, who, as I have said before, was county delegate of New York. The others who sat there had no more right to sit as delegate in a national convention of the Ancient Order of Hibernians than a man from California, from Milwaukee, or from Cincinnati, who never were members of the order at all. Now I take it, Mr. Chairman, that that statement being correct, and if it is not correct there are gentlemen present who know my connection with the movement in the past, and whom I know very well, too, and if the statement which I have made is not correct they can disprove it, or attempt to do so, and I am prepared to prove every assertion that I have made.

Let's see, then, if we are in earnest and are acting in good faith. Let's settle our differences here in America first, and then if it is necessary after we are united for the common good and the honor of Hibernianism, if after we are united here, I can assure you that we would be willing to go with a representative of our dissenting brethren, who are here, to the other side and settle and adjust any differences that might exist in Europe.

But it is not becoming to us, as a great body of American citizens, as members of the Catholic Church, a church that has always been the exemplar of unity from its very foundation—it is very unbecoming for us to begin to settle our differences by references to matters which are in dispute in Europe. Let us settle our differences here first. We are willing upon any honorable basis, if these gentlemen will make an honorable proposition to us today, we are willing to make an effort to settle our disputes.

We have the authority and the right. We are here

in good faith, and we mean business. We mean unity. In the honesty of our hearts and the honesty of our intentions we now propose, if they have the authority to do so, if they will make an honorable proposition to us here, why I am sure we will give it not only fair consideration, not only honest consideration, but we will give it such consideration as in the honesty of our hearts we are able to do, and make every effort to bring about such unity that we will satisfy them that we mean whereof we speak.

We represent an organization here that is the largest, greatest and the strongest of any organized body of our race and creed in the civilized world. We have printed reports of the proceedings of our national and state conventions, duly attested and certified; we have a constitution, a ritual printed, all of which are duly attested and certified; we have a directory, giving the names and addresses of the various state, county and division officers of the order throughout all America. If these gentlemen have an organization back of them, we are willing to submit to them our printed and attested reports. We are willing to submit to them our directory, and our constitution and ritual. Where is their directory? Where are their printed reports of their national and state conventions? Where is their constitution? Where is their ritual? Who do they represent, and what do they represent? Is it a body of men, or are they representatives of a mere rump convention, who met in Emmet Hall here, in 1884, after seceding from the main body? Show us what you represent in this country. Show us how many men you have, how many divisions you have, and where they are located. We offer you all of our printed matter. We offer you our constitution, our ritual and our various state and national reports. They are there on the table, and you may have them and inspect them now. Examine our national directory, it will speak for itself. Where are your reports? Where is your directory? Who do you represent, and how many do you represent and what do you represent? This is plain talk, but, as it occurs to me, it is only fair, and it is proper talk. If we are coming together, if we mean business, let us start at it in an honorable, straightforward and business-like manner. Again I repeat, Mr. President, that I think the first thing to do would be to ascertain with whom we are dealing, and what the authority of the gentlemen present is. We have no objection to submitting to these gentlemen our reports, showing who we represent, and what we represent, all of which they can ascertain from our reports and from our directory. There is nothing to conceal on our part. There is nothing hidden. There is nothing that we have to hide in connection with our organization. We have demanded, and have the right to ask, on the other hand, that they submit the same matter to us, or any part of the same that they may have. That is the basis of a business meeting of this kind, called for business purposes. And if they mean unity and harmony, let them submit to us what they have to offer as a basis of settlement on their side. And I move you now, that we furnish to the representatives of the dissenting wing copies of the reports of our national and state conventions, duly attested and certified as to their correctness, and that we submit to them a directory giving the names of all our national, state and division officers throughout all America; and that we ask from them as a basis of negotiation that they furnish us likewise the printed reports and the proceedings of their conventions, with their printed directory, if they have one, giving us the names and addresses of all their officers throughout America.

Mr. Clark—I desire to second the motion of Mr. Wilhere, but wish to add that I am in favor of submitting this printed matter to the gentlemen on the other side, whether they submit theirs or not.

Mr. Hagerty—Mr. President and gentlemen, I think it is taking a little advantage of myself and Mr. Donahoe at this time, as Mr. Donahoe is the only man present outside of myself. There are only two of us, and of course you can carry any motion at this meeting that you choose. But that will not make it binding upon us. I do not think that you are treating myself and my colleague fairly in putting and carrying this motion at this time. For myself I will say that I should be willing to submit to you our printed reports and proceedings. But do you think it would be just right for me to speak for the body I represent after you have sprung a trap like that on a fellow officer of the organization with which I am connected? Why can't you be fair and honest with us, and don't attempt to take advantage of us by little technicalities. It will serve you no good in the future.

Mr. Clark—Mr. Hagerty, what is there that is unfair about us giving you all of our reports and printed matter? We do not ask you for yours; if you do not want to give us yours, we will be more generous and give you ours.

Mr. Wilhere—Gentlemen, have you printed reports of your proceedings?

Mr. Hagerty—They are not yet printed. We have had the proofs of them from the printer. Now, Mr. Wilhere, I want to ask you a question. When you were national delegate, did you not send $75 to the Board of Erin in Ireland, which was returned to you? I dislike to refer to these matters, but you brought it up yourself.

Mr. Wilhere—Yes, sir.

Mr. Hagerty—Now why did they send the $75 back?

Mr. Wilhere—Because we did not owe it.

Mr. Hagerty—Do you know Mr. Kilpatrick on the other side, and did he not resign from your order with some others? Did not that happen here of late, and when there was a general election held over there, didn't he hold a yellow flag out and represent the opposite party for home rule?

Mr. Wilhere—Do you know Daniel Harkens?

Mr. Hagerty—I do.

Mr. Wilhere—Do you know in what business he is engaged? Has he ever made a living for the last fifteen or twenty years for himself?

Mr. Hagerty—The man is an old man. He is a man probably three score and ten, and would you expect a man of that age to make a living for anybody? I wish to know if the honorable Judge here would like to work at his age?

Mr. Wilhere—Did he ever make a living? Did anybody ever inform you that he made a living during the last twenty-five years?

Mr. Hagerty—I only know him through correspondence. But he is the National Secretary today.

Mr. Slattery—I trust that we will not enter into any discussion today as to the men on the other side. Let us confine our little conference here to the settlement, if possible, of any difficulties that may exist on this side of the Atlantic.

Mr. Hagerty—The honorable Judge has entered into that, and I wish to be heard. The man that he speaks of is now, and has been for twenty-five years, the National Secretary, and is the representative of the only legal body on the other side. I did not want to enter into that, but since it has been referred to I wish to say that Mr. Harkens has been the National Secretary for twenty-five years, and is today.

Mr. Wilhere—As a matter of fact that assertion is not true. He never was the National Secretary of the Board of Erin in his existence. As a matter of fact he never was, and is not today. He was not the secretary twenty-five years ago, and he is not today. If we are to go into this matter at all, let us state nothing but the truth, and the truth of the matter is, gentlemen, that Mr. Harkens never was the National Secretary.

Mr. Hagerty—I assure you that it is so, because I have it under his own handwriting; and that is what I know about it. I have come here to tell the truth, and you can swear me under oath, and after I have sworn I will repeat the same words that I have, and I doubt if the other gentleman were sworn he would state matters the same as he has.

Mr. Wilhere—There is no man who knows Daniel Harkens that would believe him.

Mr. Hagerty—Do you know him personally?

Mr. Wilhere—No, sir, I don't, and I thank God for it.

Mr. Hagerty—I do; I know him personally.

President O'Connor—Mr. Hagerty, you may proceed without further interruption.

Mr. Hagerty—Mr. Wilhere knows that when he was

national delegate Mr. Harkens was the National Secretary of the Board of Erin, and he knows that he occupies the same place today.

Mr. Wilhere—Again I repeat that that is not true. Mr. President, I am compelled when a gentleman makes an alleged statement of fact in my presence which I know is not true, I am compelled in justice to the organization of which I am a member to state that the statements by Mr. Hagerty are not true.

Mr. Hagerty—I am here, sir, to hold myself responsible for the truth of every statement that I make. We are not here to be hoodwinked. And I am surprised at the honorable gentleman getting up here and doubting the truth of my statements. And I again say that I hold myself responsible for my statements here, and I am willing to swear that this man Harkens was, and is today, the National Secretary of the Board of Erin. I did not think that we came here to be bulldozed and hoodwinked by any man. I did not seek the office which I now hold, and never did seek an office; and I dislike any notoriety whatever.

President O'Connor—Mr. Hagerty, I understand you to say that you did not know, of your own knowledge, Mr. Harkens' relation to the people on the other side; that you simply knew it through correspondence.

Mr. Hagerty—I know it from correspondence with all of the national delegates of three kingdoms, and what better proof do you wish? I did not come here to argue matters which have taken place on the other side of the water, but I came here to have you gentlemen submit to us what you wished, and to ascertain if there is any way that we can get together and unite, and I will say that there is no man among you who is more anxious for unity than myself. Bro. Slattery, the National Secretary of your order, has known me for a great many years, and will bear me out in every statement that I make in that regard. We have come here without any notice, and we are unprepared to make any statement, but we wish to hear from you. I told your honorable County President at Patchogue that I knew but one obstacle that stood in the way of unity, and that I thought that it could be removed. That is in relation to the eligibility of members, which I have spoken of before, and I want to ask the County President if that is not the truth. I said to President Sullivan there, as I said here today, that it was a mockery to call an order "Ancient Order of Hibernians" which admitted, under its constitution and bylaws, persons who were not Irish or Irish descent from both parents. We have never permitted such a thing on our side, and I do not think we ever could unite with your body until that provision of your constitution was changed.

President O'Connor—Your convention, as I understand it, fixed this eligibility of membership in your order?

Mr. Hagerty—Yes, sir.

President O'Connor—How would you and your colleague here have the right or authority to change that, even if we agreed upon it here?

Mr. Hagerty—Well, as I said when I took the floor, that I would not think it just or honorable to have to decide at this time any matter of such importance, but it would have to be submitted to our national convention. You have had plenty of time to consider these matters, and we have had no chance to consult as to what steps we might be able to take, and we were more than surprised when we received your invitation to come here. I did not even know your County President up to that time, and I do not think I was ever introduced to him in my life. You had not answered my last letter, and for that reason I did not know of your coming here.

President O'Connor—I have already stated the reason for that.

Mr. Hagerty—I was more than surprised that I did not hear from you.

President O'Connor—But, according to your statement, your hands are still tied.

Mr. Hagerty—Yes, sir, in regard to written communications. I stated that before. I stated that to Mr. Sullivan when I met him down at Patchogue, just the same as I do now. I am not backing out one inch. I certainly would not have come here if I did not have the interest of the order at heart, and if I did not desire unity, and I can assure you that our state delegate, who is here, feels the same about it as I do. We did not come here to divide Irishmen, we came here to unite them. I have no ax to grind, and I am only here for the good and welfare of our race, and I hope that you will not try to take any advantage of us, because it does no good.

Mr. Wilhere—In order to prove that we do not desire to take any advantage, I will state that we represent a body of at least 125,000 men, as can be proven by reference to our national directory, and the gentlemen who are here, to the best of my knowledge and information, I believe represent, possibly, 4,000 men to the utmost.

Mr. Hagerty—Now I object to that statement. How can the gentleman tell how many men we do represent?

Mr. Wilhere—I have general knowledge and information upon that subject, and upon that I found the belief that that is the fact. I know your strength in this locality. Your numbers were counted on last St. Patrick's Day, when every man you had turned out in the parade, and you only numbered 720 men on the streets of New York. Seven hundred and twenty men by actual count. And that can be proven by affidavits of honest and disinterested men. You represent in America about 4,000, while we represent in America about 125,000 of organized and united men. Now to show you that we do not desire to take any advantage of you at all, I move you, sir, that, as the sense of this meeting, we request Mr. Hagerty, as the representative of the dissenting wing, to place upon record at this time the conditions upon which they will reunite with this organization.

Mr. Hagerty—I am more than surprised. Here is another trap, and it is not the first time that Mr. Wilhere has misstated matters at our meeting.

Mr. Wilhere—All we desire is that he place in his own handwriting, as the representative of the organization that he represents, the terms and conditions upon which these 4,000 men will unite with the 125,000 Hibernians whom we represent. That is all we ask.

Mr. Hagerty—How do you know that we represent but 4,000 men? I am more than surprised that any intelligent man would use such remarks here, when he knows them not to be true. .

Mr. Wilhere—We want your own terms and conditions.

Mr. Hagerty—We have come here to get your proposition. We want from this honorable body the terms upon which we can settle and unite.

President O'Connor—There can be no possible objection to our requesting you to do what has been stated, but, if you are not prepared, you may take all the time that you desire.

Mr. Hagerty—We certainly are not prepared today,

and we do not think that it is either manly or upright
in you to ask us to submit anything to you today.
Don't you think it would be more honorable to give me
time to consult with my colleagues, while you have
been consulting all week together here?

President O'Connor—We want to be perfectly fair
with you. Of course I am not one of the old-timers,
and I am not familiar with things in the past, as some
of you gentlemen are, but it seems to me that we have
the right to make the request of you, and if you desire
further time to let us know whether you will comply
with the request, or time for the purpose of preparing
and submitting the terms and conditions upon which
unity can be brought about, that is a matter for you to
decide. If you will state that you are surprised and not
prepared, of course you are entitled to time for prep-
aration.

Mr. Wilhere—I move you, Mr. President, that such
time as Mr. Hagerty thinks necessary be given him to
prepare and submit a statement in writing of the terms
and conditions upon which unity and reconciliaton
may be effected.

Mr. Clark—I second the motion, Mr. Wilhere.

Mr. Hagerty—I think that is all out of place. You
people have been here long enough to consult together
as national officers from the various states of this country, while we have had no time whatever to prepare.
You must remember that it would take some time for

me to get my people together, and it would be considerable of an expense to us. We have now $21,000 in banks and in different trust companies in this city, but still we do not feel like we could bear the expense of such a meeting at this time. You people have been together for some time, and why can't you now submit your proposition while you are here? Would that not be much fairer, and would it not save expense? And then we would submit that in turn to our colleagues.

President O'Connor—Will you permit me to suggest one thing? In one of my letters I asked you to name the terms and conditions upon which a union could be predicated, and you wrote me that if I would satisfy you that we were in affiliation with the board on the other side, you would then submit to us the terms and conditions of settlement. I wrote you that we were in affiliation with what we believed was the legal, constitutional board upon the other side. Now up to the present time, with all due respect to you, I say that you have not submitted the terms and conditions upon which a union could be predicated, and that is what we request.

Mr. Hagerty—Will you please read my letter that I sent you? Were there not questions in that letter which you refused to answer? You claim that you are the legal and genuine body, and I can show it in black and white. Your people have been utterly ignored since the worthy Judge had $75 returned to him. If you were wrong then, how do you come to be right now?

Mr. Wilhere—We were not wrong then.

Mr. Clark—We are taking up a great deal of time and accomplishing nothing.

Mr. Hagerty—If you were upright and honest you would not be afraid to give the names of the men on the other side.

President O'Connor—You said that if I would do one thing you would do the other.

Mr. Clark—What do you want the names for?

Mr. Hagerty—For the simple reason that I wanted to know who you were dealing with. I probably know more than you do about what we are speaking of here. I am an older member of the order. I have been a member from boyhood, and I can prove everything I stated here to be correct. If your people on the other side are traitors, convicts and spies in the ranks, I would not want to belong to them. I want to know who they are. That is my purpose in asking for the information. This man Samuel Kilpatrick that I refer to —I have it in black and white that he tried to elect an Orangeman as member of parliament. That was my reason for asking for information. I wanted to know if there were such members in your order there.

Mr. Donahoe—I wish to answer the statement of Mr. Wilhere as to which is the genuine Board of Erin. When such attacks are made upon the men of my race, whom I know to be honorable gentlemen, then it is time for us to withdraw. Mr. Wilhere has asked if Daniel Harkens ever did an honest day's work. I want to state that I know it to be a fact that he is a shoemaker today, and has been forty-five years working at that business. I presume the statement was made because on the 11th day of May, 1887, Mr. Harkens returned Mr. Wilhere $75, stating to him that he no longer would recognize the body which he represented. I presume Mr. Wilhere is taking the statement of this man Father O'Shaughnessy, who came over here and attended the Louisville convention. This is the same man that was told by Fathers Hamon and Murphy that they would kick him from the Liffey for certain statements that he had made. He is a man without any reputation where he lives, and is not recognized by honorable men in society.

Mr. Wilhere—I object, and I am surprised, and my feelings of respect for manhood and patriotism are outraged here by slanderous statements made against the character of one of the purest and noblest of God's men, and one of the best members of the order, and one of the best Irishmen that ever stood at God's altar to offer up the sacrifice of the Mass, and you will pardon me if I speak harshly in this matter, because I cannot sit here and quietly submit to the slanderous language used by the gentleman towards Father O'Shaughnessy, because he is one of the best Irishmen, and one of the best priests that was ever ordained in the church, and I cannot sit here quietly to hear him slandered and defamed in this infamous way, and I protest against it. If we cannot carry on this controversy here, in an attempt to adjust our differences, without impuning the character of an honest Irish Sogarth Aroon, I think we had better adjourn.   I object to this attack upon the character of the gentleman, and I assert that every word of it is untrue; and I will state further that the man who furnished you that information is a man that has not earned a dollar, and that he is a disgrace to all Irishmen on the other side, and that he was nothing but a common bum, going around from tavern to tavern and from shebeen to shebeen, trying to get somebody to buy him a drink out of charity.   This is your authority to slander and defame the character of one of God's noblest men.

Mr. Donahoe—You know I have been opposed to all of that business.   You say that I have this information from Daniel Harkens.   That is not so. I will name you James Gallagher and James Dolan as my authors. I will name James McKeown and James Morgan, of Belfast, Ireland.   I never in my life said anything against the reputation of any person unless I knew the statement to be a fact.   I have as much respect as any person for the calling of a priest in the Catholic Church, but when it comes to a man going outside of his calling and taking part in such matters as this, then

I would deal with him in outside matters as I would with any other man. Now I think the sooner that this conversation is closed, the better it will be for all. When I came here I did not dream that we were to enter into such discussion as the matters brought up here.

Mr. Wilhere—I objected to your statement as a matter of fact. I did not introduce this matter at all. It grew out of Mr. Hagerty's assertion. And when an assertion is made that is not true, it is my duty to the order, and my duty to the gentlemen here, to deny that assertion, when I know it is not true.

Mr. Donahoe—We are now about to withdraw from the room, and I wish to say that I am not one of these men that will come here and then try to run away with your reputations. I wish to say that our proceedings are now in the hands of the printer, and, speaking for myself, I will say that we will have no objection to your having copies of the same as soon as they are printed. I do not see any reason for withholding it from you. There is one thing that I do hate, and that is the running down of the reputation of my fellowmen in the public press, and I hope that anything that took place here is not for publication. You gentlemen claim that you are representatives of the true Board of Erin. Now we wish you to make a proposition, and we will submit it to our colleagues. Now I am going to leave.

Mr. Wilhere—I call for the motion before Mr. Donahoe leaves.

The Chair—There is a motion that requests from Mr. Hagerty that he suggest the terms and conditions upon which his wing will reunite with ours, and if he desires further time in which to prepare his proposition that sufficient time be allowed.

Mr. Donahoe—Why don't you agree here among yourselves, and submit a proposition to me and my associates?

The motion was then put by the chair and carried.

Mr. Wilhere—We have asked Mr. Hagerty for a proposition, either now or at such time as will suit their convenience, and I now ask him if he will be kind enough to submit us such a proposition?

Mr. Hagerty—If you people mean business, why don't you submit now to us in writing your proposition, and then if there are any differences we can give and take, and probably our matters can be adjusted. I am afraid that you people don't mean unity at all. It has often been said by our people that you did not. It has been said that Judge Wilhere, of Philadelphia, was merely carrying on a game of bluff, and did not mean any settlement, and now we want a proposition from your side first. It may be possible that if a word or two were stricken out from your constitution, and making such changes as I have heretofore suggested, that, if they were submitted to our colleagues, an agreement could be brought about. But at this time we have no authority whatever. We cannot do anything until we meet in convention again. But very likely we could come together then. I cannot see that there is any wrong in asking that much of you.

Mr. Wilhere—I want to ask you gentlemen one question before you retire. Were either of you present in Jefferson Hall at Brooklyn on the 15th of February, 1891?

Mr. Donahoe—I was not.

Mr. Hagerty—I was there.

Mr. Wilhere—Here is what actually occurred, and I say it in the presence of these gentlemen and in the presence of Captain Slattery, who was present, I think. I came there under a very great disadvantage to attend the meeting, which was to be the basis of reunion, and Mr. Sherlock was official head of the seceding wing, and he sat upon the platform, and I was invited there to make a proposition as the official head of the Ancient Order of Hibernians of America. I started in to make a proposition, when I was interrupted by Mr. Sherlock, who pulled out a written document and said that it was his duty under his instructions to read this document, and that that was the proposition alone that they would abide by. He read the document and the proposition was to the effect that he and I should then, within a few weeks, leave this country and go to Europe, and there settle and adjust all differences that there were in the Hibernians of Europe. I said to him in reply to that—that was the substance of his proposition. I said in reply to that proposition just about as I have said here today. We are in America, organized for a noble and patriotic purpose, and whatever difference exist started here in America, and not in Europe; the differences originated here in America and not in Europe; and my suggestion was to settle our own differences here by arbitration, and named Monseigneur John Farley as arbitrator, and I said to Mr. Sherlock: "If you are honest in your effort to bring about unity, put on your hat and come with me; let us go to the Most Reverend Archbishop of New York as representatives of both sides of this controversy, and let these men remain in this hall until we return; let us go to the Archbishop (Laughlin) of this diocese, while these men remain here, and I pledge you on behalf of our organization that whatever the decision of these men may be as to our differences we will abide by it, and then we will come back here and announce that decision to the meeting and let it be final." That proposition was not acceded to. But I was invited to go with Mr. Sherlock to Europe in order to settle alleged differences in the Board of Erin. Bluff! You say we have been bluffing! We have been honest. We have made an honest effort every year to bring about a settlement, and you know that the bluff has been entirely on your side. It is unfair, unjust and untrue, the statement that you have made as to there being any bluff on my part. I am speaking now of what actually occurred, and I will say that the bluff has all been on your side.

Mr. Donahoe—We did not come here to be abused. It was not necessary for you to send for us to be attacked in this way. You assert that you are the only constitutional body, and we believe that we are. Now if you have any proposition to submit, we will accept it and will take up no more of your time.

Mr. Hagerty—I want to answer the Judge. There was a committee of three appointed, the very year you speak of—Mr. Powers, of Chicago, Mr. Hayes, of Brooklyn, and another—and our committee waited two or three days on you, but you claimed that you had some business and could not stay in the city and county of New York any longer.

Mr. Wilhere—That was three years before that.

The Chair—The statement of Mr. Hagerty is not true. I was a member of the committee and you refused to go with us.

Mr. Wilhere—I am glad the Chair has stated the matter as he has, for the opposition have published that falsehood throughout the length and breadth of the land.

The Chair—It is absolutely untrue.

Mr. Hagerty—I understood from Mr. Powers that the committee remained in New York two or three days after the time was up, and Mr. Wilhere was not to be found. Since I have become national delegate of our side, you have removed all obstacles except one, which I think, will have to be removed if you want union.

The Chair—Will you be kind enough to comply with the request that we have made of you?

Mr. Hagerty—I cannot see why your Board of Directors are afraid to make a proposition in writing to us. My term of office is about up, and they have stopped me from making any further propositions.

The Chair—Then you have no authority to make a proposition in writing and submit it to us?

Mr. Hagerty—I have not.

The Chair—Will you not then comply with the request?

Mr. Hagerty—You did not comply with my request. You would not answer the questions that I put to you. I am willing to throw down my office on two hours' notice, and if you people mean business you will make a proposition and send it to us, and I assure you it will receive proper consideration. I cannot see that there is anything now to keep us apart. As I said before, everything has been removed excepting one part of your constitution.

Mr. Wilhere—You agreed by your own letters to submit a proposition to us, as representative of your organization, and you have not done so. You have refused to comply with your own agreement.

Mr. Hagerty—I claim that Mr. O'Connor did not

answer the questions which I put to him, and furnish me with the names that I requested, and for that reason all further correspondence ceased.

Mr. Clark—Here are your letters in which you agreed to submit a proposition.

Mr. Hagerty—Yes, and I stand by the letters; and I want to state again that I never said to Michael Langan that I did not receive Mr. O'Connor's letter. I did say that there was a letter mislaid.

Mr. Wilhere—You have been misinformed about a great many things and lies have been told to you which you believe.

Mr. Hagerty—I have been telling exactly what occurred, and I wish to state again about Daniel Harkens, that he has been the National Secretary for twenty-five years, and is now, and there is no use denying that.

Mr. Wilhere—I have had a better chance, with all due respect to you, of knowing the facts in this matter, for I have had twenty-five years' experience in the order, and have had better opportunities than you have had of knowing the facts in relation to the matters about which I have been talking. And I know perfectly well what I have stated is true. You simply have been misinformed.

Mr. Hagerty—I have got more information about that than you have. I have got the proof, and it is in black and white, and it can be easily proven. Good day, gentlemen.

On May 11th, 1896, the A. O. H. Board of Erin national convention convened in the city of Philadelphia, Pa., and the A. O. H. of America held their national convention in the city of Detroit, Mich., July 14th to 17th, The Board of Erin elected a committee on unity with full power to act, and the A. O. H. of America gave full and discretionary power to their national officers and directors, for the purpose of bringing together both branches of the A. O. H. and to cement them into one grand United Ancient Order of Hibernians.

The Board of Erin convention adopted the following preamble and resolution, to-wit:

The Ancient Order of Hibernians, of the United States of America, in affiliation with the Board of Erin in National Convention assembled, congratulate ourselves upon the wholesome, intelligent and earnest growth of our order during the past year and, with pardonable pride, point to it as an evidence of a re-awakened desire on the part of the children of Innisfail, in this country, to win by patriotic devotion to American institutions, loyalty to the government under which we live, and for the perpetuation of which we are ever ready to risk all we hold most dear—that distinction and recognition to which our numerical strength, law-abiding disposition and mental organization, entitle us. It would be trite, if not commonplace, to recount the names of the heroic dead of Irish birth

and parentage who have, in peace and war, signalized
by burning words of attachment and a prowess that
knows no retreat, their unalterable resolve, that this
great nation of the western hemisphere shall remain
the haven of the oppressed of less favored lands and
the home of equality and liberality. It is with no vain-
glorious spirit, nor to enlist controversy, that we refer those who criticise us to the pages of impartial history to prove that our people, before and since the
revolutionary era, have been foremost in the halls of
legislation, on the fields of battle—on land and water—
among those who struggled to establish and maintain
an "indissoluble union of indestructible states." In
view of our claims to at least fair consideration from all
classes of our fellow-citizens, we cannot refrain from
expressing our surprise at and unqualified condemnation of the discrimination that is directed against us
by an organized aggregation of makeshifts who parade
under the euphonious, but misleading, name of the
American Protective Association. Knowing our honest rights in this enduring and glorious land of freedom, we are unable to learn why we should be the
objects of hatred or the subjects of persecution, nor do
we care to inquire why or seek an amnesty that we did
nothing to make possible. Presenting the foregoing
briefly summarized references as a preamble, the committee beg leave to submit the following resolutions:

Whereas, The Ancient Order of Hibernians, of the

United States of America, in affiliation with Board of Erin have, by judicious management and discretion, attained a gratifying position among the truly sincere and liberal fraternities of the United States, and

Whereas, It is the design and earnest hope of the order to ever deserve the respect and confidence of the people of this country, by leading upright lives and remaining unchangingly faithful to the imperishable principles of constitutional government:

Therefore, Be it Resolved, That we invite the co-operation of our fellow-citizens of the Irish race to the end that, as a people, we may by unity of action and unison of thought, command that esteem and consideration, as loyal American citizens, which we should receive and which is easily within our grasp, if wise and thoughtful discretion is observed and capable and trustworthy leadership is recognized and obeyed.

Resolved, That we favor the cause of Catholic education, believing that those who are trained in the ways of righteousness and learn and observe the lessons of true christianity, adorn society, make virtue lustrous, cherish integrity, ennoble humanity, render honesty priceless, enkindle patriotism and give citizenship an enduring loyalty.

Resolved, That we are in fullest accord with the suggestion that a chair be endowed in the Catholic University, at Washington, for the revival and teaching of the Irish language and that we pledge our moral support and financial aid to the accomplishment of the same.

Resolved, That we recognize the advancement of temperance as a most salutary sign and one of the greatest blessings that could come to our people. We further pledge ourselves to the encouragement of the cause of Total Abstinence and renew our respect for and allegiance to the brilliant corps of self-sacrificing men who are so ably and successfully battling against the evils of strong drink and inculcating and disseminating the noble virtues and lasting benefits of sobriety. We repeat an often stated truth when we assert that no vice has been so damaging to the moral, intellectual and physical welfare of our people as that of intoxication, and to modify, if not entirely eradicate it, is one of the most earnest desires of our order.

Resolved, That we recognize the right of suffrage as a sacred privilege, and one that should be exercised freely and with an honest purpose. As an order we do not identify ourselves with any political party, or endorse any policy that is a source of honest difference of opinion among well-meaning citizens. We, however, deprecate the unwarranted use of the name of our order by any of its representatives for the furtherance of the aspirations of any party, as such use tends to permanent disintegration and public reproach. Dissensions have often been occasioned by probably thoughtless, yet indiscreet, action of members who permitted the impression to go forth that our order partook of the nature of a chattel that was at the behests of the political organization that wielded the most potent influence and was best endowed with financial equipment. We cannot be too pronounced in our discouragement of any action that can possibly breed discontent in our ranks, or too firm in encouraging everything that will produce harmony and fraternal relations in our order.

Resolved, That a sincere amalgamation of all Irish American societies actuated by similar motives and prompted by the same design is earnestly requested. Why there should be any opposition to such a desirable coalition, is beyond the comprehension of reasonable minds. Lack of agreement, in matters of detail, ought not be permitted to defeat the primary object. "In union there is strength," and the converse of that aphorism is, inevitably, weakness. Too much cannot be done to bring about that earnest unity—which so many have long looked for and would so gladly hail as an omen that promises the realization of achievements that heretofore have existed only in the rosy vision of poetic fancy—the alluring pages of romantic creations, or in the hopeful dreams of the poor exile. The judicious and permanent uniting of the Irish people in this country on a basis of the highest integrity is an anxiously sought desideratum, for the consummation of which our best endeavors should be used, and best thoughts employed. Acting in unison we will command the admiration of our fellow-citizens, thwart illy-conceived opposition, reach a higher intellectual plane, attract friendlier consideration, wield a greater power, exercise a broader influence, be of more mutual advantage to each other, and establish a grand fraternity that will be edifying, instructive, elevating, beneficial and lasting. The necessity for such a condition is too apparent and too generally felt to need elaboration. The principles of our ancient and enduring order contemplate the betterment of their adherents and invite co-operation in their intelligent fulfilment. The time is ripe for action, and no place is so appropriate for the inauguration of such a desired resolve as here in this great historic city of brotherly love—the cradle of liberty—where first the peals of emancipation and disenthralment rung out on the air of gladness—here where the right of the masses to govern was first promulgated and which will be a place where valor may halt and freedom trim her torch.

Resolved, That we favor a leadership of men who are imbued with lofty and expanding purposes, who are proof against retrograding tendencies, and who regard the living present and promising future of paramount importance to the unfortunate occurrences and fadeless glories of the past, sad in contemplation and inspiring in reflection as the latter may be. This is essential in order that we may keep in the vanguard of the procession of progress that is marching onward to greater achievements in a nation in which equal opportunities are offered to all her worthy citizens.

Resolved, That we regard the publicly expressed hostility of the alleged American Protective Association as an emanation of bigotry, counterparts of which have been buried every century since enlightened citizenship and broad-minded statemanship blessed the domains of civilization and toleration. Believing in the unerring philosophy of history we deem their mission short-lived, and their power for mischief circumscribed and limited. We have confidence in the nobleness of American manhood and, proving ourselves worthy, we feel that no narrow-minded progeny can ever, in Fair Columbia, become successful in waging an untenable and unpatriotic crusade against any creed or race that adheres to the inimitable principles of right, and although an unholy alliance may, and unmistakably does, exist, we nevertheless counsel our adherents to patiently await the more sober and calmer judgment of these misguided people.

Resolved, That we extend to the Cuban patriots our sincere and cordial sympathy in their struggle for country and liberty, and hope and pray that their effort for home rule and home government will be successful.

Approved by National Officers and adopted by the national convention.

TERENCE DONOHUE, Chairman.
DR. T. C. FITZSIMMONS,
D. J. BARR,
JOHN QUINNAN.

At the Detroit convention of the A. O. H., of America, the following resolution was unanimously adopted:

The Ancient Order of Hibernians, in national convention assembled renews its pledge of filial obedience to our Holy Mother, the church, and since being a practical Catholic is an essential of eligibility to membership in our order and our religion teaches us that we are bound to serve our country and our government with fidelity, our duty as citizens is based not alone on sentiments of patriotism but on the substantial footing of a religious and moral obligation.

Our order never has attempted and never will attempt to dictate or control the political action of any of its members. We believe that all political questions should be discussed openly and decided by the honest ballot of all citizens, each so voting as his individual judgment will best serve the interests, integrity and honor of his country; and we denounce as inimical to free government and disloyal to American institutions all secret organizations based on race, class or religious prejudice which would deprive any American citizen of his individual political liberty or directly or indirectly require qualifications for office forbidden by the constitution of our country. American history affords all the vindication we ask of the patriotism of Irishmen or Catholics. While we love the land from which we sprung and the race from which we have descended, we hold the conscientious discharge of our individual obligations to this land of the free and the the maintenance of its laws and its government our first civil duty. In all domestic affairs our motto is "The greatest liberty to the individual consistent with the rights of all," and in all international complications we subscribe without reservation to the sentiment, "Our Country, may she always be right, but, right or wrong, Our Country."

The civil, religious and political liberty for which the people of Ireland have struggled during so many centuries of oppression, we hold to be the birthright of all peoples, and while we pray fervently and work unceasingly for the dawn of Irish independence, our sympathies and assistance are ever ready to go out to the oppressed of every other land; and in this spirit we extend to the struggling patriots of Cuba our cordial sympathy and join our prayers with theirs for the speedy arrival of the day of their deliverance.

For years the Irish people and their leaders have looked to America for material and moral support in their struggles for liberty, and such support has been freely given. Foremost of all among those who have so generously responded have been members of the Ancient Order of Hibernians. We therefore demand of the official representatives of the Irish people in parliament, unity of action and singleness of purpose, the putting aside of all personal bickerings and petty grievances, and the presentation of a united and solid front in their demands for the redress of Ireland's wrongs, and we warn all who would put individual considerations before duty to their country that history will hold them responsible for all delays and sufferings caused by their censurable inaction and want of united effort. Whenever we are assured of harmonious action on the part of the representatives of our race in Ireland we pledge them our most hearty co-operation and support.

We rejoice that our objects and purposes have so far become understood that our ancient and honorable order is now everywhere welcomed as a valuable auxiliary of the church and is denominated by his grace, Archbishop Ryan of Philadelphia, speaking for the American hierarchy, as "A most desirable society."

We commend the endeavors made by our national officers and board of directors to bring about the return of the members of the so-called B. of E. A. O. H. to this organization, and we regret that our efforts to that end have not as yet been crowned with success; but inasmuch as we desire unity and harmony with all who profess the name of Hibernians, we again authorize and empower our incoming national officers and directory to use all proper means to effect the reunion with our order of the members of the dissenting A. O. H.

In the spread of Hibernian literature we recognize a

powerful aid in the development of this organization, and we declare it to be the duty of each member and of each division, wherever the same is practicable, to accord to those journals and periodicals which are devoted to the interests of Hibernianism their generous material support.

We extend a generous and hearty godspeed to all kindred societies, organized for the promotion of Catholic charity, benevolence and all other good works looking to the spiritual good and material advancement of our people; especially do we commend those societies which like ourselves are engaged in the work of elevating the character of the Irish race in America and in promoting the sacred cause of Irish liberty.

To the end that the works of our order may become better known to our members and our fellow-citizens, we hereby empower and direct the incoming national officers and directory to take such steps as in their judgment may appear most feasible to cause to be prepared and published an authentic history of the order.

In the year 1898 will occur the centennial of the memorable battles in which our forefathers gave up their lives in their gallant struggles to wrench Ireland from the grasp of her oppressor. We are proud of the spirit which animated the heroes of that time in their determination to restore to their land the blessing of independence; and we desire to perpetuate the significance of their glorious sacrifice. To the end that this may be done we call upon the respective state and county organizations throughout the country to observe on the 21st day of June, 1898, the anniversary of the famous struggle of Vinegar Hill, in such manner as may seem meet and befitting the memories of that occasion.

Signed the adoption of resolutions:

> JAMES F. STRATTON,
> M. F. WILHERE,
> W. F. REDDY,
> PATRICK O'NEILL,
> JAMES McIVER,
> JAMES McKENNA,
> E. P. HUGHES,
> L. J. TIERNEY,
> JAMES P. BREE,
> T. J. MAHONY,
> THOS. L. CONROY,
> D. MAHER,
> DAN McGLYNN,
> CHAS. J. O'NEILL,
> MR. SHINE,
> J. E. DOLAN.

In 1896 both national conventions elected committees on unity, with full power to act.

Prior to the committee's meeting the following correspondence passed between P. McGarry, National Delegate of the B. of E., and P. J. O'Connor, National President for the B. of A.

P. McGARRY TO P. J. O'CONNOR.

Chicago, Ill., Oct. 1st, 1896.

Mr. **P. J.** O'Connor, Savannah, Ga.:

Dear Sir—At the last annual convention of the A. O. H. (Board of Erin), held in the City of Philadelphia, May 11th, 12th and 13th, 1896, a committee of five (5) were elected to act with the national officers to try and bring about unity on an honorable basis among all Hibernians. This committee has full power to act in the matter. I will be glad to hear from you at your earliest convenience and receive any suggestions which you consider likely to lead to that grand result.

Yours truly,

P. McGARRY,

N. D., A. O. H., Board of Erin.

O'CONNOR TO McGARRY.

Savannah, Ga., Oct. 12th, 1896.

Mr. P. McGarry, Chicago, Ill.:

Dear Sir—Your favor of the 3rd inst. was received and duly considered. In view of previous experience with the conference committee from your wing I insist upon a definite statement being furnished us as to the position you and your colleagues propose to occupy and the terms that will be asked before considering the matter. If you mean business send a statement to me by the 21st inst. in care of the Shoreham Hotel, Washington, D. C., and our national officers and directors will then pass thereon and you will be promptly advised of the result. Yours truly,

P. J. O'CONNOR,

N. P., A. O. H. of America.

Chicago, Ill., Oct. 17th, 1896.

P. J. O'Connor, Shoreham Hotel, Washington, D. C.:

Dear Sir—Your favor of the 12th inst. received and contents noted. I am not aware of any committee from our order having met in conference with a like committee from your order, except you mean the meeting of your board of directors in New York last August, to which you invited our N. D., James J. Hagerty, and Terence Donohue, S. D., of New York. We do not consider that meeting a conference, as those gentlemen had no power to act for our order. This committee which we have selected has full power to act and mean business to my view. There are only two debatable points in the unfortunate misunderstanding now existing among Hibernians in this country, and to try and settle those two points is the object of this committee being elected, and the terms we propose to make and settle on are: First, the recognition of the Board of Erin as the supreme head of the order so long as they do not ask to do anything which will conflict with our duties as American citizens, as Irish patriots, or as practical Catholics. Second, no person shall become a member of this order who is not Irish by birth or descent from both father and mother, and a practical Roman Catholic. We consider all other points in dispute of minor importance, and are ready at any time it will suit your convenience to meet a committee from your order and debate those two questions with the view of bringing about United Ancient Order of Hibernians. Hoping to get an early reply, I remain, yours truly,

P. McGARRY,
N. D., A. O. H., Board of Erin.

O'CONNOR TO McGARRY.

Savannah, Ga., Feb. 13th, 1897.

Mr. P. McGarry, Chicago, Ill.:

Dear Sir—Through an inexcusable blunder in my office, a letter written to you shortly after my return from Washington, D. C., last fall, was discovered to-day, and consequently not forwarded. I regret the same very much, because I wanted to be courteous, at least, to you, and all my correspondents. While there has been considerable delay on account thereof, I sincerely trust it will not prevent the pending matter from receiving due consideration. Your favor addressed to me at Washington presented two questions of differences, to which I will now reply:

First—As to the recognition of the Board of Erin, etc. In reference thereto I have this to say: We are here on American soil, and have a constitution and system of laws for our own guidance. Our obligation was taken under the constitution of the A. O. H. of the United States, and are to be guided and directed by its principles alone.

The Board of Erin, from the very foundation of the

order, occupies the same relation to our organization now as heretofore, and that is, we interchange cards, receive merchandise from them, so as to have common merchandise throughout the world, and one chief executive has concurrent jurisdiction with said board in all matters pertaining to the making of merchandise and in all national questions that may arise. If we have any differences here let us settle them first, and then if it is necessary, after we are united for the common good, we will be willing to send a representative to the other side and adjust any differences that might exist there as to our qualifications for membership. In reference thereto, I have this to say: Our order would not consent to change the same; our order has prospered greatly thereunder, and many of our best people enrolled in our column. The same were, I believe, agreed to in Cleveland before the secession took place, and the wisdom of its adoption has been shown by the success since and the hearty approval of clergy and laymen. We will be glad to get together on a basis that will not affect our present membership or deprive our people from enjoying our benefits, and will be in consonance with true Hibernianism. If necessary, I could have a committee of say three from our side to meet a similar committee from yours in New York City early in March, to discuss the entire situation and see if it is possible for us to reach an agreement that will result in an honorable union. With kindest regards, I am, fraternally,   P. J. O'CONNOR, N. P.

McGARRY TO O'CONNOR.

Chicago, Ill., Feb. 17, 1897.

Mr. P. J. O'Connor, Savannah, Ga.:

Dear Sir—I have just returned from New York and find your favor of the 13th inst. Our national officers and committee met in The Vanderbilt, New York City, on Sunday, the 14th inst., and you will be notified of the results of that meeting by our National Secretary.

Yours very truly,　　　P. McGARRY,

N. D., A. O. H., Board of Erin.

O'CONNOR TO McGARRY.

Mr. P. McGarry, N. D., A. O. H., Board of Erin,
Chicago, Ill.:

Savannah, Ga., Feb. 22nd, 1897.

Dear Sir—Your last favor received. Your National Secretary's communication arrived this morning. I replied thereto, urging a conference in Philadelphia on the 5th of March. I will address the Emmet gathering on the 4th in that city, and can arrange to have a majority of my colleagues present the day following. My engagements are of such an imperative character that unless a conference is held at the latter part of next week in a convenient place I will be unable to attend one before July or August. You will certainly have no more trouble in getting a majority of your committee present at that time than I will have with mine. I trust, therefore, you will accept my suggestion and meet them with the earnest hope that union will bless our efforts. I leave here next Monday for Washington and Philadelphia, and will be glad to hear from you before that day. With best wishes, I am, yours very truly,　　　P. J. O'CONNOR,

N. P., A. O. H. of America.

Chicago, Ill., Feb. 25th, 1897.

Mr. P. J. O'Connor, N. P., A. O. H., of America, Savannah, Ga.:

Dear Sir—Your favor of the 22nd inst. to hand and contents noted. In reply I will say I am at present President of the Confederated Irish Societies of this city, which compose a part of the great Irish organization of the Clan-na-gael. We celebrate the anniversary of the birth of Ireland's martyr patriot, Robert Emmet, annually, as becomes Irish patriots. Our arrangements for the coming 4th of March are all completed and our programmes will come from the printers today. I have been honored by being selected as chairman for that occasion, so it is impossible for me to be in Philadelphia on the day you mention (5th of March). I will add, that it is very inconvenient for me to leave my business and go East so soon after my last trip, but in view of the object of unity among all Hibernians on an honorable basis I, and as many of my colleagues as possible, will meet you and your colleagues in Philadelphia on Sunday, the 7th of March, at the hotel agreed on. I can leave here on Friday and be in Philadelphia Saturday afternoon and meet you at your hotel and make arrangements for meeting on Sunday. Had it not been for our arrangements being completed here, the 5th would answer me as well as any other date, so I hope you will make the 7th convenient, so as we can make another, and I hope, the last effort toward unity. I will send a copy of this letter to our N. S. Please advise me not later than Wednesday, the 3rd of March. Yours very truly,

P. McGARRY,

N. D., A. O. H., Board of Erin.

Savannah, Ga., Feb. 28th, 1897.

P. McGarry, 442 Seminary Avenue, Chicago, Ill.:

Your secretary wired me yesterday your committee would meet ours in Philadelphia March 5th. I immediately notified our committee. I appreciate your position and regret I am compelled to be in Savannah March 7th. If necessary we can agree for a conference at a later date. Wire me if I shall recall my notices.

P. J. O'CONNOR.

Mr. McGarry wired Mr. O'Connor as follows:

Chicago, Ill., Feb. 28th, 1897.

To P. J. O'Connor, Southern Bank Building, Savannah, Ga.:

I will not block conference. Proceed with meeting. My colleagues know my views.   McGARRY.

Mr. P. McGarry, national delegate of the A. O. H., Board of Erin, being unable to attend the conference at Philadelphia on March 5th, 1897, the Rev. E. S. Phillips, of Plains, Luzerne County, Pa., was appointed as substitute for McGarry. Mr. Terence Donohue, state delegate of New York, was requested by the national delegate to attend the Philadelphia conference, as he thought that the state delegate of Ohio could not attend. The following are the minutes of the Philadelphia conference, convened at Dooner's Hotel, March 5th, 1897:

> P. J. O'CONNOR, National President.
> JOHN C. WEADOCK, National Vice-Pres.
> JAMES O'SULLIVAN, National Secretary.
> JOHN P. MURPHY, National Director.
> MAURICE F. WILHERE, Nat'l Director.
> > *National Committee representing*
> > *the A. O. H., B. of A.*

> JAMES J. HAGERTY, Ex-Nat'l Delegate.
> REV. E. S. PHILLIPS.
> E. R. HAYES, National Secretary.
> JOHN McWILLIAMS, National Treasurer.
> JOSEPH McLAUGHLIN, State Del., Penn.
> THOMAS F. McGRATH, State Del., Ohio.
> TERENCE DONOHUE, State Del., N. Y.
> MILES McPORTLAND, County Delegate,
> > (Kings Co.) New York State.
> WILLIAM M. BARRY, State Treasurer,
> > New Jersey.
> > *National Committee representing*
> > *the A. O. H., B. of E.*

Mr. P. J. O'Connor in the chair.

By Mr. O'Connor:

During the month of February a communication was sent to the National Secretary and a similar communication was sent to me, both communications being sent by Mr. E. R. Hayes, National Secretary of the Ancient Order of Hibernians.   The communication read as follows:

New Brunswick, N. J., Feb. 16, 1897.

James O'Sullivan, Esq., Secretary:

Dear Sir—The undersigned, a committee elected at the forty-seventh annual convention of the A. O. H., have been delegated with full power from our order to unite the two bodies of the A. O. H. in this country into one, if possible.   At a meeting of this committee, held in the Vanderbilt Hotel, New York, February 14, 1897, the committee came to the conclusion that they would make one more effort to have the representatives of your order meet with them, the object being the unity of both orders.   A failure to receive a reply to this before March 1st, will be taken as a refusal on your part to unite the orders of this country, and we will act accordingly.

E. R. HAYES, N. S.

JOHN McWILLIAMS, N. D.

THOMAS McGRATH, S. D. O.

M. F. McPORTLAND, C. D. K., Co. N.Y.

PATRICK McGARRY, N. D.

JAMES J. HAGERTY, Ex-N. D.

JOSEPH McLAUGHLIN, S. D., Pa.

WILLIAM BARRY, S. T., N. J.

I replied to this communication that we were very glad to meet the gentlemen whose names have been read, on this date, for the purpose of having a conference with a view to effecting, if possible, a union among our people. We are here for the purpose of going into that conference, and for the purpose of hearing from the gentlemen who suggested it.

By the Rev. E. S. Phillips:

Mr. Chairman, has the reply been made to this letter, or is this the reply?

Mr. O'Connor—The reply was that made here at this time that we would meet them here for the purpose of having a conference, and they are here in pursuance to it.

Rev. Phillips—Are the committee willing to accept the proposition?

Mr. O'Connor—There has been no proposition made. We are here to receive and entertain any proposition that is to be made.

Mr. Hagerty—We came here to hear what proposition you will give, and we are willing and ready to give one at a recess. You know August, a year ago, Mr. Chairman, you sent a sealed letter to my country home by two messengers and the County Secretary, to meet you on short notice. In the absence of the national officers, I telegraphed to the state delegate in New York. You then asked the same question you ask today: If we were willing to give you a proposition. Now you sent your messenger down to me, the county delegate, and you were three days in session and more, and I think it will be no more than fair and just to our committee that you will give our committee a proposition to work on.

Mr. O'Connor—I understand you gentlemen asked for a conference and required an answer in a certain time?

Mr. Hagerty—Our national delegate made the terms in his first letter, and he was elected in Philadelphia, with full power to act.

Mr. O'Connor—Do I understand that you submit these terms?

Mr. Hagerty—We are willing to submit others if they are not suitable. We may add to them if the committee agrees on our side.

Mr. Hayes—I will state, Mr. Chairman, the reason why the committee came to the conclusion to send the document just read (it might seem abrupt), but our national delegate had written to you some three or four months previous to this at your request, stating some proposition, and requested that you make some proposition to work on, and while he had not time to communicate with his full committee throughout the country, he gave the proposition he first gave, that he might get a conference, and that they might make a unity. To that communication he never received a reply. You know you gave him but little time, as you were going to Washington, and he had not the time to communicate with members throughout the country. It was going on to four months (over three) and no reply. This is why these documents were read on March 1, and, of course, we determined to take some action, and as men, we had to make some definite answer to those who created us a committee, that we might act intelligently one way or another. As regards a proposition, the committee feel that there has been a grievance in the two organizations which existed before the initiation of myself and you, and others, and we think the better way is to come to an understanding intelligently under some friendly agreement with the organization's representatives on both sides, and that we could, in a nice quiet, peacable way, discover here in a general conversation what are the vital issues which either organization want us to stick to, or give way. We come here to see if it is possible to bring out in a general discussion what is really the vital point that keeps the organized Irishmen of this country apart, and if there is any way of bringing them together. Personally I object to propositions on this ground, as we could do much better work that way than submitting a proposition and having the other refuse it.

Rev. Phillips—Mr. Chairman, I wish to state in behalf of the rank and file of the Ancient Order of Hibernians, known as the Board of Erin, that unity is very much desired. But it is expected that it be without

any sacrifice of honor or principle on either side. I
have had occasion to test the sentiment of our people
in a course of lectures which I delivered, and I find
that whenever unity between the boards was mentioned, it was received with most marked evidence of
approbation.   And I have also had occasion to discover the feelings of the members constituting the two
boards in Ireland, and I know that unity is very much
desired there; in fact, it is prayed for, for the condition
of the order there, as here (and there more than here)
is quite deplorable, owing to the differences of feeling
on account of disunion.   But it was told by men high
in the councils of the board there, that the trouble is
here, and if we can adjust matters in America, that
unity will necessarily follow in Ireland, and I hope that
the discussion of this vital question of unity today will
be in accordance with our own personal desires to see
our own people reunited.   I know in the industrial sections of this state, where the mining districts are, our
people are bitterly opposed to each other, not only in
society affairs, but on other questions, and they are
presenting a great scandal and an element of discord.
Now, in regard to politics (I will use that as an illustration, without special reference), they are making
each other an object for special enmity, and are therefore doing each other considerable harm in American
affairs, and they are presenting to the people of Ireland an example for dissension that is wrecking the

hopes of the workers for the national cause in Ireland. I had the distinguished honor to represent the Board of Erin at the Irish race convention.   The objection was made to me there that my position was unsustained inasmuch as I advocated party affairs, and the society to which I belonged was opposed to unity. I deny that, as far as the Board of Erin is concerned, but as far as the A. O. H. B. of A. is concerned, that has the same motto of "Friendship, Unity and True Christian Charity," that is another matter. In any case, we are setting a very bad example to our people on the other side, and it is well for us before we take any further action in the national affairs in Ireland, to try to get together here as children of a country that is loved by our parents, and those among us who are of Irish descent, and every good man who has been forced by the sorrow of unwilling exile, to make this land his home. I trust in our deliberations today, we will forget everything like bitterness of feeling, for everyone has this matter at heart, no matter on which side he may be. But let us, at the same time, endeavor to get at the root of the difficulty so that when we ask our associates at home to adopt the views that may seem feasible to us here, we will be able to satisfy whatever scruples they may have in regard to the validity of the organization to which they belong.

Mr. O'Connor—My own judgment is that the gentlemen who have recently passed on this matter and who knew all about this conference, should certainly submit some proposition, and I assure you we will make prompt answer to it, and in such a way that there will be no question about it. My own idea is that I prefer to have a proposition submitted in writing, or a counter-proposition in writing, so that there can be no question hereafter as to what was or was not submitted.

Mr. Donohue—Mr. Chairman, we had asked for a conference and co-operation of the A. O. H. If I understand myself, you did the same at the national convention as the Board of Erin did in the City of Liberty, Philadelphia. Now, sir, if there is any point that stands in the way of unity, the sooner our people know of it the better. If there are any persons who stand in the way of uniting the sooner our people know of it the better. Having these gentlemen appointed from both sides, appointed from your own convention, certainly it must be the sentiment of both organizations that their intention was unity of the organization. Therefore, it becomes the committee on both sides, in my estimation, to submit their own terms on an amicable basis, so that the organization can unite without degrading one or the other. We as a people receive the same sacraments, we kneel at the same altar, and it is a disgrace to the civilized world to say that the Irish people are divided in the Land of Liberty, as well as in the land of persecution, which gave them birth.

We come here as one member, fully determined, if possible, to see our people united. Do not let it go broadcast that we seek office. Every officer in the Board of Erin is willing to lay down his official duties and give his friendship to his brother, and let the rank and file unite in one grand organization that will be a credit to the Irish people of this country. They have aided and assisted emigrants in this country, that was the great object of this organization. They have aided the church by building temples erected to the living God. They have aided in building schools of education that our people might compare favorably with any race on the face of the earth. They have not only subscribed in this country, but they have extended their subscriptions to Rome; they have extended them into Scotland for the education of the people. So have you. We have sent subscriptions into the four provinces in Ireland; into the districts of Pennsylvania, even as far as California; therefore, if we are to be united in this grand, charitable movement, that we can be united, come together and bury the past that it may never again be brought to the surface. Then we will go back with credit to ourselves, as well as a credit to the Irish nation.

Mr. McPartland—Mr. Chairman, I have been a member of this organization for the past ten years. Unfortunately, I was not born in Ireland, but it strikes me very forcible that an organization of this character should be united. I have heard time and time again that the members representing the American board had appealed continually for a conference committee. We were ready at all times to meet them. With that object in view, for some time I had the idea put into my mind to advocate a committee from our organization, giving them some of the powers that I was led to believe the American board had, having full power to settle all differences outside that convention. With this idea in view this committee met in Philadelphia. The intention is to unite the two orders on an honorable basis. It seems to me that the differences existing between the two bodies is very slight; it is simply a misunderstanding, and if the gentlemen of this committee representing the American board insist upon a proposition coming from our side, it is only fair and just that the same should be submitted from their side. We feel that this can be settled today, and if it cannot be settled today we are willing to go on record of having a committee leave this country, investigate who is responsible for this condition of affairs we are passing through, and whoever is responsible, let them be dealt with accordingly, and whoever is right, let the question be settled by the country at large, and unite on a basis that will be creditable to both sides. I am in favor of unity. I know that the organization has always outspoken itself of being in favor of unity. This committee has everything in their hands, and I hope before we leave this city today, if there is any way to get at this question, we will do it, and if we must submit a proposition, let us find out what proposition we can make, and then have a recess and discuss the important matters in the discussion, and I think before we leave this city, we will be able to arrive at some conclusion that will be creditable to both organizations, and return home with the one mind and one opinion that unity has been at last proclaimed in the A. O. H.

Rev. Phillips—I would like, Mr. Chairman, to have some expression of sentiment from the American Board. I think the Board of Erin has expressed itself in the matter of this conference. We have not heard from the other side except the preliminary remarks of the Chairman.

Mr. O'Connor—I presume we will hear from them. We will hear from Brother Wilhere on the subject.

Mr. Wilhere—Mr. Chairman: The reason I imagine we are so silent in reference to the particular purpose of this assemblage today is because of the fact that we were led to believe, in point of fact, are convinced of it, that this gathering is brought together for the purpose of hearing from the gentlemen representing the Board of Erin. We in America, hearing from them a definite proposition which we would consider, and which we would answer affirmatively or negatively, in a very short time. We are just as anxious for unity as any member on the other side. I

am sure my brethren are just as anxious as I am, and
I have been working on this proposition for two years.
We represent an organization of more than 100,000
men who are living and existing and have a being, and
in order to be practical about the matter, if we are going to get on a basis, we would ask you gentlemen as
to how many you represent? We are led to believe,
in fact, I have in my office a report of the convention
held in Luzerne County, Pa., a county from which our
honored Father here comes, and this report states that
some three years ago, your organization represented
less than 5,000, and I am sure they represent less than
that today. I have every reason to suppose you actually represent about 3,000 men. If I am deceived in that
we are willing to produce the documents, facts and
figures in order to sustain our assertion. If you
gentlemen represent a large body, produce the documents, give us the evidence. Outside of that, however,
laying aside the question of numbers, no matter how
many we represent, we are firmly convinced of the fact
that it is your duty, first, because you have asked for
this conference, and secondly, because you are numer-
ically inferior to us. It is your duty to submit a proposition here in writing; it will be treated with every consideration and a prompt answer will be furnished you.
Again, I say, I am sure every brother representing the
A. O. H. of America here today will concur with me
that we are as anxious as any man in America or Ireland may be.

Mr. McWilliams—Mr. Chairman, in reply to the remarks of Brother Wilhere, I will state that we did not
come here to ask about numerical business. It does
not make any difference if we had 10,000 or you had
2,000, still the split keeps on, and it looks as bad of
your 10,000 as our 2,000 in the eyes of the public, to
keep the strife going on. It has been going on for the
last ten years and what has been the result? It is an
evident fact that if it was put to a popular vote, of your
100,000, I'll bet 80,000 would vote for unity. It is because they belong to the organization; they are waiting
to see the outcome. Plenty of those on our own side
feel the very same. They are waiting to see what these
committees will do from year to year. Mr. Chairman,
it was only yesterday afternoon before I left my home,
that a committee of the American Board waited on me.
They said they heard I was coming to Philadelphia
as one of the committee on conference. I said, "Yes."
"Well," they said, "what was your idea of it?" "Well,"
said I, "you have known me a good many years?"
"Yes."   "Have you ever heard me speak against
unity?" They said: "We hope you will use every effort and means in an honorable way, provided you can
bring about the desired union." Mr. Chairman, belonging to the Board of Erin, etc., we have not heard
any remarks yet as to what was the cause of this little
dissatisfaction and trouble. As Mr. Hagerty has suggested, this thing of bringing big documents and presenting them is only a waste of time. Let the brothers

express what they wish. You have good competent stenographers to take it down. Do not be afraid to spread it broadcast to the world; do not spend unnecessary time to draw out documents, compare them with each other and then throw them into the waste basket. Let bygones be bygones. We are living in a progressive age; we come here to shake hands in friendship and fellowship; the rank and file of the whole country demands, common sense demands, everything de-demands it. Mr. Chairman, are we going to stand here on little technicalities? Are we going to stand here and keep our race divided, and say: "There are two boards on the other side?" I think the easiest way would be for this committee to appoint one on each side, and let it go over there; hold a meeting over there and tell them what transpired at this meeting here, and let the two boards meet and decide upon what is right, and we will follow them; and if our side is right, we will expect them to follow us. This is the best thing to be done. There is no use meeting in this way from time to time without getting down to business.

Mr. Weadock—I have remained quiet until this time for the reason that the section of the country from which I hail knows nothing, except by hearsay, of any difference existing between the Irish people of America. I want to say that it is my individual opinion that you gentlemen who are laboring under the impression that there are differences between the Irish people of America are mistaken. The differences do not exist between the people. I think if we applied to a consideration of the question which will be presented to us today our fair and unbiased judgments, that we would not find ourselves necessarily applying bad judgment to a question of difference existing between the people. There are differences that apparently exist elsewhere, and I think that, upon this subject, not having been associated with any parties who have had differences, that I can judge with some degree, if not a full degree of impartiality. Now, we are met here, and I want to say to you that we people in the west want when we read the proceedings of our convention (and it is about the only place that we hear of these differences), that there shall be no reference to any dissension among the Irish people, for the reason that there ought not to be any. We people in the west want absolute unity, and I want to say to you that we are not fearful of expressing our opinion. Now, the question is, how can that best be brought about? I want to say to you, sir, that time is altogether too valuable to me to spend in digging into the history of the past for the purpose of finding out what has separated somebody else. We ought to be able to grasp the situation as it is today and come together. How can that best be done? We are met here. You have not considered any proposition; my associates and superiors in office have absolutely given the question no consideration as to a question of means. I might differ with my brothers who might want to weigh questions of the past. I do not want to spend the time on it. From what I have heard you gentlemen say you are not agreed as to means. Some of you think it would be well to take one course, and some another. Now, it would seem to me a business proposition, that letting the past, as my brother has well said, "take care of itself," make a written proposition upon the express understanding that you shall have within a time limit, make it an hour if you please, two hours if you will, and reply to that proposition, and that the proposition which you shall make, as well as the discussion of that proposition, shall remain with the honor of the gentlemen associated here today, and not to be published unless such a reply is given. I will say to you, of course, such a proposition will be made, and the gentlemen here with whom I have the honor to be associated, would sit here a life-time unless you could carry out such an agreement. It would seem to me, without spending time on this discussion, to let you gentlemen get together, formulate your proposition, submit it, as I say, and we will give you an answer. Then we will see what the differences are. Then let us get together, and as Christian gentlemen discuss these differences. I am very frank to say to you that I cannot imagine that differences exist which should take any great length of time to discuss or solve.

Mr. Hagerty—I would ask for a point of information from Mr. P. J. O'Connor, President of the American board, if your organization represents the Irish race on the other side of the water and in the United States?

Mr. O'Connor—Yes, sir.

Mr. Hagerty—This is a grand issue. If we can carry this point, then we can have two or three hundred thousand people in our organization. Nothing should belong to the Ancient Order of Hibernians except by Irish birth of father and mother. I make this as a suggestion; submit a proposition. As long as you people appear to make no attempt to give us a proposition, we would like to know if we will take nothing in only those of Irish birth, making no difference whether three or four generations back, and go right along as we did in the past. It is not well to take note of nationalities. We do not find fault with nationality or creed, but when our ancestors organized this order that was the principle. I ask Mr. P. J. O'Connor or any of the delegates of the American board, how will that suggestion go? If they will agree in future to take nothing in only of Irish birth, make no difference how many generations, three or four back, in the future, we are agreed on this point, then it will be easy to settle differences across the water. You stated that you had the genuine body across the water, did you not? Yes.

And I claim the same. So it will be very easy for us to select two men, one from your side and one from ours, and bring the two together, and if you have the right side we will agree on that point, but as my term of national delegate (I had it from a large majority), I do not propose to go into that today because we want to look into the future. Now you claim you have the genuine. I will make a suggestion. If you agree and you are satisfied, here is the place to draw up a proposition to take nothing in but Irish birth. The other will be very easy to get over. There are two principles —honor above all. Now, I ask of you to answer that question, and then we will know what we are about, and not take up the time of you gentlemen today.

Mr. McLaughlin—Seeing that much time is wasted here (pretty much all the remarks coming from one side, with the exception of two from the American side), I think it is quite useless to go into a discussion of the question of numerical standing. If such a question is important in this country, and if your side claims to be the parent body in the old country, it is important to find out who has the greatest standing on the other side. Therefore, I have nothing else to say unless some of the gentlemen who have not already spoken give their views. I would suggest that no more suggestions come from our side except we hear from our friends here, Mr. O'Sullivan, or Mr. Murphy.

Mr. O'Connor—If the gentleman will put that in

writing we will give you an answer in writing, and there can be no mistake about its meaning.

Mr. McPartland—I agree with the chair on that point, but in submitting this proposition are we to understand that we can meet and discuss the proposition after being presented?

Mr. O'Connor—Yes, sir; we will meet you gentlemen any time you say after we reply to it.

Mr. McPartland—My reason for that, Mr. Chairman and gentlemen, is this: There might be things in your proposition that might possibly not meet with our approbation, and the result is, we may be able in this committee while in session, with an intelligent view of both propositions, take them just as they are read, and arrive at a better conclusion in that way, and if this is acceptable to your members, I would also like you to submit a proposition to us. The committee can take an hour's recess, and arrive at some conclusion. I think Mr. Weadock will agree that is a decisive way to arrive at a conclusion.

Mr. Weadock—It seems to me that it would be idle to submit a proposition and have it voted upon here at this time. Necessarily, without consideration, each side will be a unit. Now I am not accustomed to having my intentions questioned, and I want to say to you gentlemen that the necessity here for preliminary negotiations does not exist. I say to you as honorable gentlemen, that we are in favor of unity. You have said the same thing. I say to you that if you make a proposition, it would be considered by us and we will reply, then we will get together and discuss. It may be that some parts of your proposition may be acceded to. It may be that we may make counter-propositions. But let us take this up in an intelligent way and negotiate it. Now, we hand you a proposition, and you gentlemen hand one to us, then we would have to have a committee appointed on conference, so we could get together and answer it. It would be idle. Let us have it agreed here that you will submit to us a proposition in a time to be named by you and we will make a reply to it in one hour, and in one hour after that reply is delivered we meet in this room or elsewhere, where we can discuss matters, and discuss the proposition and reply. Now, if we have confidence in each other, there ought to be no question upon that line.

Rev. Phillips—Mr. Chairman, I am very much afraid that the gentlemen representing the American board here today have already decided to reject the proposition, having already had correspondence regarding it. As we have made advances in this matter, showing thereby a great desire for unity, I think in behalf of the end proposed, that the committee on the other side should meet us half way and submit their desire in the form of a proposition, which we will consider by ourselves, and they will, in like manner, consider ours, and it is possible we may reach a happy

medium. I think from the remarks made by Mr. Wilhere that it is a question of numerical standing in this
country more than principle. It would be hardly likely
that, under the present condition of the Board of Erin,
and that of the Board of America, that we could compete in numbers with your organization, inasmuch as
our constitution is more restricted. We do not permit membership outside of Irish descent of both
parents. The standing of the Board of Erin in Ireland,
as Brother Hagerty has remarked, appears to me as
vital in a solution of this difficulty. As I understand
it, I believe it to be the position of the A. O. H. of America, that what we might call Apostolic succession
was necessary as a matter of principle. We claim that
the Board of Erin in Ireland affiliated with the board in
America is the parent organization. The other side
claims that the Board of Erin in Ireland affiliated with
the Board of America is the parent organization. A
proposition is made to investigate the matter, and, as
advanced by Mr. Hagerty in behalf of this committee,
and as this committee is empowered to act in the matter, if you can prove that your board in Ireland is the
true representative of the organization, we are willing
to submit our case to your judgment. If we can prove
on the other hand, that the Board of Erin, which represents us in Ireland (i. e., the Board of Erin in America) is the true organization, then we expect that you
will also submit your case to our judgment, and we

will accept you as brothers, as we believe, in the other case, you would accept us as brothers. That would end the difficulty. And I think now that in order that we may reach some practical conclusion in the matter, that by these two propositions, see what is claimed by each organization, and as we desire unity very much, as we have made the advancement in this matter, and that you have accepted it, (at least the consideration of a proposition informally placed before you by Brother Hagerty), that if we can consider separately in each committee and return in a half hour or hour, and discuss them in a friendly spirit, with no determination to accept either until we hear the other side, regarding it merely as a matter of business, see where the difficulty is, remedy it if we can, and then come to an understanding, one that we believe will be acceptable to the A. O. H., regardless of sectionalism, which word I use advisedly. I hope, if you are standing on a technical basis, that you will yield this point, and give us your proposition, let us consider it a certain length of time at your discretion, and you can have the same privilege of examining our proposition, and then we may concede something to each other, and out of the two propositions we may make a third that will be acceptable to both.

Mr. Weadock—Mr. Chairman, I do not think we ought to waste much time in trying to get our place in this matter. I have the distinguished honor of hand-

ing to the gentlemen all the correspondence I ever had
on the subject.

Rev. Phillips—Mr. Chairman, I hope I will not be
understood as questioning the intentions of Mr. Weadock.

Mr. Donoghue—Mr. Chairman, the question has
been put to you very forcibly by Mr. McPartland. Do
you absolutely refuse to offer a proposition to us on behalf of unity? That is exactly the question before the
house. If it is let us know it exactly. Let it go on
record that you refuse to give your opinions. We will
give ours, and hand them in to you and consider yours,
and if I understand it, you will consider ours.

Mr. Wilhere—The Reverend Father, whom I had
had the honor and pleasure of knowing very well, and
having the highest esteem and regard, both as a man
and a clergyman, is probably not as familiar with this
matter as I am, and he is probably drawing wrong con-
clusions because of his want of knowledge of the past
in connection with this question which we are now discussing, and which I trust we will settle amicably before we adjourn. The reason why I speak now is that
it would be improper that our organization should be
put in a position, or attempt to be put in a position by
any gentleman, either clerical or lay, of not having
gone to every extreme in order to effect a unity long,
long ago. Ten years ago a committee representing our
organization in New York came to me, and I had the

pleasure and honor at that time of being the executive head of the A. O. H., with a proposition from the Board of Erin convention, asking me to go there and meet them in order to consider this question, and to effect unity. I went there. The proposition that I submitted then (and there is a gentleman who was present at that time in this room, probably more. Mr. Donoghue I remember very well on that occasion. I met them in Tammany Hall, where the convention met), and the proposition I submitted that night and which our convention and my colleagues from time to time indorsed, and which our order indorsed from time to time, was to submit all alleged differences to any Bishop, Archbishop or Priest, to be appointed at the joint request of our committee, or of those representing the organization. At the request of our committee the Most Rev. Archbishop Corrigan, of New York, appointed the Rt. Rev. Mgr. Farley as the referee in this matter. We agreed and submitted to him in writing an agreement. After he would hear both sides of the question we would submit to his decision, no matter what it might be. The other side, the party whom you gentlemen represent, would not agree to any proposition of that character. On subsequent occasions (and I remember very well when I was called to Brooklyn on a Sunday), the same proposition that was made here today was made by gentlemen representing your side, that we go to Ireland in order to settle our differences. I said, as you very properly said, Father, too, that from your information, even received in Ireland, that the differences occurred here in America. I submitted a proposition to the representative, who was the national delegate on the National Board of Erin wing, of men on both sides at that time. We will not go to Ireland to settle the differences that have occurred in America, but if you are honest and mean unity, put on your hat, sir, and you and I will go to Archbishop Corrigan, or the Rt. Rev. Bishop McLaughlin. He represents both sides. Let them be in session and I pledge you that whatever either one of these Right Reverend prelates say, we will abide by it. That will not be adhered to. You wanted your party, represented by Mr. Sherlock, to send a delegate to Ireland in order to settle the differences which you stated yourself had originated in America, and which largely existed in this country. During all these ten years, and I have had some little part to play in it, we have done everything in our power to effect unity. I will not say how we have been met; I won't say what would be absolutely true, that we were not met in good faith, and that good faith and honesty was never kept with us. We come here today with the same spirit. I do not believe in recounting these things. You are familiar with them. Starting out ten years ago the Rt. Rev. Bishop of New York will verify to you the statement I make in your presence here, and he has the cor-

respondence and the document. We have done everything that Irishmen could do, and men who are not
professional Irishmen, but men who are honest in their
loyalty to their motherland, and loyal to the A. O. H.,
and have done everything that honest men could do to
settle their grievances. When I mentioned numbers,
Father, I mentioned them advisedly, because I had
thought, without going into the merits of the case,
without going into the question of our secession, that
our organization was justified in 1884. I do say that
when the organization was united in 1884 in Cleveland,
Ohio, I do say that we had about 43,000 members in
the entire United States of America. We have gone
along and whatever success we have had it is because
of our honest endeavor, and God has blessed our labor
and we have and represent today more than 100,000
active, living, breathing men. We are proud of that.
Thank God for it, and when gentlemen come and ask
for a conference with the purpose that we all have dear
to our hearts of taking back those who have strayed
from us long ago, and of uniting those who have come
into the organization without knowing the issue since
then, when they come here with that honest purpose,
they represent a very insignificant minority. I do not
think we are asking them too much to submit a proposition because they are represented in this conference,
when we asked them to submit it in writing so that we
may give it honest, fair, thoughtful consideration ; that

we will give it consideration with but one purpose, with one view, with one object, and that is the unity of the men in America, in Ireland and throughout the civilized world who call themselves Hibernians. If you submit that proposition the sentiments in our hearts will make it simple to effect, through that proposition, a basis of settlement for those grievances and unite all men throughout the civilized world who call themselves members of the A. O. H.

Mr. Hayes—Mr. Chairman, I would like to say that what the gentleman has said who has just preceded me I have heard for years back. Numerical strength has been quite important in the controversy. I have heard that same from the officials of the state, and while the statements may be true, I think they are wrong to the extent of 30,000 to 50,000. There have been inuendos thrown out that it has been a case of dishonest effort on one side. I say that the effort is honest. I say that the past must not be thrown into our teeth. Every statement I have heard has been successfully refuted. When controversies exist so many years, is it not time in the minds of all honest men to quietly place the past to one side, no matter if a man says we are an "insignificant minority." They do not say it in the public press. Your side clamors, and our side clamors, to unite. That is our purpose here today. Our friends here today are honest friends. If the past, in the minds of some men, has been dishonest, wipe it out and give us honest propositions. Let us meet as men, and we will not meet you as your numerical inferior any more than as your intellectual inferior. We meet you as men, with the object of uniting our race, and I hope in the discussion that the past effort, which has been an utter failure on our side, and an utter failure on yours, that this committee in 1897 works to close the nineteenth century, letting the dead bury its dead, so that our organization will step into the twentieth century a united body of Irishmen, and that we will not have each other by the throat. There are no differences in the West. You can step into Jersey and see there are no differences there, because in the town from which I come there are no better friends on God's footstool than members of the American Board. There are two workmen, laborers, who live in the same room, who are on opposite sides of the order, and yet live up to the spirit of the motto of our order —Friendship, Unity and True Christian Charity. Here is an instance where there is no bitterness, as a gentleman from the West has said, but there are other instances right in this city and in other sections of this state, where they would help each other in a business sense and in other senses. In all this proud land there are sons of our country living in such unity that no intelligent Irishman can find fault with. I say, cast all differences aside, and I hope in our discussion the past will be cast aside, that we of the present day who have come here to settle these questions can be honest. I say the past is buried. If you gentlemen on the American side will insist on a proposition, then I say our members here present will leave this room and offer a proposition. Let us do everything that is possible in an honorable way so that we may leave this city with one vast step towards advancement, towards that unity for which all have been publicly crying; that any man, whether it is Mr. Wilhere or any other, let us make one more honest effort that we can throw away the past and make at least one grand, last step of advancement towards unity before the sun sets on us this evening.

Mr. McLaughlin—I have never yet heard the gentlemen representing the American Board declare that they are in favor of unity, or even declare that they are in favor of any one act to insure it. If a man is going to accomplish anything does he not make an effort to do so? I believe we also have a right to demand a proposition. When the question was referred to the Rt. Rev. Bishops is it not a fact that the B. of A. was stated to be purely an American order, and not in communication with people in Ireland? Those two statements have been thrown out.

Mr. Weadock—That is true. We have a treaty with the Board of Erin which we made ten years ago, and I defy the members of your organization to produce any similar treaty. We have a treaty that can be produced by which recognition was given to us by the Board of Erin, and that was that they governed the organization in Europe, and that we would govern the organization in America according to our own ideas. The principle of Home Rule was established in the treaty made ten years ago, and has since been adhered to. Our National President is in now for ten years and has been receiving the communications and merchandise under the terms and conditions of that treaty.

Mr. Phillips—Has it ever been told to an American Bishop that there is no connection whatever between the American Board and any foreign organization?

Mr. O'Connor—Not to my knowledge.

Mr. Phillips—I will make this statement: The Bishop of Rochester has said that the American board represented to him that they had no affiliation whatever with any foreign organization, with any board in Ireland. I made it my business to question Mr. Crilley, of Belfast, Ireland, who was last year the chairman of what he called the "O'Connor Party," and he said to me that if any member of the American board has made a statement of that kind, he told an untruth, and when I told him that it was a dreadful thing to think that a Bishop would willingly stultify himself by making a statement in a church which could be so easily corrected, he said "perhaps he was misinformed." As to the O'Connor Party, I have it on statement of Mr. Crilley that through all these years of difficulty the

American Board of America had an affiliation with the American Board he represented last summer in Ireland, with which I believe he is still connected.

Mr. O'Connor—There was no such statement made to Bishop McQuaide.

Rev. Phillips—I think then the whole question is this: If the party represented by Mr. Crilley in Ireland be the original Ancient Order of Hibernians, then we are willing if the party represented by Harkens at the time of the difficulty be the original board, and we are affiliated with that, that it repudiates the Crilley board, then we are right. If we settle the difficulty here in America they will be only too glad to submit, and I have it also on the authority of a prominent member of the Board of Erin in Ireland that they are anxious, most anxious, for the settlement of the difficulty here, so they can have cause for unity in Ireland. Unity is desired there, and is earnestly desired here, and I believe Mr. Wilhere's statement of an "insignificant minority" is wrong, but we will pass that over. Let the past be the past and let the dead bury its dead. We are not here to resurrect trouble. If we can settle the difficulty here today, and we are authorized, I believe, on both sides, to act as a final deliberative body in this matter, we will have done remarkable good to the people of this country, and also to our suffering brethren in Ireland, and their condition there is most deplorable. They are struggling with difficulties of church and state in Ireland, and it was a proud moment in my life when I proclaimed myself as an American representative of the A. O. H. and stated it to be, as I believed, from my knowledge of the history of the organization in Ireland, the most patriotic organization there, and there is no reason why we should not consider it so in America, but as long as we are divided this way and do not meet as brothers, by fighting each other, we cannot fight the common foe of our country. If we can meet together as brethren we shall be one grand common phalanx. Now, I hope, gentlemen, that the proposition that we will probably make to you, as one of our gentlemen has remarked, will go even further than that stated in the beginning. We are willing to make a proposition to you. We hope you will consider it deliberately, as coming from brothers who desire to take your hand in friendship and all good fellowship.

Mr. O'Connor—I take pleasure in saying that, as the head of the order, that I will give any proposition you submit that comes from your side, fair and honest consideration.

Rev. Phillips—Do we consider, Mr. Chairman, that your answer is final; that you will not give us a proposition?

Mr. O'Connor—My judgment is that you should submit one first; then we will act fairly on that proposition.

Rev. Phillips—Then, with your permission, Mr. Chairman, we will retire for a few moments to see whether we consider the advisability of placing a proposition before you, knowing that you will not submit a proposition to us.

Mr. Hagerty—I see that the gentlemen think they should not offer as a basis of settlement. I do not see how unity could be effected if that is absolutely refused. As a man of intelligence, Mr. Chairman, and Mr. Wilhere is a man of intelligence, and I am sure the man from Michigan is, I ask you is there any more difference in the idea of our committee asking your co-operation by presenting to us your terms, than it was for you and your associates last August a year ago when we arrived in your session, you asked us the same question to offer you a proposition as you do now after sending for us? Now, here is the same thing repeating itself over again. Mr. Chairman, I simply say that I think we had better adhere to the suggestion of our friend and not dig up the past, because it will require quite an answer to your remarks in reference to that matter. There is no question that cannot be answered peacably and quietly. Gentlemen, was there any proposition or statement laid before the Right Rev. Bishops of the United States?

Mr. O'Connor—I presented no statement to the conference of the Right Rev. Bishops. Probably the gentleman from Philadelphia can answer that?

Mr. Wilhere—I will state positively and without any question, no such statement as that was ever made by any representative of the order to my knowledge; certainly not by me.

Mr. Donoghue—Well, then, let us get to business in a businesslike manner.

Mr. Hagerty—I beg to differ with Mr. Wilhere. Probably Mr. Wilhere is not aware of the fact that I waited on Archbishop Corrigan, and he had been told by some of the officers of the American board that they had no affiliation across the water. I was told that personally.

Mr. Wilhere—I want to state that this is absolutely unreliable and untrue, and Brother O'Connor was my colleague and he was present, and we remained there about three days.

(The conference then, at 3:30 p. m., adjourned until 4:15 p. m., to consider a proposition to be presented by the committee of the A. O. H., B. of E.)

(At 4:30 p. m. the conference re-convened and the following proposition was submitted):

To the Officers and National Directors of the A. O. H., B. of A.:

Gentlemen—We, the undersigned committee, offer you the following proposition for the settlement of the differences that exist between the Hibernians of this country:

"Resolved, That we, the representatives of the A. O. H., B. of E., do hereby agree that we will unite the organization known as the A. O. H., B. of E., in this country, with the organization known as the A. O. H., B. of A., under the Board in Europe, which can be proven to be the orthodox Board of Erin in Great Britain and Ireland, with the understanding that the members of the irregular board be accorded membership in the true board, and that one member of each body be sent to Europe to take evidence from both boards in Great Britain and Ireland, and submit the evidence to the presiding officer of the late convention of the Irish race, the Most Reverend Patrick O'Donnel, Lord Bishop of Raphoe, Ireland, the decision of the three to be final."

(Signed)

JAMES J. HAGERTY, Chairman.
E. R. HAYES, Secretary.

On behalf of the committee of the A. O. H., B. of E. Dated at Philadelphia, Pa., March 5, 1897.

ANSWER TO FIRST PROPOSITION.

To the Committee Representing the Board of Erin, Ancient Order of Hibernians:

Gentlemen—We beg to acknowledge the receipt of your communication of this date, and in reply thereto will say that the proposition made by you is not acceptable for the reason, among others, that it is predicated upon a theory not founded on fact.

Our understanding of the situation is that the committee was appointed for the purpose of adjusting the differences among Hibernians, and the first step in that direction is the adjustment of those existing in America, and we are aided in coming to this conclusion by the very apt statement of the Rev. E. S. Phillips, a member of your committee, made during the negotiations today, which, to quote his own language in reference to that subject, was as follows: "I was told by men high in the councils of the board there (Ireland) that the trouble is here (America) and that if we can adjust matters in America, unity will necessarily follow in Europe."

We are unanimously in favor of taking some action as will result in the Hibernians belonging to one organization. The highest of our good faith is the fact that we are representing a body of more than 100,000 members that has, by its strict adherence to the constitution of the order, attained the highest possible standard in America. It has, by its magnificent record as a Catholic organization, received, and at present enjoys, the approval of the Catholic hierarchy of our country, and by the devotion and sacrifices of our members in the sacred cause of Irish liberty, our order has been accorded a distinguished place in the front rank of Irish patriotic organizations in this land, yet, for the sake of unity, we are willing to throw the mantle of charity over all class differences, and the occasion of them. As a further evidence of our good faith, and as a basis upon which the results which we all desire to attain shall be brought about, we submit for your consideration and under agreement with you, for an answer, the following proposition, viz.:

1. The Ancient Order of Hibernians of America will accept all divisions of the now-called Board of Erin, Ancient Order of Hibernians, which are now in good standing according to the constitution and bylaws of such B. of E., A. O. H., which medical examination or aids test, upon the express understanding that the constituent members of such divisions at the time of their admission therein were within the age limit and of such physical condition as the said constitution and bylaws provided at the time of their admission. The provision relative to the acceptance of divisions shall apply in all states except those where an insurance or special death benefit other than that provided in the constitution is paid; there the members of the respective divisions shall be accepted only after such medical examination as may be required by the bylaws in such states.

2. All such divisions shall be obligated according to the present ritual of the Ancient Order of Hibernians of America.

3. The County President elected by the Ancient

Order of Hibernians of America shall be and remain the County Presidents for their respective counties until the next regular election; provided, however, that in case there are no county presidents of the A. O. H. of America in any county, then, if there are in such counties any organization of the B. of E., A. O. H., their county delegates shall be the County Presidents for such counties.

4.   The National President of the A. O. H. of America and the President and National Delegate of the B. of E., A. O. H., shall be a committee to negotiate with the respective organizations with which we are affiliated in Europe for the purpose of adjusting any differences which may exist there, and if, at the next national convention of the A. O. H. of A., to be held in Boston on the second Tuesday of July, 1898, such differences shall not then have been adjusted, and in the opinion of such national convention, there is no immediate hope of adjusting, then a committee of two shall be appointed with authority to visit Europe for the purpose of adjusting such differences, and one member of said committee shall be chosen from among those who are now members of the B. of E., A. O. H.

5.   The above, when embodied in an agreement, shall take effect and be binding immediately upon its promulgation by the parties subscribing thereto.

P. J. O'CONNOR,

(Signed)   N. P., A. O. H. of America.

JAMES O'SULLIVAN,

Nat'l Sec'y A. O. H. of America.

Dated Philadelphia, Pa., March 5, 1897.

COUNTER-PROPOSITION.

To the National Officers and Directors representing the Board of America, Ancient Order of Hibernians:

Gentlemen—We have received and duly considered your reply to the proposition we honestly made in the interest of unity. We deny that it is "predicated upon a theory not founded on fact." We, in common with the majority of the members of the board, regarded it as the question which must be first settled before anything can be done in regard to unity. You are either regular or you are not. We have nothing to fear in the honest and impartial investigation we have unanimously proposed. Your evasive position is simply ridiculous when you quote with a false interpretation the language of one of our committee who distinctly conveyed the important information that "the trouble in the way of union," that is to say, the obstacle or opposition to union, "is here in America," as the boards in Ireland are practically dependent on the boards in America. This is best evidenced by the fact that the Board of America element of the A. O. H. in Ireland speak for themselves and the B. of A. in America as the O'Connor party. The virtual repudiation of the board, or the O'Connor party, in Ireland, is a confession of illegality, and your quotation of a remark, without regard to context of the discussion, is, if not dishonest, to say the least, a lawyer's quibble. We quote the subsequent remarks of the same member of the committee, Rev. E. S. Phillips, as clearly expressive of his meaning in the sentence quoted, and our position in the proposition made:

(Ad verbatim from stenographic notes):

"Mr. Chairman—I am very much afraid that the gentlemen representing the American Board here to-day have already decided to reject the proposition, having already had correspondence regarding it. As we have made the advances in the matter, showing thereby a great desire for unity, I think, in behalf of the end proposed that the committee on the other side may meet us half way and submit their desire in the form of a proposition which we will consider by ourselves, and they, in like manner, will consider ours, and it is possible that we may reach a happy medium. I think, from the remarks made by Mr. Wilhere, that it is more a question of numerical standing in this country than principle. It would hardly be likely that under the present constitution of the Board of Erin we could compete in numbers with your organization, inasmuch as our constitution is more restricted. We do not permit membership outside of Irish descent of both parents. The standing of the Board of Erin in Ireland, as Brother Hagerty has remarked, appears to me vital in the solution of this difficulty. As I understand it, I believe it to be the position of the Ancient Order of Hibernians in America that what we might call the Apostolic succession was necessary as a matter of principle. We claim that the Board of Erin in Ireland, affiliated with the Board of Erin in America is the parent organization. The other side claim that the Board of Erin in Ireland, affiliated with the Board of America, is the parent organization. A proposition is made to investigate the matter, as advanced by Mr. Hagerty in behalf of this committee, and as this committee is empowered to act in this matter, if you can prove that your board in Ireland is the true representative of the organization, we are willing to submit our case to your judgment. If we can prove, on the other hand, that the Board of Erin which represents us in Ireland (that is, the Board of Erin in America) is the true organization, then we expect that you will also submit your case to our judgment, and we will accept you as brothers, as we believe in the other case, you would accept us as brothers. That would end the difficulty. And I think now, that in order that we may give some practical results in the matter by these two propositions which are claimed by each organization and as we desire unity very much, inasmuch as we have made the advancement in this matter, and that you have accepted it (at least, the proposition informally placed before you by Brother Hagerty), that if we consider separately in each committee and return in a half hour or hour and discuss them in a friendly spirit with no determination to accept either until we hear the other side, regarding it merely as a matter of business, see where the difficulty is, remedy it, if we can, and then come to an understanding, one that we believe will be acceptable to the Ancient Order of Hibernians regardless of sectionalism, which word I use advisedly. I hope if you are standing on a technical basis that you will yield this point and give us your proposition and let us consider it a certain length of time at your discretion, and you will have the same privilege of examining our proposition, and then we may concede something to each other, and out of the two propositions we may make a third, which will be acceptable to both."

Comparing the above with your reply to our proposition, we do not hesitate to state what was felt from the beginning of the discussion, that the committee representing the Board of America do not desire to unite. What follows in your report is unworthy of serious discussion, and is hereby dismissed. We again and finally say, that it would be the opinion of this committee that until the O'Connor Party, calling itself the Ancient Order of Hibernians, Board of America, proves its lineal descent from the old Board of Erin in Ireland, it will not, because it cannot, be entitled to call itself the Ancient Order of Hibernians of America, or even in Ireland. We are regretfully, but inevitably forced to the conclusion that the motto of our order, Friendship, Unity and True Christian Charity was not the motive that dictated an evasive and (because it demanded from us an unconditional surrender) insulting reply to our just and honorable proposition, which in charity, we again make as the only basis of union.

(Signed)

JAMES J. HAGERTY, Chairman.

E. R. HAYES, N. S., A. O. H., B. of E.

On behalf of the committee representing the A. O. H. Board of Erin.

Dated at Philadelphia, Pa., March 5, 1897.

REPLY TO COUNTER-PROPOSITION.

To the Committee representing the Board of Erin, A. O. H.:

Gentlemen—Your reply to our note is acknowledged. Did we regard it as well-considered, we might very properly dismiss the subject, but we do not; neither shall we endeavor to fittingly characterize it, because that will be done for us by those who are seriously interested in the subject matter under discussion, unless upon consideration, you recede from your untenable position.

We proposed a feasible plan for a United Brotherhood of Hibernians, first, and a settlement in a fair manner of the minor questions afterwards. We evaded nothing. If our quotation from the speech of one of your members, (the literal accuracy of which you do not question), was unfortunate for you, it was because of its truthfulness.

We are unable to understand how we are to be aided by repetition. The extended quotation from the remarks of your committee-man may gratify your personal pride, but does not tend to further elucidate the vital questions, for, as you know, we had the benefit of hearing his discourse and have it preserved in the notes of our stenographer. For an answer to anything material contained therein, we refer you to the remarks of our National Director, M. F. Wilhere, made at our conference and in your hearing today. You forget contemporaneous history, if not yourselves, when you connect our organization with any of its members. It is too broad to be controlled by any individual or set of individuals, and there are none such seeking to do so. The gentleman you name takes a just pride in his connection with our honorable order, which has made its impress upon the history of the century by its Catholicity, its patriotism and its intelligent devotion to its cardinal principles of Friendship, Unity and True Christian Charity.

You admit that your constitution retards your growth. We charged you with having less than 3,000 members in America, and challenged you to prove a greater number. While we offer to prove to you that we had upward of 100,000, yet you ask us to adopt your relic of past ages as a guide for an organization that happily threw off the incubus of narrow-mindedness, to which you refer, so many years ago. Insofar as the question of regularity is concerned we beg leave to remind you of the fact that your organization did not exist until August 12th, 1884, when a seceding meeting was held in New York City, while our order can trace its direct and legitimate descent from the first division of the Ancient Order of Hibernians, founded and established in America in the year 1836. We beg leave also to remind you that we are by solemn treaty, entered into in 1887, in affiliation with the true legal and genuine Board of Erin in Europe, and that any or all other bodies claiming that title are, like your society, irregular and without a just or honest claim thereto. After your secession we immediately began negotiations with you looking to your return, and at the request of a committee representing our order and the seceders, His Grace, Archbishop Corrigan, appointed the then Mgr. Farley, now the Right Rev. Bishop John M. Farley, his worthy coadjutor, to arbitrate all differences. He required each of us to submit an agreement in writing to abide by his determination, which we promptly complied with, and your organization neglected and refused to do so, and we have his acknowledgment that the receipt of our pledge of good faith and his advice that you had failed to comply to his very proper and now self-evident wise requirement. In conclusion, we reaffirm our proposition to you, which present the most honorable opportunity for you to return to the true A. O. H., and one which we be-

lieve your membership will gladly avail themselves of
if you give our proposition your earnest consideration
and them a chance to do so.   We are sincere tonight,
as we have been for the past ten years.   We ask no
humiliation, and for the sake of unity, not to turn our
extended hand aside or refuse to accept our grasp of
honorable friendship, which is proffered in good faith,
as you have hitherto declined our liberal and christian
arbitration of all alleged differences.   We will await
your timely consideration of this matter here.

Respectfully,

P. J. O'CONNOR, N. P., A. O. H. of A.

JAMES O'SULLIVAN, N. S., A. O. H. of A.

Dated at Philadelphia, Pa., March 5, 1897.

FINAL REPLY.

To the National Officers and Directors of the Board of
America, A. O. H.:

Gentlemen—Your second reply to our renewed
proposition is received and hereby acknowledged.   As
you persist in refusing to concur in our simple, and, as
we believe, most feasible plan of union, we do not think
a further conference will promote its success.   Your
claim to "Catholicity, patriotism and intelligent devotion to the principles of the order: Friendship, Unity
and True Christian Charity," we do not question insofar as it regards your own particular organization; nor

do we think it necessary to put forth a similar claim for ourselves. Your allusion to your past efforts in favor of harmony and union cannot bring much comfort to the unfortunate position in which you have placed the well-meaning but misguided members of your order by your final rejection of our proposition to rest our case and yours in the hands of three gentlemen, one of whom would be the noble and patriotic son of Tyrconnel, the learned and saintly Lord Bishop of Raphoe. It is useless for us to continue our fruitless efforts of the past seventeen hours to induce you to unite with us on a basis that would bring honor and joy to all sincere members of the B. of A., A. O. H., in America and Europe.

With these parting words we now close a discussion which, though it promised little on your part from the beginning, has at least served to place you on record as not being sincere in your desire for union; or, in other words, to quote yourselves as being as "sincere tonight as you have been for the past ten years."

Respectfully,

JAMES J. HAGERTY, Chairman.

E. R. HAYES, N. S., A. O. H., B. of E.

On behalf of the National Committee representing the Ancient Order of Hibernians, Board of Erin.

Dated at Philadelphia, Pa., March 6, 1897.

(The conference then, at 5:45 a. m., March 6, adjourned sine die.)

The breach now appeared to be greater than ever. The committees had met and failed to agree and unity seemed an impossibility in the A. O. H. The members of the committee representing the Board of Erin left Philadelphia feeling that they had done everything in their power to effect a union on an honorable basis, but the committee representing the A. O. H. of America seemed to have decided to reject every proposition offered by the Board of Erin and appeared determined in every way to obstruct every honest effort towards unity. In May, 1897, the Rev. E. S. Phillips, at the national convention of the A. O. H., Board of Erin, held at Tammany Hall, New York, stated that he had received a letter from the President of the A. O. H. of America, asking that the Board of Erin elect a committee with full power to act finally and decisively on the union of both branches of the A. O. H. The communication was acted upon and the following resolution adopted and committee elected to confer with a like committee from the A. O. H. of America.

RESOLUTION.

Whereas, We have been informed, through a communication received since the opening of this convention by Rev. E. S. Phillips, of Plains, Pa., that the President of the A. O. H., B. of A., awaits the appointment of a committee from this body, with full power to act, finally and decisively, on the union of both orders in this country, and

Whereas, Such suggestion should meet our hearty and immediate approval, therefore be it

Resolved, That a conference committee of six delegates in this convention be elected forthwith, to meet a similar committee of the B. of A.; that such joint committee shall meet within ninety days from the approval of this resolution at a place agreed upon and selected by the respective chairmen of the conference committees; that immediately upon assembling, written agreements on the issue in question shall be agreed upon and signed by the conferees, copies of which they shall retain, and said agreements shall be final, binding all parties concerned to their contents; that upon the signing of agreements and the interchange thereof, the conferences shall proceed to select an arbitrator from the hierarchy of the United States, who shall have full and judicial power to investigate and determine the solution of the existing differences; that nothing short of a full, final and deliberate decision from the arbitration shall be accepted by this order; that the committee elected by this convention shall insist, so far as reasonable, in the formation of agreements upon an equitable adjustication of differences, on a basis which will be binding, honorable and to the best interests of all members at present of both orders, and at the same time using discretion and vigilance, by making due provision for the future membership and general internal management of the reunited order.

E. S. PHILLIPS,

C. J. McCARTHY,

WM. MALLOY.

Committee—E. S. Phillips, E. R. Hayes, John P. Quinnan, Joseph McLaughlin, Miles McPartland and James H. Murphy.

This committee met the committee representing the A. O. H. of America on August 3rd, 1897, at the Central Hotel, Atlantic City, N. J., and after formulating a plan of union they agreed upon the Right Rev. James A. McFaul, Bishop of Trenton, N. J., as arbitrator, and he consented to act. He summoned both parties to the agreement before him and heard all testimony bearing upon the case. Not satisfied with this he had Terence Donoghue, ex-State delegate of New York, and P. McGarry, of Chicago, ex-National delegate of the Board of Erin, appear before him. On December 11th, 1897, the Rt. Rev. Bishop rendered the following decision, which has been accepted by both branches of the order, which leaves today a united A. O. H. in America.

DECISION OF THE RT. REV. JAMES A. Mc-
FAUL, ARBITRATOR BETWEEN THE A. O.
H. OF AMERICA, AND THE A. O. H. of U. S.
A. IN AFFILIATION WITH THE B. of E.

Messrs. P. J. O'Connor, National President; John
C. Weadock, National Vice President; Maurice F.
Wilhere, National Director; John P. Murphy, National
Director; James O'Sullivan, National Secretary; Rev.
William T. McLaughlin, a Committee representing
"The A. O. H. of America;" and Rev. E. S. Phillips,
National Delegate; E. R. Hayes, National Secretary;
John P. Quinnan, Joseph McLaughlin, Miles F. Mc-
Partland, James H. Murphy, a committee represent-
ing "The A. O. H. of the U. S. of America," in affilia-
tion with the Board of Erin.

Gentlemen—In virtue of powers delegated to you by
the organizations which you represent, you entered into the following agreement at Atlantic City, N. J., on
the third day of August, 1897:—

"Whereas, there is an almost unanimous desire
among the members of the above named organizations
for the unification of both bodies, and believing that
the interests of our race and religion can be best sub-
served by such a union, and also believing that the
most efficacious manner of settling differences between
our respective organizations is by arbitration;

"Now, therefore, the said committees, hereby mutually covenant and agree, each committee with each other, and each organization, through its committee, with the other organization, that they will be and are hereby directed, governed and bound by the following articles:—

"First—That all questions in dispute between the two bodies be referred to an arbiter, to be chosen from the hierarchy of the United States, said arbiter to be Irish, either by birth or descent, giving, granting and delegating to him full, final and exclusive jurisdiction, and also judicial power to investigate and reconcile existing differences, constitutional and otherwise. He shall fix the time of the hearing at the earliest possible moment, and have full and discretionary power to determine the order, manner and extent of the presentation of the case of both former bodies, to summon before him such officers and members, and to order the production of such documents as he may deem expedient, to the end that he make an equitable adjustment of all differences, and formulate a plan of union which will be binding, honorable and for the best interests of the order, and for this purpose we delegate him all power and authority which we may have in the premises.

"Second—That each organization shall continue to manage its own affairs, as at present, until the arbiter shall have finished his work and announced his decision, which decision shall be binding upon all officers and members of both former orders, anything in the constitutions, laws and customs of either former order to the contrary notwithstanding; and that we hereby pledge our official honor, and the honor of the organizations we represent, to a faithful and strict obedience to the decision of the arbiter."

In pursuance of this agreement you came to my residence in Trenton, the next day, and requested me to act as arbitrator. I cheerfully consented with the understanding that my powers extended not only to the devising of a plan for uniting the two bodies, but to such a union as would clearly manifest your filial obedience to the teachings of Holy Mother Church, and your earnest desire to be known as exemplary Catholics.

I have employed every available means for thoroughly informing myself of the principles and aims of the organization, the difficulties which have arisen and their causes, and, after weighing, I believe, justly and impartially the evidence submitted, and obtained by interviews and correspondence, as the arbitrator selected by your honorable committees, I render the following decision:

1. The name by which the reunited organization shall be known is "The Ancient Order of Hibernians;" the words "in America" shall be added only to designate the country wherein the organization is located.

2.   The constitution in use previous to disunion, and adopted at the national convention held in Cleveland, Ohio, May 16th, 1884, shall be taken as the ground work to which all necessary amendments shall be made.

At the national convention, held by virtue of this decision, amendments shall be recommended by a committee of five members, appointed by the permanent chairman, and said amendments may be adopted by the convention after they shall have received the approval of the arbitrator.

3.   The qualifications for membership in the order are enumerated in Article X of the above mentioned constitution.   Among others the following will be found: "No person shall become a member of this order who is not Irish, or of Irish descent through either parent, etc."

This qualification has been the cause of much discussion in past years.   I am satisfied, nevertheless, that its retention is necessary for the continuance, growth and prosperity of the organization in this country.   A more restrictive qualification may, perhaps, be better in Europe; but, in America, it would be suicidal, owing to the frequent marriages of the Irish and their descendants with other nationalities.

It has been asserted that this qualification opens the way to objectionable membership.   I do not concur in this view.   It is by vote that a candidate is received or rejected, and, as this is a sufficient safeguard, an additional means need not be selected; and one that will lead, sooner or later, to the extinction of the order in America must be condemned by every member who has the welfare of the organization at heart.

Moreover, as the Irish have always been justly proud of the part taken by their heroic ancestors in the cause of church and motherland, during the dark ages of persecution, this organization will only be true to its best traditions when it cultivates and encourages the patriotic pulsations of every heart which circulates a single drop of Irish blood.

4. The "Quarterly Communications," after the national convention held in accordance with this decision, shall be manufactured and issued, subject to the approval of the national chaplain, by the chief executive officer of the order in America, until the European branches of the order shall have united, and a member of the Irish hierarchy shall have certified to the National Chaplain that the united body is in harmony with the teachings of the Catholic Church. Then, as provided for elsewhere in this decision, the question of receiving the "Quarterly Communications" from Europe may be considered.

You have come together like true and honorable men, willing to make any sacrifice for unity and harmony; you have resolved that all differences shall be forgotten, and you are determined to act for the best interests of your church, your race, and the general welfare of the organization. Your brothers in Europe are equally magnanimous, and will, no doubt, cheerfully follow your example. I suggest, therefore, that the chief executive officer, elected at the national convention, held by virtue of this decision, communicate with the chief executive officers of the European branches of the order, and advise them to unite by some such feasible means as you have selected.

5. A bond of Friendship, Unity and Christian Charity shall still exist between the American and European bodies. This bond shall be the "Transfer Card" from either European branch, which shall be duly honored, as hereinafter provided, by the order in America.

6. The plan of reorganization, which is hereto attached, is a part of this decision, and embraces all matters appertaining to Representation, Conventions, Credentials, Property, Transfer Card, Constitution, Ritual, Government of Organization, etc.

Allow me, gentlemen, in delivering this decision to present my thanks for the uniform courtesy shown me during these deliberations by yourselves and other members of both organizations, and to express the hope that my labors may redound to the glory of Holy Church, the best interests of America, the welfare of the Irish race, and "The Ancient Order of Hibernians" throughout the world.

JAMES A. McFAUL (Arbitrator),

Bishop of Trenton.

Trenton, N. J., Dec. 11th, 1897.

PLAN OF REORGANIZATION.

I.   DIVISIONS.

1.   The officers of all divisions shall remain in their respective positions and exercise their powers, as such officers, until the next regular election.

2.   No division formed during the period elapsing between the date of this decision and the close of the national convention, held in pursuance of this decision, shall be entitled to representation in any convention held prior to the close of the said national convention.

II.   COUNTY REORGANIZATION.

a—(Where both bodies exist.)

1.   In such counties—for the purposes of reunion and the election of one set of new officers—the county delegate and the county president of such counties shall conjointly sign and issue a call to the divisions, under their jurisdiction, for a county convention, to be held at some convenient place within two months after the date of this decision, and proceed at once to elect new county officers, who shall hold office until the next following regular county convention.

2.   The delegates to this convention shall be the county delegates, county presidents and the five officers of each division in the county.

3.   The temporary chairman, during the election of the new county officers, shall be the county delegate or the county president, as shall have been decided by lot.

The successful officer shall preside over the county convention, the other act as secretary, until the new county officers have been elected.

4.   The result of the election having been declared, the old officers shall immediately resign and the new officers assume authority over the reunited organization.

N. B.—Wherever the term "by lot" is employed in this decision, the names of the candidates shall be deposited in a box and some person shall draw them, one at a time, therefrom.

b—(Where only one of the bodies exists.)

1.   In such counties the county delegate (or the county president), as the case may be, shall sign and issue a call for a county convention to be held within the time above-mentioned in II, under 1.

2.   The delegates to such county convention shall be those corresponding to the body existing in the county, viz., those mentioned in II, under 2.

3.   The election for new county officers shall be held at the next regular county convention.

N. B.—All county conventions shall make arrangements in accordance with the Plan of National Reorganization, for sending delegates to the national convention.

III.   STATE REORGANIZATION.

a—(Where both bodies exist.)

1.   In such states the state delegate and the state president shall conjointly sign and issue to the divis-

ions under their jurisdiction, a call for a state convention, to be held at some convenient place within four months after the date of this decision, and proceed at once to elect new state officers, who shall hold office until the next following regular state convention.

2.   The delegates to this convention shall be the new county delegates (in counties where both bodies existed), and the county delegate or the county president (in counties where only one of the bodies exists), the state delegate and the state president, the state secretaries, the state treasurers, and the president of each division in the state.

3.   The temporary chairman, during the election of new state officers, shall be the state delegate or the state president, as shall have been decided by lot. The successful officer shall preside over the state convention, the other act as secretary, until the new state officers have been elected.

4.   The result of the election having been declared, the old officers shall immediately resign and the new officers assume authority over the reunited organization.

b—(Where only one of the bodies exists.)

1.   In such states, the state delegate (or the state president), as the case may be, shall sign and issue a call for a state convention to be held within the time above mentioned in III, under 1.

2.   The delegates to such state convention shall be those corresponding to the body existing in the state, viz., those mentioned in III, under 2.

3.   The election for new state officers shall be held at the next regular state convention.

N. B.—1. All state conventions shall make arrangements, in accordance with the Plan of National Reorganization, for sending delegates to the national convention.

2.   The officers elected in county and state conventions (where both bodies exist) shall be the same as mentioned in the constitution of May 16th, 1884, until said constitution has been amended to meet the requirements of the reunited order, at the national convention held in accordance with this decision.

IV. NATIONAL REORGANIZATION.

1.   The national delegate and the national president shall conjointly sign and issue a call, countersigned by the arbitrator, to those under their jurisdiction, for a national convention, to be held during the month of June, 1898, on such day and in such place as the Arbitrator shall decide.

2.   The delegates to this convention shall be the following officers of both bodies, viz.: the national president, the national treasurer, the national secretary, and the five members of the national directory, belonging to the American branch; the national delegate, the na-

tional secretary, the national treasurer, and, in order to render the national representation of both bodies equal, five other members of the Board of Erin Branch (these additional five members shall be selected by the national delegate after consultation with his national secretary and treasurer); the new state delegates elected in the reorganization of states (where both bodies existed), state secretaries, state treasurers, new county delegates elected in the reorganization of counties (where both bodies existed), the state delegates (or state presidents), state secretaries, state treasurers and county delegates (or county presidents) (where only one of the bodies exists), together with an additional delegate in each county for every one thousand members in good standing over and above the first one thousand in such county, as shall be ascertained by the reports submitted to the county conventions.

3.   The temporary chairman of this national convention shall be the arbitrator, and he shall select such temporary officers as he may judge necessary.

4.   a —In the national convention, after the committee on credentials has reported, and said report has been disposed of, the next business in order shall be the election of a permanent chairman and a permanent secretary, and such other officers as may be required for the convention, who shall act until the amended constitution shall have been adopted and approved, and the new national officers, as therein provided, shall

have been elected and installed. The result of the election having been declared, the old officers shall immediately resign and the new officers assume authority over the reunited organization.

b —In the state and county conventions provided for under this decision, after the committees on credentials have reported and said reports have been disposed of by the conventions, the next business in order shall be the election of officers, who shall hold their offices until the next regular conventions.

MISCELLANEOUS.

1.   The office of Vice President, wherever it is not mentioned in this plan of reorganization in the list of delegates to a convention, has been omitted so that there may be the same mode of representation in both bodies.

N. B.—The delegates to conventions shall be only those whose names are above mentioned for county, state and national conventions, respectively.

2.   The officers of the military organizations have not been made eligible to seats in the county, state and national conventions, with the view of equalizing the representation of both bodies; but they will be provided for in the amended constitution to be adopted at the coming national convention.

3.   In all conventions held under this decision, the officers of both bodies shall report in writing to such

conventions, and said reports shall be referred to the appropriate committees for such action as may be deemed necessary.

4. Cushing's Manual shall be the recognized parliamentary authority in all conventions.

V.   CREDENTIALS.

a—To County Conventions.

1. Credentials to the county conventions shall be signed by the president of the division and countersigned by the county delegate (or the county president) in accordance with the body to which the delegate belongs.

2. The temporary chairman of all county conventions shall appoint four members (two from each body in counties where both bodies exist) as a committee on credentials. If this committee cannot decide the admissibility of certain credentials, the dispute shall be submitted to the county convention whose decision shall be final.

b —To State Conventions.

1. The credentials to the state convention shall be signed by the county delegate (or the county president) in accordance with the body to which the delegate belongs.

2. The temporary chairman of all state conventions shall appoint four members (two from each body, where both bodies existed), as a committee on creden-

tials. If this committee cannot decide the admissibility of certain credentials, the dispute shall be submitted to the state convention, whose decision shall be final.

c —To the National Convention.

1. The credentials to the national convention shall be signed by the new state delegate and new county delegate (in states where both bodies existed previous to reorganization), and by the state delegate or state president) and county delegate (or county president), (where only one of the bodies exists), in accordance with the body to which the delegate belongs.

2 The temporary chairman of the national convention shall appoint four members (two from each of the bodies, as they existed previous to reorganization), as a committee on credentials. If this committee cannot decide the admissibility of certain credentials, the dispute shall be submitted to the national convention, whose decision shall be final.

VI. SUBSTITUTES FOR DELEGATES.

1 In case any county or state officer, mentioned above as a delegate to the national convention, is unable to attend said convention, his substitute may be selected by a majority vote of the county or state officers, respectively. Said member shall be entitled to the rights of a delegate in the national convention only upon the acceptance of his credentials in the manner already stated for that convention.

VII. Property and Funds of the Order, etc.

1.   Should two or more divisions unite, a new election for officers shall be held immediately, and the property and moneys belonging to each division shall be transferred to the new officers of the new division thus formed, and the usual bonds required shall be given by said officers.

2.   All moneys and property held by county, state or national officers shall be immediately transferred to the corresponding new officers elected in the conventions held in pursuance of this decision, and said officers shall give such bonds as may be required by their respective conventions.

3.   If two divisions in a county have the same number a special number shall be selected for each by the county board of directors.

VIII. The Quarterly Communications.

1.   From the date of this decision until the national convention held by virtue of the same, the "Quarterly Communications" shall be manufactured and issued by the arbitrator through the national president and the national delegate.

After the said national convention, the "Quarterly Communications" shall be manufactured and issued, subject to the approval of the national chaplain, by the chief executive officer in America, until such time as the European separated bodies shall have united, and placed themselves in harmony with the Catholic Church.

2. When the two bodies of the "Ancient Order of Hibernians" in Europe settle their differences, unite by some feasible means, and are able to certify through a member of the Irish hierarchy to the national chaplain of "The Ancient Order of Hibernians" in America, that they are united among themselves and in harmony with the Catholic Church, the national officers in this country may be directed by the said chaplain to consider the advisability of accepting the "Quarterly Communications" from Europe; and the said "communications" shall be accepted and used only subject to his approval and after he has received a copy of the same.

3. Until the national officers of "The Ancient Order of Hibernians" in America, with the approval of the national chaplain, have decided as above mentioned, to accept the European "Quarterly Communications," any member or division receiving the same, shall, by that act, cease to be a member of, or division of "The Ancient Order of Hibernians" in America, and shall be declared expelled and deprived of all the rights and privileges belonging to a member or division of the order.

IX. TRANSFER CARD.

1. A Transfer Card, properly executed, from either of the two bodies in Europe, shall be honored by "The Ancient Order of Hibernians" in America, and said

card shall render the lawful holder eligible to membership in any division of the order in America, provided the said member is in good standing, and has paid all dues to the division of which he was a member in Europe.

2.   For the purpose of identification this "Transfer Card" shall be countersigned by the chief executive officer of the branch in Europe to which the said member belongs.

3.   A European "Transfer Card," therefore, entitles the holder to the same privileges as the American "Transfer Card."

X. Constitution, Amendments and Ritual.

1.   The constitution, adopted by the national convention, held in Cleveland, Ohio, May 16th, 1884, has been selected as a basis for amendments, because it governed the organization previous to separation.

2.   A committee on amendments to the constitution shall be appointed at the national convention, as heretofore provided for in this decision, and it shall be the duty of the said committee to prepare such amendments to the said constitution as shall bring it up to the needs of the reorganized order.

AMENDMENTS MADE BY THE ARBITRATOR TO THE PREAMBLE AND THE CONSTITUTION OF MAY 16th, 1884.

1. Instead of the old preamble, substitute the following:

PREAMBLE.

The members of "The Ancient Order of Hibernians" in America declare that the intent and purpose of the order is to promote Friendship, Unity and Christian Charity among its members, by raising or supporting a fund of money for maintaining the aged, sick, blind and infirm members, for the legitimate expenses of the order, and for no other purpose whatsoever.

The motto of this order is "Friendship, Unity and Christian Charity."

Friendship shall consist in helping one another, and in assisting each other to the best of our power.

Unity, in combining together for mutual support in sickness and distress.

Christian Charity, in loving one another and doing to all men as we would wish that they should do unto us.

I. This order is to be formed exclusively of practical Catholics. Therefore each member is expected to comply with all his christian duties.

II. Should any of the members fail in the above, and, instead of giving edification and encouragement, become a stumbling block and a disgrace to the organization, such a one, after proper charitable admonition, unless there be an amendment to his conduct, shall be expelled from the order.

III. In order, however, that all may be done with justice, christian charity, and edification, there shall be in each county a chaplain, appointed by the ordinary of the diocese, to be consulted by the division before determining anything relating to morality or religion.

IV. The chaplain in each county shall see that nothing is done or countenanced by the order which is contrary to the laws of the Catholic Church, the decrees of the Plenary Councils of Baltimore, and the Synodical constitutions of the diocese. In any difficulty or doubt which he may not be able to solve, he shall consult the ordinary of the diocese.

V. All divisions of this order shall adopt the foregoing preamble, and their special constitutions and by-laws shall be in harmony with the constitution and by-laws of this order.

CONSTITUTION.

Article I.

Substitute the following:

Name.—1. The name by which this order shall be known and distinguished is "THE ANCIENT ORDER OF HIBERNIANS in America.

2. This order pledges itself to the cause of church and country, and to exercise, at all times, its influence in the interests of right and justice; and further, it hereby declares that its constitution and bylaws shall always be in accordance with the doctrine and laws of the Catholic Church and the decrees and instructions of the Plenary Councils of Baltimore.

Article III.

Substitute the following:

1. There shall be national, state and county chaplains of this order. All chaplains shall be approved by their respective ordinaries before holding office.

2. The national and state chaplains shall be elected respectively by the national and state boards of directors at the regular national and state conventions, and shall hold office respectively until the next regular national and state conventions, following their election.

3. The county chaplains shall be appointed by the ordinary of the diocese on the application of the county boards of directors.

4. The duty of the chaplains shall be to exercise

spiritual supervision over their respective jurisdictions, and for this purpose they shall be admitted to all meetings held herein.

Article X.

In place of "Roman" in third line, Section 1st, insert "Practical." And to the same article add a third section as follows:

"It shall be the duty of the members of this order to receive Holy Communion, at least once a year, within the Easter time."

Article XXX.

In the amended constitution insert the following:

"All disputes which cannot be disposed of in the national convention by the ordinary methods of the order shall be referred to a board of three arbitrators, selected from members of the order. Each of the disputants shall select one member of the board of arbitration, these two shall select a third. Their decision, when approved by the national chaplain, shall be final.

N. B.—The amended constitution will contain the necessary provisions relative to the military branches of the order and state insurance, and also to the Ladies' Auxiliary, provided the constitution of the latter has been previously approved by the arbitrator.

RITUAL.

I find the rituals of both branches of the order defective, and I will, therefore, revise the rituals now in use.

and prepare a new version for submission to the national convention.

XI. INTERPRETATION OF DECISION.

To obtain uniformity in the interpretation of this decision, and avoid friction in its application, all disputes regarding the same, or in any way pertaining to the Plan of Reorganization, shall be referred to the arbitrator, whose decision shall be final.

XII. GOVERNMENT OF ORGANIZATION.

1. Between the date of this decision and the election of new national officers, the national president and the national delegate shall conjointly govern the entire order, and all commands and instructions issued by them to the order shall be signed conjointly by them and countersigned by the arbitrator.

2. In states (where both bodies exist), the state delegate and the state president shall govern their jurisdictions conjointly, and all commands and instructions issued by them shall be signed conjointly until the election of new state officers.

3. In states where only one of the bodies exists the state delegate (or the state president), as the case may be, shall govern his jurisdiction.

4. In counties where both bodies exist, the county delegate and the county president shall govern their jurisdiction conjointly, and all orders and instructions issued by them shall be signed conjointly, until the election of new county officers.

5. In counties where only one of the bodies exists, the county delegate (or county president), as the case may be, shall govern his jurisdiction.

6. In all matters not otherwise provided for in this decision, or not otherwise provided for by the arbitrator, previous to the adoption of the amended constitution in the national convention, held by virtue of this decision, each division shall be governed by the constitution and bylaws under which it is at present governed; but in those matters pertaining to county, state and national government, and not otherwise provided for as above, both bodies shall be governed by the present constitution of "The A. O. H. of America," until the adoption of the said amended constitution.

7. All parts of this decision relating to state officers and to state affairs, shall apply to the District of Columbia, to the territorial and provincial officers, and to territorial and provincial affairs, in so far as such parts are applicable thereto.

*   *   *   *   *

We, the undersigned, representing the above-named committees of "The A. O. H. of America," and "The A. O. H. of the U. S. of America," in affiliation with the Board of Erin, hereby, for our respective organizations, and ourselves, accept the foregoing decision of the Rt. Rev. Arbitrator, and bind ourselves faithfully to execute the provisions of the same in the aforesaid organizations.

P. J. O'CONNOR,
N. P. A. O. H. of America.

JOHN C. WEADOCK,
*N. V.-P. A. O. H. of America,
by his attorney in fact,
P. J. O'Connor.*

JAMES O'SULLIVAN,
Nat'l Secretary.

M. F. WILHERE,
N. D.

JOHN P. MURPHY,
N. D.

WM. T. McLAUGHLIN,
Com. A. O. H. of A.

E. S. PHILLIPS,
Nat'l Delegate A. O. H. B. of E.

E. R. HAYES,
Nat'l Secretary B. of E.

JNO. P. QUINNAN,

JAMES H. MURPHY,
S. D.

JOSEPH McLAUGHLIN,

MILES McPARTLAND,

JOHN McWILLIAMS,
*Nat'l Treasurer,
Com. A. O. H., U. S. A., B. of E.*

Trenton, N. J., Dec. 11, 1897.

In issuing the call for the national convention and announcing the time and place for the same, the Rt. Rev. Bishop said:

Gentlemen—In my decision of December 11th, 1897, I reserved the right to designate the time and place for the national convention to be held by virtue of said decision, in the following words: "The national delegate and the national president shall conjointly sign and issue a call countersigned by the arbitrator, to those under their jurisdiction, for a national convention, to be held during the month of June, 1898, on such day, and in such place as the arbitrator shall decide." This clause was accepted and ratified by your honorable committees. In pursuance of this part of the decision, I have weighed the reasons which should be considered in relation to the time and place of the national convention, bearing always in mind the interests of both organizations and specially the cause of unity and harmony.

Before the selection of an arbitrator each branch of the order had selected an American city for holding its own national convention, and after arbitration had been resorted to it became at once perfectly clear that only one national convention could be held, and that this must necessarily be one of the points on which the arbitrator should exercise his judgment.

Besides, after so cordial an acceptance of my decision by your honorable committees, acting for both bodies, and its unanimous ratification—without even one discordant note from the organizations throughout the country, covering, as it did, principles which had been discussed with such divergence of opinion during many years—it is evident that the question of time and place is of minor importance. Nevertheless, I have carefully considered this question, and I find that it would be imprudent and prejudicial to the interests of unity and harmony if either of the cities designated, previous to my selection as arbitrator, for national conventions this year, were selected, I must, therefore, choose a neutral city, and be guided by its accessibility as a railway center, and its capability for accommodating the delegates. Moreover, I think it will be granted, after my long and arduous labor in behalf of unity, since I am to be temporary chairman, and my personal supervision, as arbitrator, will be needed until the close of the national convention, that my convenience should also be considered. For, I am required, in a very busy season of the year for me, to devote a great part of my time to the interests of the order, and should not be asked to leave my diocese.

It has been urged that certain American cities are replete with revolutionary memories, and that this entitles them to consideration in making a selection. Gentlemen, I most willingly concede the force of this argument. It will, indeed, be a glorious day when Irish and Irish-Americans meeting here in America, on soil rendered sacred, in revolutionary days, by the blood of our fathers, will lovingly entwine the memories of the heroic deeds of Erin and American deeds crimsoned with their hearts' blood and performed for "life, liberty and the pursuit of happiness." Therefore, I feel that providence guided the steps of your honorable committees, seeking for union, to New Jersey. For here are the historic battlefields of Princeton, Monmouth and Trenton. I love, indeed, to think that New Jersey was among the first of the sturdy colonies to raise the standard of independence; that her hills and valleys have been hallowed by the blood of revolutionary heroes, that when the destinies of this country were shrouded in darkness, when the spirits of the Fathers hung heavy and dejected, when defeat after defeat had tried their patience and taxed their endurance, the victory at Trenton gave them new strength and courage; and that in this city was seen, for the first time, the bright star of hope rising above the darkened horizon of America's brilliant future.

Familiar as we are with these glorious deeds, must not I and my devoted flock be proud of the fact that my cathedral is built on the ground first dedicated to freedom and then to religion by the Lord of Hosts and that its Gothic spire, while pointing out the way to heaven, is alike a monument to civic and christian virtue!   Yes, gentlemen, be assured Providence guided you to Trenton; here the work of union was begun and here let it be enduringly cemented.

Therefore, I hereby decide that the national convention to be called in pursuance of my decision, dated Dec. 11th, 1897, shall be held in the city of Trenton, New Jersey, and begin on the 27th day of June, 1898.

This decision shall be forwarded to both organizations by their national secretaries and a call for the said national convention shall be issued later, in the manner directed in my former decision.

With my best wishes for the new year, and my blessing to every member of the A. O. H., I am,

Very sincerely yours,

JAMES A. McFAUL, (Arbitrator),

Bishop of Trenton.

Trenton, N. J., Jany. 10, 1898.

The joint national convention called to ratify the decision of the Rt. Rev. Bishop McFaul, met at Taylor's Opera House, Trenton, N. J., Monday, June 27, 1898, when the following program of exercises was carried out:

1. THE PROGRAM OF EXERCISES.

Monday, June 27.

1. Pontifical Mass, St. Mary's Cathedral, 10.30 a.m.

   a—Sermon

2. National convention, Taylor Opera House, at 2 p. m.

   a—Address by the Rt. Rev. Bishop McFaul.

   b—Address of welcome by His Honor, the Mayor, W. G. Sickel.

   c—Addresses of national officers.

The delegates to the forty-first national convention of the Ancient Order of Hibernians assembled in St. Mary's Cathedral, where Solemn High Mass coram pontifice was celebrated. The officers of the Mass were: Celebrant, Rev. D. J. Duggan; Deacon, Rev. Joseph A. Osborne; Sub-deacon, Rev. William F. Dunphy. Rt. Rev. Bishop McFaul occupied the episcopal throne. Assistant Priest, Rev. John H. Fox; Deacons of Honor, Revs. E. S. Phillips and William J. McLaughlin; Master of Ceremonies, Rev. John M. McCloskey.

The Rt. Rev. Bishop introduced the Rev. Father Fox, the rector of the cathedral, who in part said:

"In the name of the Catholics of the city and diocese of Trenton, and in the name of our illustrious bishop, who has labored so hard and so successfully for the union of your great order, I welcome you, gentlemen of the A. O. H., here today. Here in this church I

welcome you as Catholics, as Irish Catholics, as sons
of a race that has been of all races the most loyal to the
Catholic Church.

"The object and purpose of your order, and the principles by which it is guided, commend it to all fair-
minded men. It is composed of men of Irish blood,
and professing the Catholic faith, united under a common standard, in the cause of church, country and
mutual aid, and the principles by which it is guided in
all its actions are: 'Friendship, Unity and Christian
Charity.'

"But your order is composed not only of Irishmen,
but of Catholic Irishmen. And what nation or race has
been so Catholic as the Irish? In spite of centuries of
persecution, in spite of penal laws, coercion bills, and
wholesale confiscations, Ireland has preserved its original purity in the faith as preached to it by St. Patrick
nearly fifteen hundred years ago. Follow then the
example of your Catholic forefathers; be true to the
Catholic Church; true to her teachings, teachings by
which she has converted and enlightened the nations of
the earth. Continue to be united, and listen not to
those who would even suggest disunion. Where there
is union there is strength. Disunion weakens. Labor,
then, for this unity so essential for the strength and
growth of your order. Guard it jealously; look with
suspicion on any one who would favor division. Be
true to the spirit of your constitution by which you are
united in the glorious cause of church and country,

and the blessing of God and His Church will be with you, and the good work of your order will be extended, and it will grow in influence and favor with your fellow men."

PROCEEDINGS.

June 27, 1898.

Trenton Opera House, Trenton, N. J.

The forty-first national convention and eighth biennial meeting of the Ancient Order of Hibernians was called to order at 3 o'clock at the above place and date by the Rt. Rev. Bishop McFaul, who spoke as follows:

Honorable Delegates of the Ancient Order of Hibernians:

In obedience, gentlemen, to a call issued by the National President and the National Delegate, countersigned by myself, you assemble here to begin this national convention. This enthusiastic greeting renders it impossible to repress the emotions awakened in my breast by the sight of this convention, composed of delegates from all parts of the United States and Canada, for the purpose of lastingly cementing the union so happily accomplished during the memorable year of 1898.

As a man whose pride is to have first seen the light of day beneath the genial sky of the ever-faithful Isle, as the chief pastor of the diocese of Trenton, as Bishop of the Catholic Church, the spouse of Christ and pillar and ground of truth, I bid you a thousand welcomes, and pray God to bless your deliberations.   (Applause.) Questions momentous to the integrity, the progress the prosperity of your noble order—questions whose significance and importance are far reaching, not limited merely to the interests of your own organization but co-extensive with the welfare of the Irish race —will engage your attention.   Wherever an Irishman, yea, wherever there dwells a heart in which pulsates Irish blood—and what land, visited by the sun in his majestic course around the world does not cherish the sons and daughters of Erin?—the principles of "Friendship, Unity and Christian Charity" here proclaimed by a re-united Ancient Order of Hibernians will meet a generous welcome and encourage the sea-divided Gael to unite for securing the strength and influence which, joined to that indomitable courage which has never deserted us during long ages of oppression and tyranny, will place dear old Ireland forever in possession of her long-sought liberty.   (Applause.)

Here I may be permitted to remind you that the poet, dwelling in the bitterness of his soul upon the miseries of his native land, has announced their cause in tones which must find an echo in every Irish heart:

"Let Erin remember the days of old,
    E'er her faithless sons betrayed her,
When Malachy wore the collar of gold
    Which he won from the proud invader."

Ah, yes, let us remember the days of our glory and our sorrow, and let no thoughtless word or act mar the magnificent future of the Irish nation and Irish race. Looking out into that future, I see the star of Irish freedom rising on the horizon; I behold it approaching the zenith whence it will bathe with its generous beams the hills and the vales of the "Emerald Gem of the Western World."

Concerted effort enabled us to retain that faith which we hold dearer than life; disunion caused the tears of the children of Erin to flow at home, and render it possible to describe their woes in a foreign land in the language of "The Exile of Erin."

There came to the beach a poor exile of Erin,
The dew on his thin robe was heavy and chill;
For his country he sighed, when at twilight repairing
To wander alone by the wind-beaten hill.
But the day-star attracted his eye's sad devotion,
For it rose o'er his own native isle of the ocean,
Where once, in the fire of his youthful emotion,
He sang the bold anthem of Erin go bragh.

Sad is my fate! said the heart-broken stranger,
The wild deer and wolf to a covert can flee;
But I have no refuge from famine and danger,
A home and a country remain not to me.
Never again in the green sunny bowers,
Where my forefathers lived shall I spend the sweet
    hours,

Or cover my harp with the wild woven flowers,
And strike to the numbers of Erin go bragh!

Erin my country! though sad and forsaken,
In dreams I revisit thy sea-beaten shore;
But alas! in a far foreign land I awaken,
And sigh for the friends who can meet me no more!
Oh cruel fate! wilt thou never replace me
In a mansion of peace—where no perils can chase me?
Never again shall my brothers embrace me?
They died to defend us, or live to deplore!

Where is my cabin-door, fast by the wild wood?
Sisters and sire! did ye weep for its fall?
Where is the mother that looked on my childhood?
And where is the bosom friend, dearer than all?
Oh! my sad heart! long abandoned by pleasure,
Why did it dote on a fast fading treasure!
Tears like the rain-drop, may fall without measure,
But rapture and beauty they cannot recall.

Yet, all its sad recollection suppressing,
One dying wish my lone bosom can draw;
Erin! an exile bequeaths thee his blessing!
Land of my forefathers! Erin go bragh!
Buried and cold, when my heart stills her motion,
Green be thy fields—sweetest isle of the ocean!
And thy harp-striking bards sing aloud with devotion—
Erin mavourneen! Erin go bragh!

Union among Irishmen also enabled our fathers to stand shoulder to shoulder with other nationalities while they laid deeply and firmly the foundations of free institutions in this fair land. For, does not history proclaim that one-half of the American Revolutionary army was composed of Irish Catholics and Irish Presbyterians? Here they fought and bled and died for liberty.

A memorable example is found in this city of Trenton, where the names of McConkey, the Irish Presbyterian, and Patrick Colvin, the Irish Catholic, have been rendered glorious by the assistance they gave to Washington and his army at the battle of Trenton.

This same spirit made conspicuous the labors of Irishmen and their sons as officers in the army and navy, and even in our legislative halls—for we number nine signers of the Declaration of Independence and six framers of the constitution.

These deeds prove that the Irish, when united, are invincible. Shall we not then stand together for race and fatherland? Yes, disunion shall not weaken our efforts. We have and we shall be generous enough to make sacrifices for union that Ireland may rejoice in the garlands of liberty, prosperity and peace.

Then, oh Irishmen, with union at home and union abroad, with fair Columbia extending assistance, Erin shall arise in her might, and shaking off the shackles of oppression, take her place among the nations of the earth.

Let, therefore, these deliberations be conducted in the spirit of your great fundamental principles, Friendship, Unity and Christian Charity; let all personal ambition, all jealousies and contentions be cast aside; and this will be the grandest convention known in the history of your organization and productive of most important results to the Irish race throughout the world.

*   *   *   *   *

At the close of the Rt. Rev. Bishop's remarks he was presented with a beautiful floral harp.

The Rt. Rev. Arbitrator then said:

In accordance with my decision the temporary chairman of this national convention shall be the arbitrator, and he shall elect such temporary officers as he shall judge necessary. I therefore select as the temporary officers of this organization, James O'Sullivan, national secretary, representing the Ancient Order of Hibernians of America; Edward R. Hayes, of New Brunswick, representing the Ancient Order of Hibernians of the United States of America in affiliation with the Board of Erin, and John P. Dullard, of Trenton, N. J.; and as the stenographers of the convention I appoint James J. Kerney, of Trenton, N. J., and Manus O'Donnell, of Columbus, Ohio; and as sergeant-at-arms, Jas. E. Clinton, of Trenton, N. J.; assistants, James Culliton, Edward Fitzpatrick, James Feenane, Michael Moran and Joseph O'Keefe, of Trenton, N. J.

I take great pleasure, gentlemen, in now introducing a gentleman who is an American of Americans; (applause) whose patriotism is co-extensive with the

United States—who is loved by all his people, irrespective of creed or nationality—a man who has at heart, I believe, above all other men in this city, the interests of Trenton. (Applause.) He has given to us an energetic, business-like administration, and I believe if he continues as he has began—and I am positive he will —that it will not be long until we will get Trenton out of the ruts. (Applause.) I take great pleasure, therefore, in introducing to you the Honorable Welling C. Sickel, Mayor of the City of Trenton. (Great Applause.)

*   *   *   *   *

Mayor Sickel then came forward and said:

It affords me great pleasure to extend to you the freedom of the city. I feel, as mayor of the City of Trenton, that you have paid us a great compliment by holding your convention in our city. On the very ground on which this building is erected was fought one of the decisive battles of the Revolutionary War. And, as you well know, that was the war that brought about the independence of this glorious country and caused the Stars and Stripes, which mean "Liberty, Prosperity, Peace and Good-will to all men," to float o'er our land. (Applause.)

I had the pleasure a short time ago, of visiting the country where no doubt some of you were born—Ireland. Many times did I wish for her the happy solution of her ills. While the people seem willing to accept their lot yet such a result would mean prosperity to Ireland.

I congratulate you upon having united and come together as one great body, for, as you know, "in union there is strength."

I feel that Bishop McFaul, as Arbitrator, has performed an important and manly duty in bringing you together, and I sincerely hope that the deliberations of your body, during your session here, will prove a benefit to your order, as all beneficial orders are a benefit to mankind.

While you are in this city we want to make you comfortable, and extend to you true Jersey hospitality. I want to say, on behalf of the Citizens' Committee, that every member stands ready to do anything in his power to help you and make your visit pleasant while you are here. As mayor of the city, it is particularly gratifying to me to be able to throw the doors of welcome wide open to you, that you may partake of the hospitality we are able to extend to you.

I thank you for the privilege of being present with you today, and hope that it will be my good fortune to meet every one of you personally during this week. (Applause.)

The Rt. Rev. Arbitrator then said:

I rise to introduce a gentleman whose name is familiar to every one of you. A gentleman who has had at heart the interests of the organization for years. A man who has arisen to the ranks of the highest office in one branch of the American order. I will say that he left nothing undone to bring about this reunion, (applause) and while I think of it, I may say here to you in a body what I announced in my decision, that although it has been my good fortune to meet many men of ability and distinction in this country, I never have met as many men at one time so intently interested in the welfare of their countrymen as to throw aside every ambition and willing to make every sacrifice as the gentlemen who represented both branches and who came to ask me to be their arbitrator, (applause) and I feel that under the guidance of such men that you will attain strength and influence here and in the old country; that the strong Irish-American spirit which they will infuse into your convention will produce fruit an hundredfold and that no petty quarrels or small contentions will be ever able to render you asunder again if you listen to the advice and counsel of such men. Gentlemen, it gives me great pleasure to introduce to you the Honorable P. J. O'Connor, National President of the American branch, of Savannah, Georgia. (Great applause and cheers.)

Brother P. J. O'Connor, of Savannah, Georgia, National President of the American branch, then came forward and said:

Right Rev. Bishop, Ladies and Gentlemen:—It is with great pleasure that we accept the hearty welcome

extended to us by the citizens of Trenton through His
Honor, Mayor Sickel. We feel that in so doing we
enter their hearts and homes and leave hope of flight
behind. The cordial greeting of his Lordship Bishop
McFaul, is highly appreciated. Through his earnest
and patriotic efforts we are here to complete the unification of our people and receive his blessing. The city
of Trenton is bristling with inspiring and historic memories and the grand result achieved therein for Hibernianism will always be remembered. I am glad to see
a number of the fair ladies present today. Their brilliant eyes and radiant faces charm and delight this occasion. It has been well said that the tongue of the
famous liberty bell is silent, but I am sure if some Hibernian from the east, west or south, will take to his
home a New Jersey belle he will find that her tongue
not only is not silent, but it has proven to make a music
that will sweeten his dreams, bring comfort to his heart
and add relish to his joys all the days of his life. We are
pleased to be among our golden-hearted New Jersey
brethren, whose high character, devotion to Holy
Church, loyalty to American institutions and love for
Ireland, reflect lustre and fame upon our people. (Applause.) We glory in the fact that we meet in a state
where men are measured by their merits, women are
honored, and freedom of speech and of the press and
right to worship God according to the dictates of their
own consciences, is guaranteed to all. We will carry

with us as we pass from out the gates of this fair city the kindliest recollections of the efforts of her people to make our visit one of the pleasantest experiences of our lives. We are all proud of our membership in the Ancient Order of Hibernians of America, which has for its object the promotion of practical Catholicism, the furtherance of Friendship, Unity and Christian Charity among its members, and peace and good will to all men, the advancement of our country's welfare and a cultivation of a love for the Emerald Isle. Practical Catholicism has for its effect to make our members better men as to themselves, better as to their families, better members of society, and better citizens of their country. (Applause.)

Our reports show that we have dispensed during the past term more than half a million dollars in charitable work. Our charity was not circumscribed by the domain of our own brotherhood, but was co-extensive with the world itself, and as universal as the footprints of mankind. It is the crowning piece in the brow of our society, as it is the rich jewel in the rough setting of the poor man's heart, that charity which ennobles and draws the spirit in closer communication with the eternal spirit, that part of our nature which when touched "makes the whole world kin."

Our people reverence the old land as a sainted mother while loving America as a chosen bride. We cherish and perpetuate the memories and achievements of our forefathers and we will hand down to our child-

ren a proper pride in the race from which we sprang.
The genius of that race has given to philosophy some
of its grandest thoughts; to letters the most graceful
garb it has ever worn; to poetry the sweetest music in
which its numbers has ever yet been sung; to history
its chiefest instances of heroism and valor, and which
through all the ages has made the Irish patriot to stand
as the embodied figure of unselfish consecration to the
cause of human freedom. (Applause.)

Our people may with propriety claim that they have
something to boast of in American history. Over a
hundred years ago the Pennsylvania line, composed
mostly of Irishmen and Catholics, were complimented
by George Washington as comprising the flower and
pick of his Continental army, and the Father of our
country gave testimony of his respect and admiration
by becoming a member of the Friendly Sons of St.
Patrick, of Philadelphia. Our people gave to the
revolution a Montgomery, a Barry, a Sullivan, a Jasper,
a Moylan, and other names that will forever gem the
American sky. Later on they gave to the country a
Jackson, who from behind the cotton bags of New
Orleans repulsed the whole British host, 8000 strong,
and put the finishing stroke to the war of 1812. They
gave to the country a Shields and a Kearney, who
achieved signal distinction in the Mexican war. In the
late civil conflict they were found on either side mar-
shalled in battle's stern array, whether fighting with the

blue or with the gray, beneath the starry folds of our national ensign or bearing aloft the Southern cross, their valor was equally tested on many a hard fought field. As long as the nation endures the sturdy man of the north will tell his children of Sheridan's ride to Winchester, and while the magnolia blooms and the orange groves bear their golden fruit the name of Cleburne will be loved in the Sunny South. In the present war our people are nobly doing their part. They have always been conspicuous for that true heroism, which consists in the unselfish, fearless discharge of duty at the cost of that highest and holiest of sacrifices, life; and has been, under the best forms of civilization, esteemed and ranked as the noblest virtue of a people, the choicest treasure of a state, and what purer sacrifice can be made upon the altar of human love than that of him who voluntarily lays down his life for his country. Such an oblation includes and involves the sacrifice for conscience, for right and truth. (Applause.)

It is the spirit which idealizes and transcendentalizes the social part of our being and subordinates our individual appetites and passions. It forms the life spring and is the source of power to every great commonwealth. That people who have been callous to this sentiment or dead to these instincts has invariably retrograded in the pathway of civilization. We rejoice that the war with Spain has brought all our people together, and in the future there will be no dividing lines between the north and south. We are now a united people, animated by the same patriotic impulses, and will do everything in our power to enhance the welfare and promote the success of our glorious country whose onward march of progress enlightens the world. As I was coming up the harbor of New York last week it was filled with shipping and high above the masts was a magnificent statue that gives light to the mariner by night and cheers those who come to the land of the free. Back of that statue are millions of people enjoying the blessings of liberty. Everywhere its genial rays are penetrating and the time is coming when all over the darkness of despotism will scatter before them like the mists of the morning before the sunlight of heaven. God speed the day when that statue shall light to liberty and happiness our beloved Green Isle. (Applause.)

The memories of our visit to Trenton will form a pleasant episode in our lives—a spot to which we can look back with grateful emotions and cherish as a flower that never withereth and whose fragrance will never die.

"Long, long be our hearts with such memories filled,
Like the vase in which roses have once been distilled,
You may break, you may shatter the vase if you will
But the scent of the roses will hang round it still."

(Great applause.)

Rt. Rev. Bishop McFaul then said:

I have been reminded by Mr. O'Connor that there are ladies present and I will say that we will have a reception this evening, at which I expect to have Mr.

O'Connor and other officers of both organizations present on the stage here to assist me in receiving, along with some of the clergymen, and I am sure that the ladies will then be here in sufficient numbers to give satisfaction to Mr. O'Connor. (Applause and laughter.)

I have been told that Mr. O'Connor was born in Georgia, but I believe that he has paid a visit to the Emerald Isle since then, and I don't think that it is once only that he has kissed the Blarney Stone, but a half dozen times, and I would not be surprised if he has a small portion of it in his pocket. (Laughter.) Now, lest the ladies might imagine that Mr. O'Connor had a purpose in these beautiful things which he said regarding the fair sex, I will say that I have it on the authority of Mr. O'Connor himself that he has a mother-in-law. (Applause and laughter.) But, lest this might now dampen their fervor and ardor this evening, I say that I am positively sure there are eligible single gentlemen among the delegates.

In introducing the new elected President of the organization, The Rt. Rev. Bishop John T. Keating, said: I would like to say a word to the delegates assembled. It is with pleasure that I rise at the conclusion of this magnificent convention to express my admiration at the efficiency with which it has been conducted both on the part of its officers and the assembled delegates. I am gratified beyond expression to find that Irishmen and their sons in America have made such rapid strides in acquiring parliamentary ability and eloquence within this generation. Ireland has always stood pre-eminent in forensic eloquence, and I rejoice exceedingly that this grand organization, having come across the sea, is making its influence felt in greater Ireland over which floats the flag of the free. (Applause.)

Allow me to say, gentlemen, that I am proud of the intelligence, virtue and courage of the gentlemen sent from their respective states to cement this grand old order firmly together and to declare to the world that what God had joined together no man shall put asunder. (Applause.) Let me here repeat what I said at the opening of this convention: Stand together under your noble leaders for faith and fatherland and you will be invincible, and your influence will be felt at home and abroad, and the star of Irish freedom can not set.

Conquer we must if our cause it is just,
And this be our watchword: "In God is our trust."
And the green flag of Erin in freedom shall wave
O'er the land of the Gael and the home of the brave.
Let us fight for our altars and our fires,
O'er the green graves of our sires,
For God and our native land.

3. Reception to the delegates by the Rt. Rev. Bishop McFaul, Taylor Opera House, 8 p. m.

Tuesday, June 28, Taylor Opera House.

Permanent organization and appointing of committees.

Wednesday, June 29.

Grand parade of state and visiting organizations, leaving P. R. R. depot, Clinton street, at 11 a. m.

Thursday, June 30, Taylor Opera House.

Regular work of convention.

Friday, July 1, Taylor Opera House.

Completion of business of convention.

The following national officers were elected to serve for two years:

JOHN T. KEATING, National President.

JAMES E. DOLAN, National Vice President.

JAMES O'SULLIVAN, National Secretary.

PATRICK T. MORAN, National Treasurer.

The convention adjourned, to meet in the city of Boston, Mass., in 1900.

During the years of disunion there were many debates and law suits (to all our shame as Irishmen). But during that unfortunate period neither side forgot their duty to God and His Holy Church. So by the past let us learn wisdom and in the future the Ancient Order of Hibernians will flourish under the guidance of our bishops and priests and will be a credit to our race at home and abroad.

I close with an extract from work of Dr. J. C. O'Connell of Washington, D. C., entitled "The Irish in the Revolution and in the Civil War."

Irishmen have represented the American republic abroad under all ̲dministrations. It is needless to say with distinction equal to the distinguished valor of their brethren who wrote the Declaration of Independence and quenched the fires of secession by their blood, proclaiming in thunder of artillery, this great republic to be for all time one and indissoluble. The words "Old Ireland," are carved on every tree that falls before the axe of the Irish emigrant. The smoke ascending to the clouds from the old log cabin in the center of the clearing in the virgin forests of the far west pay homage to the words, Old Ireland. The words are carved on monuments of stone in our churches, in our cemeteries, and on statues and under several signatures of the framers of the constitution and the signers of the Declaration of Independence. The emigrant depots and large towns on the Atlantic seaboard resound with the words Old Ireland. The thousands of railroads and the huge engines that rattle over them thunder forth the words. The words, Old Ireland, are emblazoned on every battlefield of the Revolution from Stony Point to Yorktown and on every fold of the starry banner from Gettysburg to Atlanta. The names of Sheridan, Sullivan, Shields, Jackson, Calhoun and Carroll are as suggestive of the words, Old Ireland, as those of Emmet, Fitzgerald and Tone. The same spirit that hanged the latter at home would have hanged the former abroad, had the patriots of 1776 been drowned in the Delaware by the hireling Hessians and Red Coats.

Statesmen and demagogues pronounce the words

with peculiar emphasis on election day when they are put in the ballot box by the tens of thousands. They lead millions to victory whether by the sword or by the ballot. May God grant that the same words, Old Ireland, will be carved in letters of gold on Erin's green banner and be swung to the breeze from Tara's old hall, proclaiming by the hosannas of her people, amid the thunders of artillery, that Ireland has again taken her station among the nations of the earth when the epitaph of the immortal Emmet will be written. "Let not my epitaph be written until my country takes her place among the nations of the earth. Then, and not till then, let my epitaph be written." Here is to dear old Ireland! brave old Ireland! Ireland! boys! hurrah!

Irishmen, you, with the sons of Irishmen, are 20,-000,000 freemen. You help to wield the destiny of the greatest republic that the world has ever seen or heard of. The country that gave you birth is writhing under the galling Saxon yoke. Her bleeding breast heaves with the breath of returning life. Why not win for her what you won for your adopted country, the inalienable rights of life, liberty and the pursuits of happiness? The golden prize for which you have yearned and toiled and suffered so long is within your grasp. Win it by one grand, great dash, shoulder to shoulder, hand in hand. All lovers of liberty will wish you God speed. The starry banner will smile encouragingly on her sister, sunburst, in grateful remembrance of the heroic bravery of her sons in the cause of American liberty. The spirit of the brave, who now languish in the tombs of tyranny, British dungeons, will be liberated and the civilized world will join in one grand chorus of jubilation as the Harp of Tara, now so mute, swells to the magic touch of freedom. Irishmen! spring to your feet, spring up from your apathy and slavery! Seize the sword, the pike, the cannon, and win for yourselves and children's children the spurs of nationhood.

In conclusion, I greet you, in the language of the flag of our country, emblematic of all the blessings conferred on the human race, and robed in the majesty of which we in this day, enjoy life, liberty and the pursuit of happiness. Under its folds our fathers of 1776 reared the fabric of this Republic. Under its fostering care it has grown to be a monument of solid sunshine, a beacon light of liberty, with the stars and stripes winding around and around it as a winding stair of light, towering into the infinite, proclaiming "liberty throughout all the land and to all the inhabitants thereof." The starry banner will become in time the flag of the universe. The future belongs to it and to it alone. It will become the emblem of the heart, the emblem of all that man holds dear; inmost poetry of each human soul. Within its folds are wrapped the interests of liberty and civilization till time will be no more. Under that banner all people will worship their Creator untrammelled. They will learn to know the destiny of their being and that the title, American citizen, is far dearer than all the patents of nobility or the diadems of the Caesars.

***

GOD SAVE IRELAND.

High upon the gallows tree,
Swung the noble hearted three,
   By the vengeful tyrant stricken in their bloom,
But they met him face to face,
With the courage of their race,
   And they went with souls undaunted to their doom.

CHORUS.

God save Ireland said the heroes,
   God save Ireland said they all,
Whether on the scaffold high or the battle field
    we die,
   O what matter when for Ireland dear we fall.

Girt around with cruel foes,
Still their courage proudly rose,
   For they thought of friends that loved them far
    and near,
Of the millions true and brave,
O'er the ocean's swelling wave,
   And the friends in holy Ireland ever dear.
      [CHORUS.]

Climb they up the rugged stair,
Rung their voices out in prayer,
Then with England's fatal cord around them cast,
    Close beneath the gallows tree,
Kissed like brothers lovingly,
    True to home, and faith, and freedom, to the last.

Never till the latest day,
Shall the memory pass away,
    Of the million lives, thus given for our land,
Ever on the cause must go,
Amidst joy, and weal or woe,
    Till we've made our Isle a nation free and grand.

[CHORUS.]

[The End.]

IRELAND VINDICATED.

ENGLISH TYRANNY AND INHUMANITY EXPOSED.

The barbarous system of warfare pursued by the Irish government. Indiscriminate murder and massacre of the Irish, men, women and children. St. Leger, Monroe, Coote, Hamilton, Grenville, Ireton, and Cromwell, bathed in blood. Five days' butchery in Drogheda. Detestable hypocrisy of Cromwell. A medal and a gold chain awarded to a Noyadist. Extermination of man and beast, for twenty-eight miles! ! !

(BY M. CAREY.)

We proceed to examine the system of warfare pursued by the Irish government; and to ascertain with what propriety or justice it could complain of murder and massacre, had the insurgents been really guilty of the crimes alleged against them. We pledge ourselves to prove, that a more murderous system of warfare never prevailed, in any age or in any country; that many of their commanders were as merciless and as bloodthirsty as Attila or Genghis Khan; and that some of the scenes of slaughter were so horrible, particularly, as will appear in the sequel, at Cashel, Drogheda and Wexford, that they never were and never could be exceeded, and have been rarely equaled.

In the long catalogue of human follies, there is none more unaccountable, more ludicrous, or more universal, than that of censuring in others those vices and crimes to which we are ourselves most prone. Who has not heard elaborate declamations against intemperance, from drunkards; against lust, from debauchees; against meanness and avarice, from misers? There is not a nation in the world that has not a variety of terse passages on this extraordinary propensity.

"Quis tulerit Gracchos de seditione querentes?
  Quis cœlum terris non misceat, et mare cœlo,
  Si fur displiceat Verri, homicida Miloni,
  Clodius accuset mæchos, Catilina Cethegum;
  In tabulam Syllæ si dicant discipuli tres?"

Juvenal, II.

The era embraced in our discussions affords a most striking illustration of this view of human nature. While the

"Starry welkin has rung"

with the hoarse din of horrible massacres said to have been perpetrated by the Irish, it will appear, as clear as the noon-day sun, that the Irish rulers, in giving these statements, were drawing their own picture; and that the poet's

"Mutato nomine de te fabula narratur,"†

was never more appropriate than to those rulers and their agents.

The leading features of the warfare carried on by the forces of the Irisn government were,

I.   The Irish, unarmed and wholly defenceless, were frequently massacred and drowned, without mercy. From this fate, neither priests, women, nor children, were exempted;

†"Change but the name, of thee the tale is told."
—(Francis.)

*"All must hear, the while,
The Gracchi rail at faction, with a smile.
Who would not swear by ev'ry awful name,
If Milo murder, Verres theft should blame;
Clodius pursue adulterers to the bar,
Caius tax Catiline with civil war;
Or Sylla's pupils, aping ev'ry deed,
Against his tables of proscription plead."

—(Gifford, p. 41.)

II.   Men who had been overcome in battle; thrown down their arms; made no further resistance; and begged for quarter; were butchered by hundreds, and sometimes by thousands.

III.   And, to crown all, after surrender made, and quarter promised, the faith pledged to the Irish was often perfidiously violated, and they were butchered in cold blood.

It was our intention to have classed the various facts, in support of these several allegations, exactly under their respective heads; but, as many of the instances of atrocity which we have collected, exemplify more than one of our positions; and as others, though of equal force, cannot properly be classed under any of them, we are not able to carry that plan fully into effect. We shall, however, adhere to it as closely as in our power. But we are convinced that their effect on the reader's mind will depend, not on their classification, but on their magnitude, importance and authenticity. If, weighed in the balance of truth, they be found wanting in these essential particulars, no accuracy of arrangement can save them from condemnation. But if they stand a scrutiny on those grand points, their deficiency in any of the minor ones will not be regarded as of material consequence.

In this investigation, we voluntarily subject ourselves to a disadvantage, of which we are persuaded, the world has hitherto afforded no precedent. We had provided a large body of authentic testimony, from Clanrickarde, Castlehaven, Walsh, Curry, and other writers on the Irish side of the question, of which we proposed to avail ourselves. But, being determined to remove all possible ground for cavil, we have laid the whole aside; and shall rely solely on two species of authorities, which must overwhelm all opposition, and settle this question eternally. The first is, the despatches and documents of the sanguinary ruffians who perpetrated the murders; and the second, the statements of the Anglo-Hibernian historians.

We thus place ourselves in the predicament of a man who has a process at law, and has prepared ample documents to establish his claims; but, finding his antagonist's documents so strong and so powerful against their owner, as to render his own unnecessary, he throws them into the fire; and, so far as respects the contents of this chapter, one of the most important in our work, we care not if every page, written in defense of the Irish, were committed to the flames.

Should we, to use the legal phraseology, make out

our case under these circumstances, as we trust we shall, it will afford the strongest proof that can be desired or conceived, of the intrinsic goodness of the cause, and of the extent of the delusion that has prevailed on the subject. We are well aware of the immense advantages we forego by this course; but we forego them cheerfully, and have no more doubt of the result than we have that the sun, which is now setting in the western horizon, will rise again, resplendent, in all its majesty and glory, to illumine a grateful and admiring world.

Those, however who wish to peruse a list of the murders and massacres perpetrated on the Irish, as recorded by the writers of that nation, are referred to the Appendix to Clarendon's "History of the Irish Rebellion," where there is a large collection to be found, with due detail of time and place.

Resting wholly on plain matter of fact, we are unfortunately debarred of the rhetorical flourishes of "lakes and rivers of blood," "spirits chanting hymns," "ghosts rising from the rivers, and shrieking out revenge," and all those other "tales of horror," and "suggestions of frenzy," which decorate the pages of the long train of historians, from Temple to Leland, who have exhausted the power of eloquence in embellishing the legends of "the execrable Irish rebellion." But we feel full confidence that our

"Round unvarnish'd tale"

will "put them down," in the estimation of every upright and candid reader.

After these preliminary observations, we enter on
the proof of the important positions we have laid down,
respecting the system of warfare pursued by the forces
of the Irish government. The first branch of No. I is,

"The Irish, unarmed and wholly defenceless, were
frequently massacred and drowned, without mercy."
Behold our proofs.

"Monroe advanced with his army into the county of
Cavan, from whence he sent parties into Westmeath
and Longford, which burnt the country, and put to the
sword all the country people they met."—(Carte, first
book Irish history.)

"Sir Charles Coote, immediately after his inhuman
executions and promiscuous murders of people in
Wicklow, was made governor of Dublin."—Idem.

"As soon as Monroe had received an account of the
cessation being concluded, he fell upon the Irish peas-
ants, who were getting in their harvest in great security,
as no longer thinking of an enemy, and made a
slaughter among them."—(Idem, Irish records.)

"They put to the sword thirty Irish, taken by them in
that vessel at Padstow."—(Whitelock, Irish history.)

"After a little dispute, the Parliament's ship boarded
the Dunkirker, and put all the Irish in her to the
sword, and took the rest prisoners."—(Idem, page
204.)

"The garrison was sent away under convoy; but, by

the disorderliness of an unpaid soldiery, they were almost all of them plundered and murdered."—(Warner, Irish history.)

"They hanged about fifty of the Irish, according to the lord general's orders."—Whitelock.

"Captain Barrow took O'Ronie's island, in Ireland, and put eighty-three to the sword."—Idem.

Douglas "marched as through an enemy's country, his men plundering and even murdering with impunity."—(Leland, fourth Irish history.)

Lord Broghill, "on the 21st August, 1642, took the castle of Ardmore, in the county of Waterford, being yielded on discretion. The women and children were spared, but the men, one hundred and forty in number, were put to the sword."—(Rushworth, fifth Irish history.)

"Sir Frederick Hamilton entered the town of Sligo, and burnt it, freed many Protestants, and slew in the streets three hundred Irish."—(Ibid, Irish history.)

"Colonel Sydenham, major Sydenham, and other forces, hastened thither, put them to flight, and pursued them almost to Wareham, slew twelve, and took sixty horses and a hundred and sixty prisoners, whereof eight being natural Irish, seven of them were immediately hanged, and the other spared, for doing execution on his fellows."—(Idem.)

"St. Leger was informed of another robbery committed on the cattle of his brother-in-law, which he revenged in a very cruel and indiscriminate manner, kill-ing near twenty people, some of them entirely innocent; and when one of his captains, who had killed nine or ten inoffensive people, destroyed their houses, and drove away their cattle, was complained of to him, instead of punishing, he seemed to approve those outrages."— (Warner.)

"Some Walloons, whom the soldiers took for Irishmen, were put to the sword."—Whitelock.

"Inchiquin commits great destruction, as far as he dares venture, about Dublin and Tredah, by burning and driving away of their cattle, and hangs all he can meet with, going to the lord lieutenant."—Idem.

"At the taking of Caermarthen, by Captain Swanley, many Irish rebels were thrown into the sea."— Idem.

The second branch of No. I is,

"From this fate [of massacre] priests, women, and children were not exempted."

Our last chapter contained the bloodthirsty orders of the lord justices and privy council, to murder "all the males able to bear arms, in places where the rebels were harbored." We now proceed to prove that these barbarous orders were fully carried into operation.

Leland and Warner inform us, that "in the **execution** of these orders, the soldiers slew all persons promiscuously."* They state this on the authority of the

---

*"The soldiers, in executing their orders, murdered all persons that came in their way promiscuously, not sparing the women, and sometimes not the children."—(Leland, III. Warner.)

lords justices themselves, whose testimony must be regarded as indisputable.

But was not this the consequence the miscreants calculated on producing? Could they have reasonably expected any other?   When the devouring sword is invited from its scabbard by public authority, for the indiscriminate slaughter of "men able to bear arms," will not the expiring and bed-rid wretch be despatched to the other world, as a man "able to bear arms?" Will his cassock protect the priest? her bonnet or shawl the pity-inspiring female? or its cradle and tender cries the helpless infant? No; he must be a mere novice in human nature and human affairs who entertains a doubt on the subject.

"Monroe put sixty men, eighteen women and two priests to death, in Newry."—(Leland, page 201.)

"The lord president of Munster, St. Leger, is so cruel and merciless that he causes honest men and women to be most execrably executed, and amongst the rest caused a woman great in child to be ript up, and babes to be taken out of her womb, and then thrust every of the babes with weapons through their little bodies. This act of the lord president hath set many in a sort of desperation."—Lord of Upper Ossory's Letter to the Earl of Ormond.—Carte's history.

"Sir Theophilus Jones had taken a castle, put some men to the sword, and thirteen priests, having with them two thousand pounds."—Whitelock.

"Their friars and priests were knocked on the head promiscuously with the others, who were in arms."—Idem.

"Letters from Ireland, that the Lord Inchiquin relieved some garrisons of the English in Tipperary, entered Carricke and fortified a pass to make good his retreat, blew open the gate of Cullen by a petard, entered the town, took two castles by assault, and put three hundred soldiers to the sword, and some women, notwithstanding order to the contrary."—Idem.

"Sir William Parsons hath by late letters advised the governor to the burning of Corn, and to put man, woman and child to the sword; and Sir Adam Loftus hath written in the same strain."—Ormond's letters.

Our second position is,

II. "Men who had been overcome in battle; thrown down their arms; made no further resistance; and begged for quarter were butchered by hundreds, and sometimes by thousands."

"A neighboring bog tempted the Irish foot to retire thither for refuge, while their horse marched off with very little loss, and unmolested. The bog was too small to afford them protection. Jones surrounded it with his horse, whilst his foot entered it, and attacked the Irish, who threw down their arms and begged for quarter. About three thousand of them were put to the sword."—Carte.

"They defeated and pursued them with great slaughter, granting quarters to none but officers. About two thousand fell by the weapons of an enemy transported by zeal and resentment, about five hundred plunged into lake Erne, and but one of all the multitude escaped."—Leland.

"As no quarter was given, except to Colonel Richard Butler, son to the lord Ikerin (who was the last man of the Irish army that retired) few prisoners were taken." —Smith.

"The left, commanded by Mac-Allisdrum, consisting of brave northern Irish, stood their ground; but were at last forced to yield to the conquerers; their commander giving up his sword to Colonel Purden. But lord Inchiquin having, before the battle, ordered that no quarter should be given to the enemy, the brave Mac-Allisdrum and most of his men were put to the sword in cold blood."—Idem.

"Lieutenant Colonel Sanderson, at the same time, and Sir Francis Hamilton coming in the nick of time with his troop, they had all execution upon them for five miles."—Rushworth.

"Colonel Mathews, at Dromore, getting together a body of two hundred men, attacked five hundred of the rebels; and, having killed three hundred of them without the loss of a man, the next day he pursued the rest, who had hid themselves about in the bushes, and, starting them like hares out of their formes, killed a hundred and fifty more."—Warner.

"The lord Inchiquin took Pilborne castle by storm, and put all in it but eight to the sword."—Whitelock.

"His men had the pursuit of the rebels seven miles, three several ways, as long as the day lasted, and in the flight and pursuit, were slain of the rebels about four thousand."—Idem.

"The rebels were pursued without mercy; and, in their flight, spread a general consternation through all their adherents."—Leland.

"In the battle, and a bloody pursuit of three miles, 7,000 of the Irish were slain. The unrelenting fury of the victors appeared in the number of their prisoners, which amounted only to 450."—Leland.

Our third position is:

III. "After surrender made, and quarter promised, the faith pledged to the Irish was perfidiously violated, and they were butchered in cold blood."*

"The army, I am sure, was not eight thousand effective men; and of them it is certain there were not above six hundred killed; and the most of them that were killed were butchered after they had laid down their arms, and had been almost an hour prisoners, and divers of them murdered after they were brought within the works of Dublin."—Ormond.

---

*A most striking instance, in proof of this accusation, is afforded by the slaughter at Drogheda; of which an account will be found at the close of this chapter.

The bishop of Clogher "having detached Colonel Swiney with a strong party, to make an attempt upon Castledoe, in the county Donegal, he ventured, contrary to the advice of the most experienced officers, with 3,000 men, to fight Sir Charles Coote, with near double his number, at Letterkenny. Major General O'Cahan, many of his principal officers, and fifteen hundred common soldiers were killed on the spot; and the colonels Henry Roe and Phelim M'Tuol O'Neile, Hugh Macguire, Hugh Mac-Mahon and others, slain after quarter given."—Carte.

We cannot allow ourselves to doubt for a moment that we have fully established our positions on the most impregnable ground. Limiting ourselves, as we have done, to the accounts of the perpetrators of the murders, and their historians, it is a matter of astonishment that we have been able to adduce such strong evidence. But it is a peculiar feature in this history that the criminals narrate their crimes, with as little ceremony as if they claimed glory from them. A few circumstances, of peculiar atrocity, which add strong corroboration to the testimony, are reserved for the close of this chapter.

The pretences on which the Irish were slaughtered were, in many instances, of the most frivolous and contemptible character; but it is a trite observation, that those who are wicked enough to perpetrate crimes, are never without a plea to justify, or at least to palliate, their guilt. Sir S. Harcourt besieged a castle in the vicinity of Dublin, where, venturing too near, he was shot. The barbarian besiegers, when they took the castle, to revenge the death of their general, slaughtered every man, woman and child it contained.* Warner relates this atrocious act, not merely without censure, but with "apparent" justification, or at least extenuation. He says, "the soldiers were so enraged at the cowardly manner in which he was killed, that they put all within to the sword." This was probably the pretext the murderers assigned at the time, and which the doctor copied without reflection. It would appear that the reverend historian supposed there was some ceremony necessary to be observed by the garrison of a besieged castle, before they shot at their enemies. Perhaps he thought that they ought to have sent a herald to Harcourt, to warn him to beware of the bullet. This is sheer nonsense. Who would dare to censure for cow-

---

*"Sir S. Harcourt was sent out with a small party in order to dislodge them. But being obliged to send back for some battering cannon, whilst he waited for these and was giving his soldiers some orders, one of the rebels perceiving him, discharged his piece at him and gave him a mortal wound, of which he died the next day, to the prejudice of the service and the great grief of the English. His men, who loved him greatly, were so enraged at the cowardly manner in which he was killed, that when the cannon came up, and had made a breach sufficient for them to take the castle by storm, they put all within to the sword, without sparing man, woman or child."—Warner.

ardice the man who shot General Wolfe or General Montgomery at Quebec; General Mercer at Princeton; General Ross at Baltimore; or General Packenham at New Orleans? In a word, lives there a man absurd enough to aver that there is any owardice in sending a whizzing bullet to salute a besieging enemy who ventures within reach of a shot?

That "straws show which way the wind blows," is an adage of more sound sense than eloquence. An occurrence which Ludlow narrates, with great naivete, affords a strong confirmation of the various proofs we have already adduced of the murderous spirit by which the forces of the Irish government were actuated. It evinces that no raging bloodhounds were ever more ravenous after their prey than they were for the slaughter of the devoted Irish.

A few wretched fugitives, who had escaped from their enemies, had taken refuge in a cave, and were discovered by Ludlow's army on his march. Thirsting for their lives, he spent nearly two days in the effort to smother them by smoke; but his endeavors failed of success. At length, some of his soldiers forced their way into the cave, where they found about twenty defenceless wretches, whose forlorn state would have almost excited the pity of a band of ruthless Creeks or Cherokees; but humanity or pity for the Irish formed no part of the system then pursued. Fifteen of them were butchered in the cave; and four or five brought out alive, who probably shared a similar fate, although the writer is silent as to the issue.*

This single fact, narrated by the master butcher himself, would, if it stood alone, be sufficient to establish the infernal spirit with which the armies of the government were actuated. It is easy to conceive that those whose thirst of blood induced them to arrest a considerable army in its march, and spend two days in the hope of glutting their rage with a few human victims who had sought security in a cavern, would flesh their swords indiscriminately in all they met in human

---

*"From hence I went to visit the garrison of Dundalk, and being upon my return, I found a party of the enemy retired within a hollow rock, which was discovered by one of ours, who saw five or six of them standing before a narrow passage at the mouth of the cave. The rock was so thick that we thought it impossible to dig it down upon them, and therefore resolved to try to reduce them by smoke. After some of our men had spent most part of the day in endeavoring to smother those within, by fire placed at the mouth of the cave, they withdrew the fire, and the next morning, supposing the Irish to be made incapable of resistance by the smoke, some of them with a candle before them crawled into the rock. One of the enemy, who lay in the middle of the entrance, fired his pistol, and shot the first of our men in the head, by whose loss we found that the smoke had not taken the designed effect. But seeing no other way to reduce them, I caused the trial to be repeated, and upon examination found that though a great smoke went into the cavity of the rock, yet it came out again at other crevices; upon which I ordered those places to be closely stopped, and another

form, male or female, old or young, bearing the hated Irish name. This very rational conclusion is fully established by the mass of revolting facts contained in the present chapter.

A circumstance which occurred in consequence of the murderous ordinance of the Long Parliament to give no quarter to Irish prisoners, evinces such transcendent injustice and folly that it deserves to be put on record to display the temper of the times, and to prove that the slaughter of the Irish was regarded as perfectly innocent.

The army of the parliament had taken a number of

smother made. About an hour and a half after this, one of them was heard to groan very strongly, and afterwards more weakly, whereby we presumed that the work was done; yet the fire was continued till about midnight, and then taken away, that the place might be cool enough for ours to enter the next morning. At which time some went in armed with back, breast and head-piece, to prevent such another accident as fell out at their first attempt; but they had not gone above six yards before they found the man that had been heard to groan, who was the same that had killed one of our men with his pistol, and who, resolving not to quit his post, had been, upon stopping the holes of the rock, choked by the smoke. Our soldiers put a rope about his neck and drew him out. The passage being cleared, they entered, and having put about fifteen to the sword, brought four or five out alive, with the priest's robes, a crucifix, chalice and other furniture of that kind. Those within preserved themselves by laying their heads close to a water that ran through the rock."—Ludlow, Vol. I, page 422.

prisoners, among whom were thirteen Irishmen, who, in pursuance of the above ordinarce, were immediately executed. Prince Rupert, bold, brave, and determined, took measures to ascertain the fact; and, as soon as all doubt of it was removed, singled out an equal number of prisoners belonging to the enemy, and, as right and justice required, in order to arrest the progress of this murderous system, retaliated on them the cruelty of which their officers had set such a terrible example.

It is incredible what an outcry this laudable, because necessary, measure of severity excited. Had the prince hanged these men in retaliation for the slaughter of an equal number of cats or dogs, his cruelty and injustice could not have been more severely execrated than it was by the parliament, whose army was with difficulty prevented from butchering their English prisoners; as if they had not been themselves the original aggressors.* The carnage of the Irish, being sanctioned by

*"To the worthy and honored William Lenthal, Esq., Speaker of the Honorable House of Commons.
"Right Honorable,
"According to the ordinance of parliament on that behalf, we caused some Irish rebels, to the number of thirteen, to be put to death; and since Prince Rupert's coming into these parts, it happened that some of our men were taken by some of his commanders; and, as is verified to us, after quarter given them, were, by the prince's command, executed; which we hearing of, sent a trumpet to know the truth of the report, and the cause why they so suffered, by whom he returned us the letter enclosed for answer. The death of these soldiers being known in our several garrisons, hath so incensed the soldiery, that they vow revenge, and we

the ordinance of parliament, they regarded as lawful and innocent: but the retaliatory execution of their associates was, forsooth, abominable murder.

Prince Rupert was made of too "stern stuff" to be terrified out of his manly purpose. He announced his determination to pursue the system of *lex talionis*, and to murder man for man.* There do not appear any data whereon to ground an opinion of the ultimate issue of this sanguinary rivalry; but it is more than

found it difficult to prevent their violent falling upon the prisoners in our custody; whereof we thought good to certify this honorable house, and humbly pray your advice how we shall prevent the acting the like cruelty upon our soldiers for the future.

JOHN MACKWORTH,
ANDREW LLOYD,
SAMUEL MOORE,
ROBERT CHARLTON,
ROBERT OLIVE,
THOMAS HART,
LEIGH OWEN.

Salop, March 24, 1644."

—Parliamentary History.

*Extracts from a letter of Prince Rupert to the Earl of Essex.
"Those soldiers of mine, that were barbarously murdered in cold blood, after quarter given them at Shrewsbury, were such as, during the time they were in Ireland, served his majesty stoutly, constantly, and faithfully, against the rebels of that kingdom; and, after the cessation there, were, by his majesty's command, transported to serve him in this, where they honestly

probable that the energy and spirit of the prince stayed the progress of the devouring sword and rescued many an unfortunate Irishman from the horrible proscription of their enemies. Such a system, pursued steadily, as it ought to have been, by General Washington, would have snatched thousands of brave and noble victims from the horrors of the Jersey prisonship. Any other system sacrifices our best friends for our worst enemies, than which a more miserable policy cannot be conceived.

A murderous ruffian, commander of one of the vessels belonging to the English parliament, took a vessel with a number of Irish soldiers on board, who were not only not insurgents, but had served under the Duke of Ormond against them, and, after the cessation of hostilities in Ireland, were going to England, to be incorporated in the royal army. In pursuance of the or-

performed the duty of soldiers."—Parliamentary History.

"If the same course shall be held, and any prisoners under my command shall be taken, executed and murdered in cold blood, under what senseless and unjust pretense whatsoever; for every officer and soldier, so causelessly and barbarously murdered, I will cause so many of the prisoners remaining in my power to be put to death in the same manner; and I do not in the least doubt but the blood of those miserable men, who shall so suffer by my order, as well as those who shall be so butchered by that ordinance your lordship mentions, shall be required at their hands, who by their cruel examples impose a necessity upon other men to observe the rules they lay down."—Idem, Parliamentary history, vol. 3, page 445.

dinance for giving no quarter to Irish prisoners, he tied seventy of them back to back, and threw them into the sea. For this cruel act, and other congenial exploits, the parliament of England ordered him to be presented with a medal and a gold chain, of the value of two hundred pounds.*

Barbarous and murderous as were the commanders of the forces against the Irish, in general, there were some of them who far exceeded their colleagues in the dreadful trade of slaughter. Of these, St. Leger, Monroe, Inchiquin, Sir Richard Grenville, Sir Charles Coote, Tichbourne, Ireton, and Cromwell stand proudly pre-eminent as prime ministers of Satan, in the horrid work of extermination.

Grenville was naturally ferocious and bloodthirsty; but his native ferocity was whetted by avarice and rapacity, which goaded him to deeds of horror of the blackest dye. He hung old and bed-ridden men for not discovering wealth which they did not possess; and, with equal barbarity, hung women, frequently of quality, because they had not as much money as he had

---

*"June 4, 1644. Ordered, That Captain Swanly have the thanks of this house returned unto him for his faithful service and valiant actions, performed by him for the good of the public, both at the Isle of Wight, Pembrokeshire and Caermarthenshire, and that a chain of gold of two hundred pounds price, with a medal annexed unto it, be bestowed upon him."— Journals, III.

expected.* This barbarian, having been ordered to England, pursued the same system of rapine and murder there.†

A few of the characteristic feats of St. Leger,‡ Inchiquin, Monroe, and Coote, grace the foregoing pages. Honorable mention remains to be made of Tichbourne, Ireton and Cromwell—a bloody triumvirate, whose names ought to be held in eternal reprobation by Irishmen and descendants of Irishmen.

*Sir Richard Grenville, upon the fame of being a good officer, was sent over with a very good troop of horse; was major of the Earl of Leicester's own regiment of horse, and was very much esteemed by him, and the more by the parliament, for the signal acts of cruelty he did every day commit upon the Irish; which were of so many kinds upon both sexes, young and old, hanging old men who were bed-ridden, because they would not discover where their money was, that he believed they had; and old women, some of quality, after he had plundered them, and found less than he expected; that they can hardly be believed, though notoriously known to be true."—Clarendon.

†"He made one of them hang all the rest; which, to save his own life, he was contented to do; so strong his appetite to those executions he had been accustomed to in Ireland, without any kind of commission, or pretense of authority."—Idem.

‡"If, in the execution of martial law, he (St. Leger) spared neither sex nor age, his countrymen frequently expressed a generous indignation and horror at his barbarity."—Leland.

Henry Tichbourne, governor of Drodheda, signalized for his sanguinary career, merited the distinction we have accorded him, to be ranked with the destroyers, Ireton and Cromwell. In a familiar letter to his wife, as a matter of course, he communicates the information that, finding he could not induce the Irish to hazard the fortune of a battle, he had concluded "they were in another sort to be dealt with;" and accordingly the wretch sallied out "every other morning, for several weeks," slaughtering all he met, without mercy; so that he left "neither man nor beast alive," for sixteen miles from the garrison.*   And one of his coadjutors in this business of destruction perpetrated the same havoc, for twelve miles on the other side; thus filling the country with carnage, for twenty-eight miles, and "not leaving man nor beast alive!"   In another part of

*"Finding that they did not put themselves in arms, and would no more now than formerly forsake their strength, to draw into equality of ground, notwith-withstanding their advantage of numbers, I concluded they were in another sort to be dealt with; and from thenceforth, for the most part, I fell every other morning into their quarters, and continued those visitations for several weeks together, with the slaughter of very many of them, especially the new plantation in the county of Monaghan, and at the taking in of Harry O'Neal's house, in the Fews; insomuch that by this course, and the like acted often by the garrison at Drogheda, there was neither man nor beast to be found in sixteen miles, between the two towns of Drogheda and Dundalk, nor on the other side of Dundalk, in the county of Monaghan, nearer than Carrick Mac-Cross, a strong pile, twelve miles distant."—Idem.

this letter, he informs her of one of his murderous expeditions, in which he says, "he took no account of the slain; but there was little mercy shown in those times." —(Tichbourne.)   What a hideous picture of incarnate demons do these horrible facts present to the mind's eye!   And what effrontery must not Temple and his followers have possessed, when they dared to raise such an outcry against the Irish, for the crimes which they themselves perpetrated!

Of all the cases of murderous cruelty that marked the career of the government forces in Ireland, the most atrocious occurred at the surrender of Drogheda.   The history of the Huns, Vandals, Goths, and Ostrogoths, or of those scourges of the human race, the successors of Mahomet, may be searched in vain for anything more shocking.   In fact, it is not in the power of man, were he possessed by all the furies of the heathen mythology, to exceed these frightful scenes.   They may be equaled—but can never be surpassed.

Cromwell had besieged this town for some time; and was finally admitted, on promise of quarter.   The garrison consisted of the flower of the Irish army, and might have beaten him back, had they not been seduced by his solemn promise of mercy, which was observed till the whole had laid down their arms.   Then the merciless wretch commanded his soldiers to begin a slaughter of the entire garrison, which slaughter continued for five days! with every circumstance of brutal and sanguinary violence that the most cruel savages could conceive or perpetrate.*

"No age was spar'd; no sex, nay no degree;
Not infants in the porch of life were free.
The sick, the old, who could but hope a day
Longer by Nature's bounty, not let stay:
Virgins and widows, matrons, pregnant wives,
All died. 'Twas crime enough that they had lives."
                                        —Ben Jonson.

*"The assault was given, and his (Cromwell's) men twice repulsed; but in the third attack, Colonel Wall being unhappily killed at the head of his regiment, his men were so dismayed thereby, as to listen, before they had any need, to the enemy offering them quarter, admitting them upon those terms and thereby betraying themselves and their fellow-soldiers to the slaughter. All the officers and soldiers of Cromwell's army promised quarter to such as would lay down their arms, and performed it as long as any place held out; which encouraged others to yield. But when they had once all in their power, and feared no hurt that could be done them, Cromwell, being told by Jones that he had now all the flower of the Irish army in his hands, gave orders that no quarter should be given; so that his soldiers were forced, many of them against their will, to kill their prisoners. The brave governor Sir A. Aston, Sir Edm. Verney, the colonels Warren, Fleming and Byrne, were killed in cold blood; and indeed all the officers, except some few of least consideration, that escaped by miracle. The Marquis of Ormond, in his letters to the king and Lord Byron, says, 'that on this occasion Cromwell exceeded himself and anything he had ever heard of, in breach of faith and bloody inhumanity; and that the cruelties exercised there, for five days after the town was taken, would make as many several pictures of inhumanity, as are to be found in the book of martyrs, or in the relation of Amboyna.'"
—Carte.

This canting and hypocritical imposter, in his despatches to the parliament, had the shameless impudence to ascribe "the glory" of this bloody deed to God, "to whom indeed the praise of this mercy belongs!"*

*"Sir,—It has pleased God to bless our endeavors at Drogheda; after battering, we stormed it. The enemy were about three thousand strong in the town. They made a stout resistance, and near one thousand of our men being entered, the enemy forced them out again. But God giving a new courage to our men, they attempted again, and entered, beating the enemy from their defences. The enemy had made three retrenchments, both to the right and left, where we entered, all which they were forced to quit; being thus entered, we refused them quarter, having the day before summoned the town. I believe we put to the sword the whole number of the defendants. I do not think thirty of the whole number escaped with their lives; those that did are in safe custody, for the Barbadoes. Since that time the enemy quitted to us Trim and Dundalk; in Trim they were in such haste that they left their guns behind them. This hath been a marvellous great mercy! The enemy being not willing to put an issue upon a field battle, had put into this garrison almost all of their prime soldiers, being about three thousand horse and foot, under the command of their best officers, Sir Arthur Ashton being made governor. They were some seven or eight regiments, Ormond's being one, under the command of Sir Edmund Verney. I do not believe, neither do I hear, that any officer escaped with his life, save only one lieutenant, who, I hear, going to the enemy, said that he was the only man that escaped of all the garrison. The enemy were filled upon this with much terror, and truly I believe this bitterness

And such was the delusion of those times, that in all the churches in London, thanks were returned to the God of mercy, for this barbarous slaughter of his creatures.*

History furnishes no circumstance more disgusting, revolting, or hideous, than this nauseous compound of base perfidy, murderous cruelty, and abominable hypocrisy. Never was the throne of the Living God more egregiously insulted, than by these impious offerings of thanksgiving; and never were the thunders of heaven more loudly called for, than to blast the Pharisaical wretches who made such a mockery of all the calls and duties of humanity and religion.

Some time afterwards Cromwell gained possession of Wexford, by treachery; where a carnage was perpetrated, not far inferior to that which had taken place at Drogheda.†

will save much effusion of blood, through the goodness of God!

"I wish that all honest hearts may give the glory of this to God alone, to whom indeed the praise of this mercy belongs, for instruments they were very inconsiderable, the work throughout.

O. CROMWELL."
—Whitelock.

*"The ministers of London acquainted the people with the great success of the parliament forces in Ireland, and returned thanks to God for the same."—Ibid.

†"As soon as Cromwell had ordered his batteries to play on a distant quarter of the town, (Wexford) Strafford admitted his men into the castle, from whence is-

There is an important passage in the preface or introduction to Nalson's Collections, which we extracted and intended to quote, but have mislaid. We are therefore obliged to refer to it from memory; as the work has been returned to the New York library, whence it was procured, and there is no copy in this city. The reverend author states, that one of those Herodists, worthy disciples of the Idumean, whose deeds are recorded by St. Matthew, having been engaged in the humane employment of slaughtering children, defended the practice by saying that "nits would be lice." This was an attempt to carry completely into operation the horrible plan of extirpating the whole race, the deliberate adoption of which we have proved, in a preceding part of this work, and which was for some time acted upon by the ruling powers. For the accomplishment of this grand object the slaughter of the "lice," that is, the full-grown men and women, was not deemed sufficient; the destruction of the "nits," or children, was necessary to complete the magnificent scheme of a new plantation of the kingdom.

Ireton, apparently sated with slaughter, gave protection to the remnant of the inhabitants of a certain barony. But "being informed that they had broken

suing suddenly, and attacking the wall and gate adjoining, they were admitted, either through the treachery of the townsmen or the cowardice of the soldiers, or perhaps both; and the slaughter was almost as great as at Drogheda."—Warner.

the articles," he, without inquiry, issued orders to slaughter every "man, woman and child" it contained.* Lord Broghill, though a sanguinary man, shuddered at the barbarity of these terrible orders; remonstrated with Ireton; and at length, with considerable difficulty, prevailed on him to confine the massacre to persons found in arms, or who made resistance.† Those who consider the awe which a ferocious army inspires, the reluctance which, without the most grievous outrage, the peasantry must have felt to encounter the swords of a victorious enemy, as well as the violence and rapacity of such an enemy, will be led to believe that the provocation was of a similar character with that which, according to Phædrus, was given by the lamb, drinking at the lower part of the stream, to the wolf, who was allaying his thirst above, and who charged the innocent

*"Soon after Ireton had the command of the army he was informed that a certain barony had broken the articles in consideration of which they had been protected. He marched therefore against this barony, and gave immediate orders to his soldiers to kill man, woman and child; but before these orders were executed, Lord Broghill expostulated with him upon the cruelty of such proceedings."—Orrery.

†"He was therefore humbly of opinion that it would be more just, reasonable and honorable to order the soldiers to kill none but who were found in arms or made any opposition. With these words, Ireton was at last, though hardly, persuaded to revoke his bloody commands."—Idem.

animal with muddying the waters. The strong probability is that some individual resisted the rape of his wife or daughter, or the plunder of his property, and that the foiled ruffians magnified the affair into a violation of the protection. But be that as it may, it does not diminish our horror of the merciless Ireton, who issued the murderous mandate to slaughter "man, woman and child;" as it must be obvious that, if there were really a violation of the articles, a large portion of the men were probably wholly innocent, and, at all events, the women, and more especially the children, could not have deserved the extermination from which they were so hardly rescued.

To the wretched Irish, neither caves, nor castles, nor churches afforded any security. The murderous spirit of their enemies pursued them in every quarter, with as little mercy as the tiger displays towards the bleating lamb.

Three thousand men, women and children, of all ranks and ages, took refuge in the cathedral of Cashel, hoping the temple of the Living God would afford them a sanctuary from the butcheries that were laying the whole country desolate. The barbarian, Ireton, forced the gates of the church, and let loose his blood-hounds among them, who soon convinced them how vain was their reliance on the temple or the altar of God. They were slaughtered, without discrimination.* Neither rank, dignity, nor character saved the nobleman, the bishop or the priest; nor decrepitude, nor his hoary head, the venerable sage, bending down into the grave; nor her charms, the virgin; nor her virtues, the respectable matron; nor its helplessness, the smiling infant. Butchery was the order of the day—and all shared the common fate.

"Behold the furious and unpitying soldier,
Pulling his reeking dagger from the bosoms
Of gasping wretches. Death in ev'ry quarter,
With all that sad disorder can produce,
To make a spectacle of horror.
     "Distracted mothers
Kneeling before their feet, and begging pity;
Their naked, mangled breasts besmeared with blood,
And ev'n the milk, with which their fondled babes
Softly they hush'd, drop in anguish from them."
        —Otway.

That the leaders of the forces of the government perpetrated the most atrocious cruelties, we have fully proved. We shall now give a few strong facts, to satisfy the reader that they gloried in their guilt and regarded the extent of their murders as constituting their merits. The sanguinary Lord Orrery, bending down

*"Having brought together an army, he marched into the county of Tipperary, and hearing that many priests and gentry about Cashel had retired with their goods into the church, he stormed it, and being entered, put three thousand of them to the sword, taking the priests even from under the altar."—Ludlow.

into the grave, being seventy-six years of age, in urging the claims of the Earl of Barrymore and his two sons on the speaker of the English House of Commons, appears to lay his chief dependence for success on the desolation they had perpetrated. The first, he says, lately hung up "forty-three notable rebels for a breakfast."* It is not difficult to conceive what hideous havoc and carnage the constant repetition of these breakfasts, and of dinners and suppers of the same character, must have produced.

The merit of the two sons of Lord Orrery far transcended that of Lord Barrymore; as they, in the course of a few months, destroyed above three thousand of the Irish.† This afforded them a sure claim to the favor and protection of government.

Sir William Cole, with one regiment of foot, of five hundred men, and one troop of horse, is recorded by

*"The Earl of Barrymore hath nothing but what he fighteth with the rebels for, and getteth by his sword, he having lately hanged forty-three notable rebels for a breakfast."—Orrery.

†"I do affirm, and will make good this undeniable truth, that my two sons, Kynalmeaky and Broghill, with those forces that I have raised and satisfied, and they command, have been the destruction of above three thousand rebels, since the beginning of the insurrection."—(Idem). This letter is dated Aug. 25, 1642; and the insurrection had not spread into Munster until December, 1641. This affords a clew towards forming an estimate of the horrible carnage perpetrated throughout the kingdom on the wretched Irish.

Borlase to have slain 2,417 swordsmen, in various skirmishes and battles, and to have "starved and famished of the vulgar sort," whose property they had previously plundered, no less than "7,000 persons; (Borlace) and thus, adds he "the English in all parts fought, so as indeed the rebels lost, in the general, many men, and much of their substance." That they lost "much of their substance," and that their enemies were as justly celebrated for their skill in plunder as for their thirst of blood, is beyond doubt. The following circumstance will shed additional light on this subject.

Sir Richard Cox, in the subsequent war between James II and William, boasted that he had, in the single county of Cork, killed and hanged three thousand of the Irish;* made preys to the amount of twelve thousand pounds; and divided three hundred and eighty pounds among one troop. This, it is to be pre-

---

*"As for the enemy, I used them like nettles, and squeezed them (I mean their vagabond parties) so hard that they could seldom sting; having, as I believe, killed and hanged not less than three thousand of them, whilst I stayed in the county of Cork; and taken from them, in cattle and plunder, at least to the value of 12,000£ which you will easily believe when you know that I divided 380£ between one troop (colonel Townsend's) in the beginning of August. After which colonel Beecher and the western gentlemen got a prey worth 3,000£ besides several other lesser preys, taken by small parties, that are not taken notice of." (Sydney Papers M. I.) 168.

sumed, is a pretty fair specimen of the slaughter and rapine that extended throughout the kingdom.

When a view is taken of the various thousands which we have gleaned up in the preceding pages; 3,000 in one place; 7,000 in another; 4,000 in another; 3,000 in another, and so on in succession; and when regard is had to the novel circumstance of our utterly excluding all the histories on the Irish side of the question, no man can doubt, that in this war of extermination, originally founded on the manifest perjury of O'Conally, provoked by the most savage cruelty, and protracted by the combined influence of devouring avarice, religious bigotry, and the most rancorous national hostility, there were, as we have already stated, from Sir William Petty, above FIVE HUNDRED THOUSAND OF THE IRISH "wasted by the sword, plague, famine, hardship, and banishment, between the 23d October, 1641, and the same day, 1652;" (Petty, 18. Sir William states the precise number of 504,000.) that Ireland, during that war, exhibited as dreadful a scene of rapine and slaughter as either Mexico or Peru, when invaded by the Spaniards; and that none of the sanguinary exploits of Cortes or Pizarro could exceed, for atrocity, the deeds of Coote, St. Leger, Monroe, Inchiquin, Grenville, Hamilton, Tichbourne, Ireton, and Cromwell.

The horrible scenes we have depicted were not confined to Ireland. The war was carried on, in England

and Scotland, with similar rapine, desolation, and carnage on both sides, royalist and republican. It is not necessary, nor would it be proper, to enter here into detail respecting the affairs of the sister island. A few instances will be sufficient for our present purpose, merely to display the spirit of the age, the humanity of its warfare, and the peculiar propriety of the eternal reproaches, with which "the welkin has rung," against the barbarity of the Irish.

Lord Clarendon, in various parts of his history, narrates the ruthless ferocity that reigned in battle and after defeat, when neither age nor sex was spared. In particular, he states, that, in the pursuit of the royalists, after the battle of Edgehill, there were about one hundred women slaughtered, and among them the wives of some of the officers.*

According to Burnet, prisoners were slaughtered in cold blood, and after quarter given; and the preachers, from the pulpit, deprecated the extension of mercy towards them, and denounced all those who were for moderate measures.†

*"The enemy left no manner of cruelty unexercised that day; and in the pursuit killed about one hundred women, whereof some were the wives of officers of quality." (Clarendon, IV.)

†"Upon this occasion, many prisoners that had quarter given them, were murdered in cold blood. The preachers thundered in their pulpits against all that were for moderate proceedings, as guilty of the blood

We conclude with an account, from Rushworth, of the ruthless and savage progress of Montross, in Scotland, anno 1644, which may stand a parallel with the murderous exploits of Ireton or Cromwell. For six weeks, he acted the part of a demon incarnate, as far as his power extended, laying the whole country in flames, and, in imitation of the sanguinary orders of the lords justices of Ireland, slaughtering all the males able to carry arms, or, in other words, "fit for war."*

The unceasing efforts that have been employed to stifle the truth, and to keep the world in a state of darkness on the subject of barbarous carnage perpetrated on the Irish, are incredible. They have unfortunately been but too successful. One instance displays such profligacy, that it only requires to be stated, to excite the indignation of every honorable mind.

that had been shed. 'Thine eye shall not pity, and thou shalt not spare,' were often inculcated after every execution." (Burnet, I.)

*"Montross dividing his army into three brigades, ranged over the whole country, and laid it waste; as many as they find in arms, going to the rendezvous, they slay, and spared no man fit for war; and so destroyed, or drove out of the country, or into holes unknown, all the service, and fired the villages and cottages, and drove away and destroyed all their cattle. These things lasted from the 13th of December, 1644, to the end of January following." (Rushworth V.)

The government forces in Ulster had committed some frightful massacres on the Irish, of which an account was published in London. The House of Commons, which was actuated by the most rancorous spirit of hostility towards the Irish, took the alarm. They had the printers committed to prison, without trial; ordered the book to be burned by the hands of the common hangman; and directed the Stationers' Company to seize all the copies that could be found, which were to be committed to the flames.* Thus early began the work of deception; thus early was the veil thrown over the enormities of which the Irish were the victims; and thus early were the streams of history poisoned by public authority.

*"June 8, 1642. Ordered, That the book, entitled 'A True Relation of the Proceedings of the Scots and English Forces in the North of Ireland,' shall be burnt by the hands of the common hangman, in the New Palace yard, at Westminster: and the master and wardens of the Company of Stationers are required to seize all such of these books as are anywhere to be had, that they may be burnt accordingly.

"Resolved, That Robert White shall be forthwith committed prisoner to the King's Bench prison, for printing and publishing of a scandalous libel, to the dishonor of the Scots nation; and he be referred to the King's Bench, to be proceeded with there according to law." (Journals, II.)

CHAPTER II.

Means by which subjugated countries are held in chains. Protestant ascendency. Code of demoralization, tyranny, oppression, rapine, and murder. Robbery of father, mother, sister, and brother, invited by acts of Parliament. Prohibition of education. Horse thieves excited and protected by law.

In every subjugated country, there is always a small body of the natives, who make a regular contract, not written, but well understood, and duly carried into effect, by which they sell the nation to its oppressors, and themselves as slaves, for the sorry privilege of tyrannizing over their fellow slaves. This has ever been the surest foundation on which the dominion of one country over another is perpetuated. The base and miserable oligarchs who subserve the interests of the ruling nation, indemnify themselves for the chains which they drag about, by the superior weight and pressure of those they impose.

When the English Henrys overran and subdued France; had the crown placed on their heads, in Paris; and enjoyed a flattering prospect of permanently securing its descent to their posterity, it was not by any means through the force of English skill or English valor, though both were of the highest grade at that period, that they achieved the conquest. They had at all times in their armies hosts of traitorous Frenchmen, who paved the way for the conquest and slavery

of their country. Such, too, was the Roman policy,—
such the means whereby that all-grasping and devas-
tating government extended its empire over the then
known world.

But the case of Ireland is probably among the most
forcible illustrations of this maxim that history affords.
A herd of wretched oligarchs have for centuries existed
there, who have bartered their country's dearest rights
and interests, for the privilege of trampling down their
countrymen, over whom they have exercised the most
galling tyranny that the mind of man can conceive.

Whenever an attempt has been made to shake off
the yoke of foreign power, to emancipate the nation,
this oligarchy has always had its spies, and pimps, and
informers, among the friends of their country, by
whose agency the attempt was baffled, and the patriots
betrayed to the gallows.

> "Oh for a tongue to curse the slave,
>   Whose treason, like a deadly blight,
> Comes o'er the councils of the brave,
>   And blasts them in their hour of might!
> May life's unblessed cup for him
> Be drugg'd with treacheries to the brim,
> With hopes, that but allure to fly,
>   With joys, that vanish while he sips,
> Like Dead-Sea fruits, that tempt the eye,
>   But turn to ashes on the lips!
> His country's curse, his children's shame,
> Outcast of virtue, peace, and fame,
> May he, at last with lips of flame,
> On the parch'd desert thirsting die,—
> While lakes, that shone in mockery nigh,

Are fading off, untouch'd, untasted,
Like the once glorious hopes he blasted!
And, when from earth his spirit flies,
 Just Prophet, let the damned one dwell
Full in the sight of **Paradise,**
 Beholding heaven, and feeling hell!"
        (Lalla Rookh.)

This oligarchy now styles itself, as we have more than once stated, "the Protestant ascendency;" and is composed of the professors of the established religion. Its oppression has always extended over the Protestant dissenters, as well as over the Roman Catholics; but with very great disparity of effect. The principal grievance of the Protestant dissenter, which he bears in common with the Catholic, is, that he is obliged to support the ministers of two different religions,—his own and the dominant one. In other respects, he stands on nearly the same ground as the professor of the established religion.

The tyranny exercised by this oligarchy over the Catholics, has displayed itself in the form of a barbarous code of laws, the professed object of which was "to prevent the growth of Popery;" but the real one, to plunder those on whom they were to operate, of their property, and to divest them of their most sacred rights and privileges; and the direct effect of which was to demoralize the nation; to reduce it to a state of the most deplorable wretchedness and misery, not exceeded throughout the wide world; and to legalize an odious system of rapine and fraud.

"Just Alla! what must by thy look,
　　When such a wretch before thee stands
Unblushing, with thy Sacred Book,
　　Turning the leaves with blood-stained hands,
And wresting from its page sublime
His creed of lust and hate and crime!
Ev'n as those bees of Trebizond,
　　Which from the sunniest flowers that glad
With their pure smile the gardens round,
　　Draw venom forth that drives men mad!"
　　　　　　　　　　　　(Lalla Rookh.)

This odious and oppressive system was about a century in maturing. Hardly a session of the Irish Parliament took place, in which there was not devised some new penalty, some new forfeiture, or some new disqualification, to crush, to prey on, and to immolate the wretched Roman Catholics. The utmost ingenuity of fraud and rapine was constantly tortured, to add to the weight of their clanking chains.

The most odious and wicked provisions of this code have been repealed; and an opinion too generally prevails, that it is nearly annihilated. This is a most egregious error. There are numberless harassing and vexatious disqualifications and incapacities still in full force. There is a most valuable volume now before us, of above three hundred and fifty pages, which contains a detail of those disqualifications, and is wholly confined to that subject. It was our intention to have given a sketch of them: but our limits forbid the fulfilment of this purpose.

Various causes conspired to produce the salutary effect of mitigating the severity of this vile code. The first stroke it received arose from the spirit of volunteering in Ireland, which was the consequence of the declared inability of the British government to protect that country, during the war against the United States, France, Spain, and Holland. Every description of religionists mixed in the ranks of the volunteers, which gave rise to an enlarged and liberal spirit of national feeling. The Irish Catholic and the Irish Protestant, as well as the Protestant dissenter, were amalgamated into one common mass of friends to their common country. Many links of the chains of the nation at large, as well as of the proscribed Catholics, were then knocked off. The increasing liberality of the age has successively removed others. But it is disgraceful and dishonorable, that much remains yet to be done.

It may be thought a work of supererogation, at this time, to revive the remembrance of a code so odious, so detestable, and so infamous. But this work would be very incomplete, and the reader would have a very imperfect idea of the state of Ireland, and the horrible tyranny under which the mass of the population has groaned, did we not give some sketch of this system.

Hundreds of thousands of pages have been written and printed, in discussing the question, Who and what is Antichrist, the beast with seven heads and ten horns? Various solutions have been given to the world. We are not very learned in this kind of lore ; but flatter ourselves that we have made the discovery, which we freely communicate :—we are convinced that religious persecution is the real and genuine Antichrist. There is nothing of the wickedness of man so opposite to the spirit displayed in the words and actions of Jesus Christ.

Antichrist obtained a glorious triumph over the spirit of Jesus, when the Inquisition was established at Madrid, at Lisbon, at Goa, and elsewhere: and his reign has been coeval with the existence of those execrable tribunals. He reigned at Paris, in full splendor, at the massacre of St. Bartholomew's ; in England, under the reign of Mary ; and he has reigned throughout all Christendom, from the commencement of the Christian era, in the persecutions, more or less severe, of the unfortunate Jews.*

Nothing, however, but gross ignorance and bigotry, can suppose that the reign of the Antichrist of persecution has been confined to Madrid, Lisbon, Goa, Paris, or the other places usually allotted to him. The most superficial glance at history must evince the

---

*It is inexpressibly painful to state, that an attempt to meliorate the condition of the Jews, has, to the disgrace and opprobrium of our common country, and of the age, recently failed, in the state of Maryland ! So powerful is inveterate prejudice, so slow the progress of illumination, and so much easier is it to rivet chains than to knock them off !

egregious folly of such an opinion. Antichrist reigned in Geneva, when Calvin sanctioned the death of Servetus; in London, when Henry VIII and Elizabeth erected their gibbets, to immolate those opposed to their opinions; in Scotland, when the Covenanters were shot down in the fields; in Holland, when the Remonstrants were plundered, and banished, and immolated, for their dissent from the established creed; in Boston, when the Quakers were persecuted and hanged; and he exercised a most rigorous sway in Ireland, for above a century, during the operation of the barbarous code "to prevent the growth of Popery."

We stand pledged to trace, at a future day, the progress of Antichrist in various parts of Christendom.* At present, the nature of this work confines us to his proceedings in Ireland.

We assume this position as undeniable:

Every man has a sacred and indefeasible right to worship God according to his judgment, provided such worship do not tend to any breach of the fundamental laws of morality. Corollaries from this maxim are:

I.　Every disqualification, on account of religious opinions or worship, is tyranny and oppression;

II.　Every pecuniary penalty is robbery; and

III.　Every capital punishment is murder.

*In the religious Olive Branch.

Let us, by these principles, test the code in question; and we shall be satisfied that it was one unvarying tissue of oppression, robbery, and murder. It awarded capital punishments, as will appear by the subsequent detail, against about twenty different acts, all of them innocent, and many absolutely meritorious. The strength of the term, murder, may startle some readers: but we hold the position self-evident—that those who suffer death, for acts not only not immoral or unjust, but absolutely laudable, are murdered, though their execution be sanctioned by all the legislatures and all the pretended courts of justice in the world.

All Roman Catholic archbishops, bishops, vicars general, deans, or any other persons of that religion, exercising ecclesiastical jurisdiction, were liable to imprisonment and transportation; and, in case of returning, were guilty of high treason, and were to be punished accordingly.*

*"All Popish archbishops, bishops, vicars general, deans, Jesuits, monks, friars, and all other regular Popish clergy, and all Papists exercising any ecclesiastical jurisdiction, shall depart this kingdom before the 1st of May, 1698. And if any of them shall be, at any time after the said day, in this kingdom, they shall be imprisoned and remain there without bail till they be transported beyond the seas, out of the king's dominion, wherever the king, his heirs or successors, or chief governors of this kingdom shall think fit; and if any so transported shall return again into this kingdom, then to be guilty of high treason, and to suffer accordingly." (Robins.)

In the year 1704, a law was passed, ordering all the Roman Catholic priests in Ireland to register themselves in the parishes to which they respectively belonged; and to give security for their good behavior, and for their non-removal from the county where they then resided.*

When a priest officiated in any other parish than the one wherein he was registered, he was liable to transportation; and, in case of return, to be hanged without benefit of clergy.†

Every Roman Catholic clergyman in the kingdom

---

*"Every Popish priest, who is now in this kingdom, shall, at the next Quarter Sessions, to be held in the several counties, or counties of cities or towns, next after the feast of St. John the Baptist, 1704, return his name and place he resides, together with his age, the parish of which he pretends to be Popish priest, the time and place of his receiving Popish orders, and from whom; and shall then enter into recognizance, with two sufficient sureties, each of the penalty of fifty pounds, to be of peaceable behavior, and not remove out of such county where his abode is, into any other part of this kingdom." (Idem.)

†"No Popish priest shall exercise the function or office of a Popish priest, but in the parish where the said Popish priest did officiate at the time of registering the Popish clergy, and for which parish also he was registered, and in no other parish whatsoever, under the penalties as any Popish regular convict is liable unto." (Idem.)

not registered ;* every one afterwards coming into it from abroad ;† every one who kept a curate or assistant ;‡ and every such curate or assistant,§ was also liable to transportation, and eventually to the gallows, if he returned.

Two justices might summon any Roman Catholic, sixteen years old, to appear before them, to give testimony when and where he heard mass; who were present, and who celebrated it; and all such other matters and things, touching the priest, as might be necessary to his conviction. In case of refusal, he was subject to a fine of twenty pounds, or imprisonment for one year. (Robins.)

*"Every person whatsoever, exercising the office or function of a Popish priest, found in this kingdom, after the 24th of June, 1705, other than such as are registered pursuant to the above act, shall be liable to such penalties, forfeitures, and punishments, as are imposed on Popish archbishops, bishops, etc." (Idem, p. 459.)

†"Every Popish clergyman coming into this kingdom after the 1st of January, 1703, shall be liable to such penalties, forfeitures and punishments as are imposed on Popish archbishops and bishops." (Idem, p. 453.)

‡"Every Popish parish priest, that shall keep any Popish curate, assistant, or coadjutor, shall lose the benefit of having been registered, and shall incur all the penalties of a Popish regular, and shall be prosecuted as such; § and every such Popish curate, assistant, or coadjutor shall be deemed as a Popish regular, and prosecuted as such." (Idem, p. 462.)

Any Roman Catholic priest, celebrating marriage between two Protestants, or between a Protestant and Roman Catholic, was guilty of felony,* and liable to suffer death without benefit of clergy.†

No Roman Catholic was allowed to have in his own possession, or the possession of any other person for his use, any horse, mare, or gelding, of the value of five pounds.‡ Any Protestant, discovering to any two justices that a Roman Catholic had a horse of that value, might, with a constable and assistant, break open any door; seize such horse; bring him before the

*"If any Popish priest, or reputed Popish priest, or any person pretending to be a Popish priest, or any degraded clergyman, or any layman pretending to be a clergyman of the church of Ireland, as by law established, shall, after the 25th day of April, 1726, celebrate any marriage between two Protestants, or reputed Protestants, or between a Protestant or reputed Protestant and a Papist, such Popish priest, etc., shall be guilty of felony, and shall suffer death as a felon, without benefit of clergy, or of the statute!" (Robins.)

†The writer of this recollects an instance in his youth of the execution of a Catholic clergyman, under this execrable statute.

‡"No Papist, after the 20th of January, 1695, shall be capable to have, or keep in his possession, or in the possession of any other, to his use, or at his disposition, any horse, gelding, or mare, of the value of 5£. or more; and if any person of the Protestant religion, shall make discovery thereof upon oath, to any two justices of the peace, or to the chief magistrate of any city or town corporate, they may within their respec-

justices ; and, on paying five pounds five shillings, have the property of such horse, "as if bought in market overt."*

Any person concealing such horse, was liable to be imprisoned three months, and pay treble the value. (Robins.)

Civil officers were authorized to seize the horses of Roman Catholics, on certain contingencies. If returned, the owners were to pay the expenses of seizing and keeping them. (Idem.)

To increase the profligacy and turpitude of this code, a large portion of its provisions were ex post facto,

tive limits, by warrant under their hands and seals, authorize such person, in the day-time only, to search for and secure all such horses : and in case of resistance to break open any door, and bring such horse or horses before them, and such discoverer, (being of the Protestant religion), paying or making tender before such justices, mayor, etc., of the sum of 5£ 5s. to the owner or possessor of such horse, after such payment, or tender and refusal, the property of such horse or horses, shall be vested in the person making such discovery and tender, as if the same had been bought and sold in market overt."   (Idem.)

* This clause had nearly proved fatal to a rascal who took advantage of it, about forty years since. He forcibly seized a horse, saddled and bridled, belonging to a Roman Catholic. But, though the law sanctioned the robbery of horses, it did not authorize that of saddles and bridles. The felon was prosecuted for the plunder of the harness, and narrowly escaped the gallows, which he so richly deserved. One other circumstance, arising from this law, may merit attention. A Catholic, who owned one of the most celebrated racers

and operated the work of rapine and depredation for years antecedent to their enaction. In 1710, an act was passed, annulling fines, recoveries, and settlements, made for seven years preceding.*

All collateral and other securities, by mortgages, judgments, statutes merchant, or of the staple, or otherwise howsoever, to cover, support, or make good any bargain, sale, confirmation, release, or other conveyance, were rendered null and void. And any Protestant might sue out such mortgages, or sue for such lands, in any court of law, and obtain a verdict, and have execution to be put in possession thereof.†

in Ireland, worth two hundred guineas, being informed that a person was about to seize him, and pay him the price fixed by law, mounted the horse, and presented him to a Protestant friend; thus defeating the miscreant of his vile purpose.

*"All settlements, fines, common recoveries, and other conveyances had or made since the 1st of January, 1703, of any lands, etc., by any Papist, or by any Protestant who turned Papist since the said 1st of January, 1703, or by any such Papist with his then Protestant wife, who hath turned Papist as aforesaid, whereby any Protestant is barred of any estate, in reversion or remainder, whereunto such Protestant is entitled at the time of levying such fine, suffering such recovery, or making such conveyance, shall as to such Protestant be null and void." (Robins.)

†"All collateral and other securities, by mortgages, judgments, statutes merchant, or of the staple or otherwise, which have been!! or hereafter shall be,

This provision was retrospective; thus, if a Roman Catholic had lent ten thousand pounds, and, as a security for payment, taken a mortgage on real estate, any Protestant might sue out such mortgage, and rob the lender of his property! None of the legislators of Tripoli or Algiers—none of the ferocious followers of Blackbeard, or Morgan, the pirates—none of the banditti whose trade is rapine and plunder, ever conceived a more piratical or plundering act than this. It may be fairly said to have converted the seat of legislation into "a den of thieves."

made or entered into, to cover, support, or secure, and make good any bargain, sale, confirmation, release, feoffment, lease, or other conveyance, contrary to 2 An. Sess. 1. c. 6. are void to the purchaser of any the said lands or tenements in trust for, or for the benefit of, any Papist, as likewise to any such Papist, his heirs and assigns, and all such lands, etc., so conveyed or leased, or to be conveyed or leased to any Papist, or to the use of, or in trust for, any Papist, contrary to the said act, and all such collateral securities as are or shall be made or entered into, to cover, support, secure or make good the same, may be sued for by any Protestant, by his proper action, real, personal, or mixed, founded on this act, in any of her majesty's courts of law or equity, if the nature of the case shall require it.

"Provided any Protestant may prefer one or more bill or bills in the chancery, or chancery of exchequer, against any such sale, lease, mortgage, or incumbrance, and against all persons privy to such trust for Papists; and to compel such person to discover such trusts, and answer all matters relating thereunto, as by such bill shall be required: to which bill no plea or

If any Protestant woman, possessed of real estate of any description whatever, or personal estate to the value of five hundred pounds, married, without a previous certificate that her intended husband was a Protestant, she forfeited her whole estate, which went to the next Protestant heir.*

To outrage the feelings of the wretched Helots, they were forbidden, under a penalty of ten pounds, to bury their dead in the grave yards of any suppressed con-

demurrer shall be allowed: but the defendant shall answer the same at large on oath, which answer shall be good evidence against the defendant, in actions brought upon this act: and all issues, in any suit founded on this act, shall be tried by none but known Protestants!!" (Robins.)

*"If any Protestant maid, or woman unmarried, being heir apparent to her ancestor, or having a sole or joint estate or interest in fee-simple or in fee-tail, or being seized in fee-simple or in coparcenary, or in common, or being seized of an estate for life or lives, by way of jointure, dower, or otherwise, or being possessed of, or entitled to any personal estate, either in money, stock, plate, jewels, or other goods and chattels, in law or equity, to the value of 500£ or more, shall at any time after the first of January next, (1704) marry or take to husband any person whatsoever, without having first obtained a certificate in writing, under the hand of the minister of the parish, bishop of the diocese, and some justice of the peace living near the place (or any two of them), where such person shall be resident, at the time of such marriage, that he is a known Protestant, that then, and from the time of such marriage, such Protestant person so marrying, and the person she shall so marry, shall be forever afterwards

vent, abbey, or monastery,* where rested the remains of their ancestors!

In order to secure impartial justice, in England, foreigners, accused of petit treason, murder, or felony, are tried by a jury composed of an equal number of natives and foreigners; and juries are thus constituted in civil actions between denizens and foreigners. But, as if nothing were too sacred or holy to be trampled under foot, in Ireland, in all the cases arising under the laws "to prevent the growth of Popery," Catholics were expressly excluded from juries;† and their honor, their property, and their lives, were thus exposed to the mercy of their envenomed enemies.

disabled and rendered incapable of having or enjoying all or any of the aforesaid estates or interests; and that the same shall go to, and be deemed to be the right and estate of the next Protestant of the kin, to whom the same would descend by law, were such Protestant maid or woman, and all other intervening Popish heirs, executors or administrators, really dead and intestate at the time of such marriage." (Robins.)

*"None shall, from the said 29th of December, bury any dead, in any suppressed monastery, abbey, or convent, that is not made use of for celebrating divine service according to the liturgy of the church of Ireland by the law established, or within the precincts thereof, upon pain of ten pounds." (Robins.)

†"From the first of Michaelmas-Term, 1708, no Papist shall serve or be returned to serve on any grand jury in the Queen's Bench, or before justices of assize, oyer and terminer, or gaol delivery, or Quarter Sessions, unless it appear to the court that a sufficient

If a Catholic child were sent abroad without license, it was presumed by law that he was sent to be educated in a foreign seminary; by which a forfeiture of his personal and of the income of his real estate was incurred. On his return, he might apply to court, and prove the cause of his absence to have been innocent: in which case, he was entitled to the future income of his real estate, but could not be restored to the proceeds during his absence, nor to any part of his personal estate.*

number of Protestants cannot then be had for the service; and in all trials of issues, on any presentment, indictment, or information or action on any statute, for any offense committed by Papists, in breach of such laws, the plaintiff or prosecutor may challenge any Papist returned as juror, and assign as a cause that he is a Papist, which challenge shall be allowed of!!" (Idem, p. 459.)

*"If any of the king's subjects of this realm, at any time after this session of Parliament, shall pass or go, or shall convey or send, or cause to be conveyed or sent, any child or other person, into any parts beyond the seas, out of the king's obedience, to the intent to enter into, or be resident, or trained up, in any priory, abbey, nunnery, Popish university, college, or school, or house of Jesuits or priests, or in any Popish private family there; and shall be by any Popish person instructed, persuaded or strengthened in the Popish religion, in any sort to profess the same; or shall send or convey, or cause to be conveyed or sent, any money or other thing towards the maintenance of any child or other person already sent, or that shall hereafter go or be sent, to be trained up and instructed as aforesaid; or (under the name or color of charity) towards the relief of any religious houses whatsoever; every

Roman Catholics were prohibited from acting as guardians. An infraction of this law subjected the party to a penalty of five hundred pounds.*

*"No Papist shall be guardian unto, or have the tuition or custody of, any orphan or child under the age of twenty-one years: but the same (where the person entitled to, or having the guardianship of, such child, is or shall be a Papist) shall be disposed of by chancery to some near relation of such orphan, etc., being a Protestant, to whom the estate cannot descend.

"If any Papist shall take upon him the guardianship or tuition of any orphan or child, contrary to this act, he shall forfeit 500£ to be recovered by action of debt." (Robins, p. 454.)

such offender, being thereof lawfully convicted, or upon any information, presentment or indictment for any the offenses aforesaid, to be found by a jury of the county, city, or town corporate, where such offender shall have any estate of inheritance at the time of the offense committed, shall be forever (after such finding) disabled to sue or prosecute any action, bill, plaint, or information, in course of law, or to sue in any court of equity, or to be guardian or executor, or administrator to any person, or capable of any legacy or deed of gift, or to bear any office within this realm, and shall forfeit all their goods and chattels, and also all their lands, tenements and hereditaments, rents, annuities, offices and estate of freehold, during their natural lives." (Robins, p. 185.)

"And if any person be convicted of being sent beyond the seas, contrary to this act, by the conviction of the person sending or conveying him only, such person, upon his return into this kingdom, shall, at any time within twelve months after, or within twelve months after attaining the age of twenty-one years, upon prayer, by motion to the king's bench in this

Roman Catholic house-keepers were obliged to find fit Protestant substitutes for militia duty; and, in case of neglect or refusal, to pay double the fine imposed on Protestants;* and likewise to pay, towards the sup-

*"The lieutenants, etc., or the major part of them, may cause to be raised upon the Popish inhabitants, and upon every person who shall refuse to take the oath of abjuration, (which oath any justice of the peace may administer) double the sum they should have paid by virtue of this act, in case they had been Protestants." (Idem, p. 409.)

kingdom, be admitted to his trial; and the judges of the said court, upon such prayer, shall cause an information to be exhibited against him, to which he shall plead; and the court shall proceed to trial thereupon, by a jury of the county where the said court shall then sit; and the defendant, at the trial, shall be obliged to prove to what intent he was sent or conveyed beyond the seas, and unless he makes it appear that he was not sent or conveyed contrary to this act, it shall be taken for granted that he was sent to the contrary, as though the same had been fully proved. And in case, upon trial, the party shall be acquitted, then he shall be discharged of all the disabilities, penalties and forfeitures in this act, except his goods and chattels, and the profits of his lands incurred, received before such acquittal.

"And every such person, sent or conveyed as aforesaid, that shall, within six months after his return into this kingdom, in the chancery or king's bench, in the term time, between the hours of eight and twelve in the morning, take the oaths," etc., "shall from thenceforth be discharged of all the disabilities aforesaid; and shall from such time be restored to the receipt of the future growing rents, and profits of his said real estate only, but shall nevertheless lose all those past and all his personal estate." (Idem, p. 186.)

port of the militia, double what the Protestants paid.*
No Catholics were allowed to purchase any part of the
forfeited estates; nor to inherit, take, make title to, by
descent, purchase, limitation, devise, or other conveyance, or to have, hold, or enjoy any such estates.†
They were even prohibited from taking them on
leases for lives or years.

Roman Catholics were prohibited, in 1702, from
buying or purchasing, in their own names, or in the
names of others to their use, any lands, or rents and
profits out of the same, other than for a term not exceeding thirty-one years.‡

*"In case such Papist shall neglect or refuse to find
such sufficient man, he shall forfeit double the sum as
a Protestant should forfeit, in case such Prostestant
should neglect to attend the service of the militia,
when thereunto required, by beat of drum or sound of
trumpet, as aforesaid." (Idem, p. 407.)

†"Leases of the premises to be made to Protestants
only, at the full improved rent, without any fine.
Leases to or in trust for Papists, or assigned to them,
to be void, and the lessor, assignor, and lessee or as-
signee, accepting or occupying such lands, to forfeit
treble the yearly value." (Robins, p. 26.)

‡"Every Papist, after the time aforesaid, shall be
disabled to purchase, either in his own name or in the
name of any other, to his use or in trust for him, any
manors, lands, hereditaments, or any rents or profits
out of the same, or any leases or terms thereof, other
than for a term of years not exceeding thirty-one
years, whereon a rent, not less than two-thirds of the
improved yearly value at the time of making such
lease, shall be reserved and made payable during such
term." (Idem, p. 454.)

No Roman Catholic could be elected mayor, bailiff, sovereign, portrieff, burgomaster, recorder, sheriff, treasurer, alderman, town clerk, burgess, common councilman, within any city, walled town, or corporation; nor be nominated, appointed, presented, or sworn, as high constable, in any barony or half-barony; or as petty constable, in any manor, ward, parish, constablewick, or place within the kingdom: but was to be proportionably taxed to support the same. (2 Geo. I.)

Some portions of this code appear so gratuitously wicked and profligate, that it is difficult even to conjecture what could have been the object of the miscreants by whom they were enacted. So late as the year 1745, it was provided, that all marriages celebrated by a Roman Catholic clergyman, between two Protestants, or between a Protestant and a Roman Catholic, should be null and void, to all intents and purposes, without any process, judgment, or sentence of the law whatsoever.* To what a hideous flood of licentiousness; what overwhelming immorality; what bastardizing of children; what uncertainty of inheritance, must this vile law have given rise!

* "After the first of May, 1746, every marriage celebrated by a Popish priest, between a Papist and any person who hath been, or hath professed himself or herself to be a Protestant, at any time within twelve months of such celebration of marriage, or between

Justices of peace might summon any person, suspected of having been married by a Roman Catholic priest, or been present at such marriage; and if such person refused to attend, or to be examined, or to enter into recognizance to prosecute, he was liable to three years inprisonment. (Robins, p. 389.)

Dreading lest the piratical and sanguinary system they were establishing should lead to insurrection, in which they might meet the fate their tyranny deserved, the "ascendency" early determined to secure themselves from that consequence, by robbing and plundering the Catholics of their arms;* thus in a manner tying them neck and heels, and laying them prostrate at their mercy.

two Protestants, shall be null and void, to all intents and purposes, without any process, judgment, or sentence of the law whatsoever." (2 Geo. II.)

*"All Papists within this kingdom of Ireland, before the 1st of March next, shall discover and deliver up to some justice of the peace, all their arms, armor, and ammunition, of what kind soever, in their possession; and after that time, any two or more justices of the peace, within their respective limits, and all mayors, sheriffs and chief officers of cities, etc., in their liberties, by themselves or their warrants, under their hands and seals, may search for, seize, or cause to be searched for and seized, and take into their custody, all such arms, etc., as shall be concealed in any house, lodging or other places where they suspect any such to be." (Robins, p. 448.)

The laws on this point, which was regarded as vital to the security of the tyrants, were of the most extraordinary rigor. Two justices of the peace might summon before them any Catholics, from the peer or peeress to the lowest peasant, and examine them, on oath, not merely on the subject of arms in their own possession, but oblige them to turn informers against their parents, children, friends, and neighbors; and if they refused to appear, or, on appearing, refused to give evidence, or turn informers, peers and peeresses were subject to a penalty of three hundred pounds, for the first offense; and for the second, to imprisonment for life, and forfeiture of all their goods!!*

By this law, the best man in the land might be summoned by two justices of the peace, at the instance of the lowest scoundrel, and an oath tendered to him to

*"Two justices of peace, or the magistrate of any corporation, are empowered to summon before them any persons whatsoever, to tender them an oath, by which they oblige them to discover all persons who have any arms concealed, contrary to law. Their refusal or declining to appear, or, on appearing, their refusal to inform, subjects them to the severest penalties. If peers or peeresses are summoned (for they may be summoned by the bailiff of a corporation of six cottages), to perform this honorable service, and they refuse to inform, the first offense is 300£ penalty the second is premunire, that is to say, imprisonment for life, and forfeiture of all their goods. Persons of an inferior order are for the first offense fined 30£ for the second, they too are subjected to premunire." (Burke, V, p. 195.)

inform against his nearest or dearest friend. The same oath might be tendered to him a second time, within an hour; and if he refused both times, he was, ipse facto, liable to be robbed of his goods, and subject to imprisonment for life!!

Lest there should be any scruples of conscience among the justices, which might prevent their activity in the enforcement of such a system of rapine, any magistrate who should neglect or refuse to perform the duties it imposed on him, was subject to fifty pounds penalty.*

All wise legislators justly hold, that one of their most important duties is to provide for the instruction and illumination of the people, under a conviction that public instruction and virtue, ignorance and vice, grow to maturity together. But the Irish Parliament doomed five-sixths of the nation, to which it was given as a curse, to perpetual and invincible ignorance! To brutalize and barbarize those Helots, to plunge them into the abysses of Cimmerian darkness, they were, at one stroke, cut off from education. The law punished the man who

> "Taught the young idea how to shoot,"

who assisted to remove that brutal ignorance which

---

*"If any justice or justices of peace, mayor, etc., neglect or refuse to execute any the powers which they are required by this act to put in execution, every such justice shall forfeit, for every such offense, the sum of 50£." (Robins, p. 459.)

prepares the mind for every species of vice and crime, as severely as the man who robbed altars, burned houses, or murdered his father or mother!

This never-enough-to-be-execrated code was far worse than Draco's, which is

"Damn'd to everlasting fame."

Draco, barbarous and cruel as he was, in his sanguinary code, which punished all crimes with death, has never been accused of punishing any thing but crimes. But the worse than Draconian Irish legislature denounced banishment, and, in case of return, death, against any Catholic guilty of the offense of teaching school; instructing children in learning, in a private house; or officiating as usher to a Protestant school master!*

The eternal laws of humanity, imprinted on our hearts by our great Creator, command sympathy for our suffering fellow creatures, and, when in our power, the extension of relief to their miseries. The rudest savages are not insensible to the sway of this universal and sovereign law. They share their slender pittance with the distressed and suffering stranger. Christ Jesus himself, in the most emphatical language he ever

---

*"If any Papist shall publicly teach school, or instruct youth in learning in any private house, or shall be entertained to instruct youth, as usher or assistant to any Protestant school master, he shall be esteemed a Popish regular clergyman, and prosecuted as such, and shall incur such penalties and forfeitures as any Popish regular convict is liable unto." (Robins, p. 612.)

Throughout the whole habitable globe, even among the most barbarous of the human race, respect and reverence for parents have been universally inculcated, except in devoted Ireland. The fifth command of the decalogue explicitly orders,

"Honor thy father and thy mother, that thy days may be long upon the land which the Lord thy God giveth thee."

This is "the first command with a promise of reward" for its observance; but no punishment is annexed to the violation. Deuteronomy, however, goes further, and pronounces a curse on those who even slight their parents:

"Cursed be he that setteth light by his father or mother."

And Jesus Christ, the light of whose Gospel the Irish legislators pretended to spread, renewed and enforced the command,

"Honor thy father and thy mother." (Matth. xix, 19.)

But what was the dictate of the hideous code "to prevent the growth of Popery?" Did it support or countenance the observance of this holy law of Moses and of Jesus Christ? No: it said, in language fit for pirates

kingdom, shall, for the first offense, forfeit twenty pounds; for the second, double that sum; and if he offend the third time, shall forfeit all his lands and tenements of freehold or inheritance during his life; and also all his goods and chattels!!" (Robins, p. 452.)

and robbers, Forswear your religion, and then you have legal sanction to plunder your father and mother, and bring their gray hairs with sorrow to the grave.* In return for all their cares, their solicitudes, their pains, their affection, strip them of that property which ought to support your brothers and sisters. This was the unequivocal spirit of Irish legislation, on the subject of filial duty.

When any child or children of any Roman Catholic, other than the eldest son, whose case was provided for before,. conformed to the Protestant religion, the father was obliged to give in, upon oath, to the court of chancery, a statement of the real and bona fide value of all his estate, real and personal; and make such provision for the present and future maintenance of the conforming child or children, as the court might order. (Robins, p. 459.)

Of this code of laws, it may be fairly averred, that, had all the penitentiaries in Europe been ransacked, to form a legislature for Ireland,—had Cartouche and his gang taken possession of the Parliament house, they

*"The eldest son, so conforming, immediately acquires, and in the life time of his father, the permanent part, what our law calls the reversion and inheritance of the estate, and he discharges it by retrospect; and annuls every sort of voluntary settlement made by the father ever so long before his conversion. This he may sell or dispose of immediately, and alienate it from the family forever." (Burke, V, p. 187.)

could not have devised a more rapacious or cruel system.

There is hardly a code in the world, that does not afford some instances of unjust and immoral laws, enacted in moments of delusion or faction. But this is the only one universally and undeviatingly profligate and depraved,—of which every provision and paragraph violated some law of God or man, and the plainest dictates of eternal justice,—and which legalized robbery, and punished with death acts of humanity, teaching schools, the celebration of marriage, etc.

The professed object of the hypocritical tyrants who framed this "ferocious system," as Burke appropriately styles it, was to rescue the objects of its rapacity from the darkness of Popish idolatry. But they might worship Jupiter Ammon, Juno, Venus, Mars, Bacchus, and Apollo, with the Romans; the sun, with the Guebres; or Apis, with the Egyptians; they might even disbelieve in God altogether.* Provided they forswore transubstantiation and the Pope's authority, they became pure and immaculate; their property and persons were secure; and, under the forms and ceremonies of the law of the land, they then acquired a right to rob and plunder the blind idolatrous Papists whom they had abandoned.

Whoever has travelled through these pages, and duly considered the villainy of those statutes, and of

*See Burke's view of the subject.

the legislators by whom they were enacted; the horrible scenes of oppression, fraud, and murder, which they could not fail to produce; the universal demoralization that must have followed their operation,—cannot fail to agree with Tillotson, that, so far as respected the devoted island whose fate we deplore, it were .

"Better there were no revealed religion, and that human nature were left to the conduct of its own principles and inclinations, which are much more mild and merciful, much more for the peace and happiness of human society, than to be actuated by a religion that inspires men with so vile a fury, and prompts them to commit such outrages." (Tillotson, III, p. 19.)

Tillotson applied this strong position to other parts of Christendom; but shut his eyes to the wickedness, the profligacy, and the immorality of the code in force in his native country;*—so much easier is it to take the mote out of our neighbor's eye, than the beam out of our own.

We have now, however, in this enlightened country, bigoted clergymen, who cant, and whine, and turn up the whites of their eyes, deploring and reviling the persecuting spirit of Madrid, and Lisbon, and Paris, and Rome, and Goa; but, like Tillotson, deaf, and blind, and dumb, to the atrocious system of persecution for ages in operation in England and Ireland. If they attend to the maxim of Jesus Christ, "Let him

*The English laws on this subject were as wicked and cruel as the Irish.

that is without sin cast the first stone," they will lay an eternal embargo on their tongues, upon this odious, this detestable subject. Sat verbum.

Here we close—and ask the reader, to whatever nation, religion, party, or faction, he may belong, whether there ever existed a much more horrible system of tyranny? And whether resistance to it, in any of its stages, whatever might have been the result, would not have deserved a nobler name than the odious one of Rebellion?

> "Rebellion! foul, dishonoring word,
>   Whose wrongful blight so oft has stain'd
> The holiest cause that tongue or sword
>   Of mortal ever lost or gain'd.
> How many a spirit, born to bless,
>   Has sunk beneath that withering name,
> Whom but a day's, an hour's success
>   Had wafted to eternal fame!
> As exhalations, when they burst
> From the warm earth, if chill'd at first,
> If check'd in soaring from the plain,
> Darken to fogs and sink again;
> But, if they once triumphant spread
> Their wings above the mountain-head,
> Become enthron'd in upper air,
> And turn to sun-bright glories there!"
>   (Lalla Rookh.)

89017612854

b89017612854a